Advance Praise for UnCommon Bonds

"At a time in history where hate, violence, and division have returned us, full speed, to pre–Civil Rights America, along comes this remarkable and bridge-building anthology, UnCommon Bonds. From the Women's March to the #MeToo movement, from Barack Obama to Donald Trump, from Black Lives Matter to intersectionality, this is a collection of unapologetically free writings from some of the most visionary leaders and thinkers in the world today. Read them, hear them, feel them, and be prepared to follow them, too, because their hope and challenges are the path to our wokeness, and our salvation."

Kevin Powell, author of The Education of Kevin Powell: A Boy's Journey to Manhood

"UnCommon Bonds is a brave, thoughtful, complicated and honest examination of the challenges and rewards of building and sustaining authentic cross-race friendships. The book examines the issue in a range of creative and engaging ways—through autobiographical narratives, essays, dialogues, letters and critical social analysis linked to personal experience. The result is a provocative and urgent exploration of why this effort can be so hard, as well as a testament to how life affirming and essential cross-race relationships can be. Unlike other books that focus only on cross-race alliances between women of color and white women, this book also looks at the challenges and opportunities in the bonds created among women of color from diverse racial groups. Further, it attends to the intersections of class, gender, generation, transnational location and other aspects of identity that impact such relationships—all the while keeping race central to the dialogue. The book offers breathtaking honesty and courageous truth telling from women of color about the damage white ignorance and cowardice can do to relationships—even within multiracial families. It also offers a wake-up call and some excellent modeling for white women about the commitment, humility, self-reflection and vulnerability necessary for being trustworthy partners/allies to women of color. The writing is vivid, strong and deeply moving with many powerful lessons to offer readers who struggle to create meaningful relationships across race. The hard-won knowledge reflected in this book is a gift to us all."

Lee Anne Bell, Professor Emerita, Barnard College, and author of
Storytelling for Social Justice: Connecting Narrative and the Arts in Antiracist Teaching

"Kersha Smith and Marcella Runell Hall have curated a touching set of essays that invite us to think with nuance about the challenges and rewards of interracial and cross-cultural friendships. The works bristle with honesty, digging deep into the challenges of forming rare 'uncommon bonds' of sisterhood across differences that are not merely descriptive, but imbricated in the asymmetrical power relations that shape the world we share. If you are looking for a rousing chorus of Kumbaya, look elsewhere—this book reveals the complicated, difficult, self-reflective, and transformative work that makes it possible for adult women to call some few true loves, sista-friends."

Deva Woodly-Davis, Associate Professor of Politics,
The New School, and author of *The Politics of Common Sense*

"Into a cultural landscape sorely lacking in representations of cross-racial friendships between women, *UnCommon Bonds* arrives as both revelation and gift—an uncommonly candid, nuanced guide to nurturing those bonds in the name of personal growth and social justice."

Emily Lordi, Associate Professor, University of Massachusetts Amherst,
and author of *Black Resonance: Iconic Women Singers and*
African American Literature **and** *Donny Hathaway Live*

"*UnCommon Bonds* is just the book we need to read right now. The 2016 Presidential campaign revealed deep fissures across and between women along racial lines that captured news headlines. This collection of essays, however, gets to the heart of uncommon bonds—those bonds of deep friendship between women across race. Race matters. It bonds, and it breaks. In essays that shift seamlessly from the personal and the systemic, *UnCommon Bonds* shows how central love, trust, and commitment are to navigating broader systems informing sisterhood and race. These beautiful and brave accounts move beyond simplistic assumptions to uncover the messy and meaningful dynamics of interracial friendships between women."

Nitasha Tamar Sharma, Associate Professor,
African American Studies and Asian American Studies,
Northwestern University, and author of *Hip Hop Desis:*
South Asian Americans, Blackness, and a Global Racial Consciousness

UnCommon Bonds

Studies in Criticality

Shirley R. Steinberg
General Editor

Vol. 372

The Counterpoints series is part of the Peter Lang Education list.
Every volume is peer reviewed and meets
the highest quality standards for content and production.

PETER LANG
New York • Bern • Berlin
Brussels • Vienna • Oxford • Warsaw

UnCommon Bonds

Women Reflect on Race and Friendship

Edited by
Kersha Smith
Marcella Runell Hall

PETER LANG
New York • Bern • Berlin
Brussels • Vienna • Oxford • Warsaw

Library of Congress Cataloging-in-Publication Data

Names: Smith, Kersha, editor. | Hall, Marcella Runell, editor.
Title: Uncommon bonds: women reflect on race and friendship /
edited by Kersha Smith and Marcella Runell Hall.
Description: New York: Peter Lang, 2018.
Series: Counterpoints: studies in criticality; v. 372 | ISSN 1058-1634
Includes bibliographical references.
Identifiers: LCCN 2017047409 | ISBN 978-1-4331-4877-4 (hardback: alk. paper)
ISBN 978-1-4331-4874-3 (paperback: alk. paper) | ISBN 978-1-4331-4878-1 (ebook pdf)
ISBN 978-1-4331-4879-8 (epub) | ISBN 978-1-4331-4880-4 (mobi)
Subjects: LCSH: Female friendship. | Interracial friendship.
Race relations. | African American women. | Women.
Classification: LCC BF575.F66 .U53 2017 | DDC 305.4—dc23
LC record available at https://lccn.loc.gov/2017047409
DOI 10.3726/b11731

Bibliographic information published by **Die Deutsche Nationalbibliothek**.
Die Deutsche Nationalbibliothek lists this publication in the "Deutsche
Nationalbibliografie"; detailed bibliographic data are available
on the Internet at http://dnb.d-nb.de/.

The paper in this book meets the guidelines for permanence and durability
of the Committee on Production Guidelines for Book Longevity
of the Council of Library Resources.

To my beautiful, bold, and brave daughters, Aaliyah and Ava. Thank you for choosing me as your Mama on this journey called life, and for inspiring me every single day to put love at the center of all my relationships, especially those that nurture and support "uncommon bonds." And to my beloved Mommy, thank you for being my first best friend and supporting my journey— in this life and beyond.

—MRH

This book is dedicated to my mother, Barbara, and grandmother, Reatter, who have always upheld and sang the praises of other women. And to my husband, James, and our sons, Julian and Ellison, for encouraging my Queendom.

—KS

CONTENTS

ACKNOWLEDGMENTS

This project was indeed a labor of love, through all of the seasons, and the ups and downs of life. A huge thank you to Shirley R. Steinberg for believing in this book right from its inception and to the whole team at Peter Lang, including Patty Mulrane and our production editor, Janell Harris. Thank you to all of the contributors who shared their stories, accepted our feedback with loving kindness, and stayed with us as the project came to life. Thank you to Sonia Nieto for penning a beautiful foreword to the book and for being so authentic in every way. Thank you to all of our colleagues who offered advance praise for UnCommon Bonds; your support and belief in this project are above and beyond what we could have hoped for.

Big thanks to Christy Herbes for bringing to life the cover design. A special thanks to April Graham for serving as our beloved intern. Your passion and dedication to the project was a godsend. Thanks to April Silver for believing in us and assisting with the press release and sharing our project with the world. Thank you, Loryn Engelbrecht, for co-creating a beautiful web presence.

Thank you to our colleagues at Mount Holyoke, NYU, and CUNY and in particular Annette, Alicia, Beth, Brenda, Elena, Erin, Karen, Latrina, Michelle, Monroe, Leah, and Rachel.

To all our sister friends in Amherst, Aurora, Brooklyn, Chicago, and Ocean City, especially Allana, Amy, Ann, Anne (RIP), Ayana, Bindi, Claudine, Dana, Daniella, Debora, Deva, Dottie, Edwina, Elaine, Elisha, Ella, Emily, Felicia, Fran, Giselle, Heather, JC, JLove, Jamielle, Jessica, Jill, Joicelyn, Julie, Heather, Hiabiba, Karen, Karyn, Keisha, Kelly, Landi, Lara, Linda, Lisa, Liza, Lori, Lynda, Marit, Mario, Marjorie, Martha, Mary, Melissa, Meghan, Michelle, Millicent, Monica, Nadine, Naima, Nicole, Nitasha, Oya's Elements, Pat, Patty, Piper, Rachel, Rani, Rha, Romina, Rosa, Sally, Sara, Seble, Shadia, Shaurnee, Shireen, Sofia, Tanesha, Tara, Vanessa, Whitney, Yael, Yolanda, Xiomara, and Zahra. To the Esdaile, Hall, Runell, Smith, and Toney families, thank you for your warmth and unconditional love. Finally, thank you to our husbands, James and Dave, for being our biggest champions and sources of support.

FOREWORD

Sonia Nieto

As is abundantly clear from the chapters in this book, forming and sustaining friendships across racial, cultural, generational, and other social differences is not easy. Reading these narratives helped me reflect on the friendships I've had over the years, some with Puerto Rican women like me, and others with women of different backgrounds. Given the communities in which I've lived—Brooklyn for most of my youth and young adulthood, Manhattan for a year shortly after I married, Queens for three years as a young wife and mother, and for the past 40-plus years, a small town in Massachusetts—I realized that although my friendships have been quite diverse, the closest ones have often been with other Puerto Rican women. I remember a day a couple of decades ago after a particularly thorny racial incident in town when I was asked to address an assembly in our local high school. After speaking with the students about the significance of cross-racial and cross-cultural friendships, a student asked me, "Who are *your* best friends?" I've always counted a very diverse group among my closest friendships. But the question made me think more deeply about this issue. I answered that my closest friend was another Puerto Rican woman and that my other close friends were African American, Jewish, Italian American, and women of other backgrounds. What we had in common was that most of us now living in Massachusetts had been raised in

New York. Sometimes geography is just as binding as race or ethnicity. At the same time, I'm happy to say that after all these years of living in Massachusetts, I have friends who fall outside of those perimeters as well.

But race and culture *do* matter, and they often matter a great deal. As I explained to the students that day, it's far easier to make friends with people who are like you, who share your ethnicity, race, language, and social class, among other differences. When that's the case, there's little need to explain things; you can speak in shorthand. For instance, with my Puerto Rican friends, we can switch back and forth from English to Spanish to Spanglish, and we can be pretty sure that we'll easily understand one another. I don't need to explain to other Puerto Rican women why my parents were upset the first time I went out for New Year's Eve rather than spend it at their home—and I was 24 years old, married, and with a baby! Other Puerto Rican women of my generation would have immediately understood why: holidays are sacrosanct in most Puerto Rican families and females especially are expected to be with their families on those days. I also don't need to explain why I never learned to ride a bike. Many Puerto Rican females who grew up in New York during the 1950s and before had the same experience, a combination of overprotective parents and an ingrained sexism that "girls don't ride bikes" (largely absent nowadays, I'm glad to say).

Yes, same-culture relationships tend to be easier, as familiar as old slippers and just as comfortable. However, it is far too simplistic to leave it at that because there's more to it than ethnicity or race. Being of the same background doesn't necessarily mean that other differences don't exist or matter. My best friend is Puerto Rican, true, but while she had a relatively privileged childhood, mine was definitely working class. Even after over 40 years of friendship, I don't "get" some of her experiences and she doesn't understand some of mine. Other Puerto Rican friends are also quite different from me in different ways: some were raised in Puerto Rico, whereas I was raised in New York, and this alone helps define starkly different childhoods. And there are numerous other differences that fall outside of race and ethnicity, including sexual orientation, family structure, and others that influence us differently.

But the fact that same-race/ethnic relationships are usually easier doesn't mean that the "uncommon bonds" of cross-racial/ethnic relationships are not also meaningful and can even be glorious. I don't know where I'd be—in my head, in my values, in my actions—without the friendships I've had over the years with women of backgrounds different from mine. These friends have been my teachers and mentors, opening my eyes to new sights, sounds, tastes, and perspectives. They have questioned my preconceptions and shattered my stereotypes (we all have them, after all, regardless of our identity). These friends have expanded my mind, introducing me to different ways of being and thinking. They have, in so many ways, enriched my life, and I hope I have done the same for them.

Of course, it generally takes more work and no small measure of patience and empathy to form and sustain cross-racial/ethnic relationships because, just like new shoes, they need a breaking-in period. An offhand remark or a hurtful comment—as you'll read in a number of these chapters—can permanently destroy or critically wound such friendships. But once they've been broken in, with years of sisterhood and struggle to strengthen whatever may shake them, these friendships are often just as comfortable as the friendships we have with our co-ethnics. But it takes time and hard work.

The chapters in this book are powerful, heartfelt, endearing, and sometimes painful to read. Often, race takes center stage. At other times, race is rarely mentioned. This can be negative, according to Millicent Jackson, as when white privilege, the "very thing that can murky the waters of an interracial friendship," goes unacknowledged. Or it can be positive, as Thembisa Mishaka writes in her chapter, "to see difference and acknowledge difference, without racializing every interaction." Sometimes—but not often—such friendships can transcend race, as suggested in some of the chapters.

What brings all these chapters together is what Jeff Duncan-Andrade has called "critical hope" (see Duncan-Andrade, 2009). Though he has used the concept to refer to urban youths and their teachers, his message is equally significant for women engaged in cross-racial, cross-cultural friendships. Duncan-Andrade contrasts the concept of false hope with critical hope, that is, a hope that rejects hopelessness and demands active struggle and commitment. Critical hope, then, is founded on the idea that regardless of difficult and sometimes even seemingly insurmountable barriers, women's friendships across boundaries of race, ethnicity, and other differences can thrive.

As you will see in the narratives that follow, in spite of what may seem to be intractable cultural differences and difficult historical realities, women of different backgrounds can nevertheless create mutually nurturing "uncommon bonds." The friendships they describe—for all their love and sisterhood, and despite their warts and problems—can serve as examples for all of us, men, women, and children, who want to forge a path to a new reality in our nation.

Sonia Nieto
Professor Emerita,
Language, Literacy, and Culture,
College of Education
University of Massachusetts, Amherst

Reference

Duncan-Andrade, J. (2009). Note to educators: Hope required when growing flowers in concrete. *Harvard Educational Review*, 79(2), 181–194.

INTRODUCTION

Kersha Smith and Marcella Runell Hall

It was never our intention to edit a book advocating for cross-racial friendship among women. In fact, asking others to write about their friendships came with some apprehension. Putting together a collection of stories about the complex, intimate relationships between women that provide sanctity and sacred spaces for reflection and growth is tricky business. We treasure our friendships and fiercely guard them. Amplifying race as a lens by which to think about our friendships was perhaps an even bigger risk. Inviting women to reflect honestly on what friendship and race mean to them was loaded, and we knew that. However, we felt that posing questions and compiling stories could provide important insight into relationships that are not easily defined.

We also did not want to edit a book that privileged a particular narrative. We guarded against positioning the book as a collective Kumbaya moment. That felt false to us because we understood the deep fissures that often get swept under the rug and outright ignored in relationships that fail to acknowledge the history of racism and the vibrancy of privilege. Fixating on the challenges of cross-racial friendships didn't do it for us either. We considered that inauthentic to our experiences. Yes, we could recall instances where racial privilege went unchecked, resentment built up, and relationships dissolved. We retell these stories with clear fault and uncomplicated characters. Except those are not true portrayals of relationships. Friendships, in their development and sometimes in their demise, are rarely linear, nor are they ever effortless.

In our country, coalitions among women of differing races are deeply fractured. They have been this way seemingly forever. Even amid gains in our collective struggle to support one another, divisions persist. History documents the contentious relationship between white women and women of color (particularly Black women). Too many times white women have been accused of prioritizing their own agenda at the expense of others, failing to acknowledge the benefits afforded to them because of their skin color, and deemphasizing the stereotypes, discrimination, and acrimony that remain a part of women of color's experience. Even with full knowledge of the discord, our aim was not to foster simple "us against them" stories.

This book contributes to the conversation about race that continues to be male centered and lacking in intimacy. Writers in this collection challenge the notion of "get-along feminism." They understand that gender parity can't simply be a fight toward equity with men, but a denouncement of and battle against injustice for all people. We have a long way to go in the wake of blatantly brutal assaults on people of color, and a presidential election and subsequent Women's March that highlighted clear divides among women. It is a long way to go indeed as we delve deeper into nuanced lived experiences and our understanding of intersectionality.

In addition, the chapters in this volume are a response to social science research on cross-racial friendships. Studies on cross-racial friendships usually concentrate on relationships formed during early and late adolescence (Bowman & Park, 2014; Fischer, 2008; Rude & Herda, 2010). Research highlights emotional and identity development in educational environments and often oversimplifies the benefits of integration and its role in developing and maintaining cross-racial friendships (Aboud, Mendelson, & Purdy, 2003; Joyner & Kao, 2000). While there is no denying the closeness that might develop between classmates, evidence suggests that cross-racial friendships are unstable and terminable (Hallinan & Williams, 1987).

Most of the research in the social sciences nearly exclusively focuses on cisgender, postsecondary relationships. In doing this, the research misses an important observation—that is, adults (postcollege) typically do not have close, meaningful relationships with people who are racially different from themselves. One exception is presented by Berry (2006), who looks at the number of cross-racial friendships adults have beyond relationships developed in school. The study gives an interesting account in the discrepancy between how cross-racial friendships are self-reported and how they are actualized. Berry finds that most people declare to have friends outside of their own racial category. However, when this assertion is tested, in this case using wedding photographs as a measure of close friendships, most people do not have friends outside of their race.

As we began to gather narratives for this volume, we realized that more than anything we wanted to provide a space for women to write about their experiences with trust, disappointment, timing, and possibility. We wanted to acknowledge that, unlike in childhood, as adult women we get to make more conscious choices about our friendships. We wanted to understand why our friends become more narrow and homogeneous as we age. Are there windows at different moments in life that are more conducive to developing racially diverse friendships? Do those windows close at certain points and remain shut? Is there value to doing the work to maintain intentional cross-racial friendships? Or is it a place of extreme vulnerability and never-ending exhaustion? The writers whose chapters we ultimately selected found a way to answer some of these questions. Their stories are honest, bold, unapologetic, and intricate. They explore the difference between maintaining a parallel partnership and developing a genuinely meaningful reciprocal friendship.

The work of transitioning to a deep mutual friendship is no small feat. We (the editors) maintained a parallel partnership for years. We knew many of the same people, ran in the same education circles, and even lived right around the corner from one another. Despite our similar experiences, we didn't actually become friends until the birth of our children. We think that bonding over motherhood provided an impetus for us to push toward a genuine friendship. It was our Sunday afternoon playdates, sipping wine and listening to music as the kids rumbled in the other room, where we found a true connection. In these moments, we talked about growing up in the Midwest and on the East Coast, the trials of being leaders within our respective institutions, raising our children, loving our spouses, and everything in between. When race came up, we talked about that too. We talked about how Marcella had so many cross-racial friendships and how Kersha had so few. We talked about the difficulties that many Black women have with white women, the suspicion, the disconnect, and exhaustion of having to teach and to explain. We talked about tokenism and authenticity. In dealing with these subjects, head on, a real relationship formed. The friendship has endured. We have judged, critiqued, and hoped. We love each other. But we know the sting of racism and privilege, history, and ignorance might prove stronger than any sense of affinity we feel for each other.

No matter how much we want to characterize them as rock solid, friendships are tenuous. They require a constant give and take. They need time and patience. They thrive in environments that support clear communication. They are founded on trust. They expect variety in conveying emotion. When we give ourselves to our friends, we make vulnerable our desires. We reveal our goals and unleash plans to fulfill our dreams. We shudder from our fears and curse ill intent. We relax into our truest self and depend on our partners to do the same. Those are the breezy moments of friendships, moments where we are carefree without judgment and discontent. Moments when our friends are the baddest women we have ever had the pleasure to know. These are moments when we think of her, see her, talk with her, and a colossal YAASSS fills our soul.

Perhaps with certain women, one never develops sisterhood. You have things in common, but there is something, a chasm, that is tough to name. Your friend is cool. She is not ignorant. There is never a drama-filled blowout between you and her. Yet the friendship fades. Every bone in your body wants to believe that race isn't just a tiny bit responsible for your disconnect. But you know that's a lie. Somewhere along the way, you both realize that growing and maintaining your friendship is going to command both of you to extend beyond what you have created with your closest sistren and neither of you is invested in doing that work. So you don't.

The narratives presented in this book color the notion that authentic, reciprocal, long-lasting cross-racial friendship between women is uncommon. Writers present letters, personal accounts, and partnered writings that convey the subtleties of cross-racial friendships. These women understand that authentically deep friendships are different from acquaintances we have in our neighborhoods and our workplaces. They challenge the convention that proximity breeds acceptance. Many of us thrive in integrated workplaces; we go to integrated schools, we might even have family members who are racially different from ourselves. But lazy thinking would have us assume that familiarity precludes us from doing the hard work of acknowledging our roles in keeping privilege and disenfranchisement alive.

Authentic representation was a tall order that none of the authors took lightly. As editors, we endeavored to keep the genuine voice of each story and at the same time push the authors to consider alternative points of view. We might have overstepped boundaries and created friction, as there were authors who after consideration decided that they could not continue with the project. We had to consistently remind ourselves that these are the stories of others and the beauty of the project relies on the diversity of voice. Authors appear in a way that seeks to preserve each distinct experience and reflection. We elected to eschew themes because we wanted to honor the uniqueness of each story while uniting them under a common bond that exposes the conflicts, celebrations, and everything in between of cross-racial friendships. In the end, we believe these first-person accounts challenge assumptions, disclose struggles, and celebrate sisterhood.

References

Aboud, F. E., Mendelson, M. J., & Purdy, K. T. (2003). Cross-race peer relations and friendship quality. *International Journal of Behavioral Development, 27*, 165–173.

Berry, B. (2006). Friends for better or for worse: Interracial friendship in the United States as seen through wedding party photos. *Demography, 43*(3), 491–510.

Bowman, N., & Park, J. (2014). Interracial contact on college campuses: Comparing and contrasting predictors of cross-racial interaction and interracial friendship. *The Journal of Higher Education, 85*(5), 660–690.

Fischer, M. (2008). Does campus diversity promote friendship diversity? A look at interracial friendships in college. *Social Science Quarterly, 89*(3), 631–655.

Hallinan, M. T., & Williams, R. A. (1987). The stability of students' interracial friendships. *American Sociological Review, 52*, 653–664.

Joyner, K., & Kao, G. (2000). School racial composition and adolescent racial homophily. *Social Science Quarterly, 81*, 810–825.

Rude, J., & Herda, D. (2010). Best friends forever: Race and stability of adolescent friendships. *Social Forces, 89*(2), 585–608.

· 1 ·

OF MY PURPLE LIFE

Joicelyn Dingle

Sisterhood among women is an honor I take seriously. I cherish those "women only" moments that happen even when you meet a new one. Those color-less notes that give the impression, maybe we—Black and white—can "be women and be friends." This is a sophisticated connection. I desire my friend-ships with all women to vibrate high and authentically with wisdom, humor, and mutual benefit. Cultural confusion, insensitivity, and disregard are the chances one takes when race is at hand. The sophisticated part comes upon deciding who is integral to the journey and who is not. What will you go through with a woman of another race and discern when it is beneficial to remain connected and open?

Being the daughter of people whose formative years were shaped through segregation and the civil rights movement, I am not a person who claims not to see color. People who claim such nonsense get the proverbial side-eye. Girlhood bonding in my Black neighborhood growing up in the 1980s was more like a rite of passage perfecting rhythmic cheers and hand games, a roller skating crew, personalizing the latest dances, committing to Janet Jackson video routines, choosing with your soul between Michael Jackson or Prince and the flyest b-boys. It was a Black thing, a time when our culture was still a mystery and solely ours.

White people didn't ask to touch our hair or use our slang or colloqui-alisms. I saw a white girl on the internet selling a T-shirt that said, "I want Felicia's life. She's always going somewhere," referring to the overrun "Bye Felisha" with no clue that Felisha is a crackhead from the movie *Friday* that everyone wanted to avoid. White girls did not get cornrows and attempt to rename them *boxer braids*. But the Kardashians tried it: "Khloe you look like a boxer." Bye Felisha. I don't have a problem with exploring African culture; just don't try to reinvent the wheel; our wagons hold history.

Going to predominately white schools, I was on sports teams of girls—Black and white—who had the collective goal of winning. I was a starting guard in basketball. Strategy from point was my mindset and my position. I didn't pass the ball to my teammate because we shared a color, history, and perhaps a lifestyle. Trusting she knew the play—Black or white—it's about passing the ball to the player who is open and ready.

When the all-white newspaper staff at my all-girl's Catholic high school wrote senior predictions, mine went something like this: Joicelyn Dingle will move to New York and write a book entitled "1001 Stupid Questions White People Have Asked Me About Black People." The girls I went to school with were Ellen Degenerous–Michelle Collins funny. I had been unreserved to their questions over our teenage years. I wasn't eager for them, but I was open, even curious. I figured my unseasoned answers were better than their unsettling assumptions. The questions would eventually help me under-stand our differences. After I chuckled at the prediction, my 17-year-old self pondered: I would never write a book solely about white folks. Not for fun. Not for money. Not for nothing. But here, in an effort toward the woman-piece, I am open.

Race matters, even in the first grade. Sabrina was crying in class, like all day. She wanted to invite a few of the Black girls in our class to her birthday party. Eventually, she broke down and told us that she was upset because she couldn't invite us to her party. "Why Sabrina?" Blurting in an emphatic sob, "Because you're Black! My daddy doesn't like Black people!" Sabrina was dis-traught, embarrassed and disappointed in her father. Six years old, we, the three Black girls in the class comforted her. We didn't know how to be angry at that moment. However, the transference was made; the idea of race and prejudice had found its way into our little girl world.

As an adult in Savannah, Georgia, I'd met Reese, a Midwestern girl, who was funny and irreverent. Our friendship rode on cobblestone for about two years. She was the type of person who was thrown off if any woman was prettier or smarter or had experienced more life. One day she walked in, her waist-long hair dyed a shocking but beautiful red. After complimenting her, she said, "One day, we can sit and I'll let you brush it." Like it was gift. I laughed and said, "Did you say brush your hair? Girl, I don't want to brush your hair. Ever. You twisted that compliment in your mind." That baffled me. If a white girlfriend had complimented her hair, would she have offered to "let" her brush it? Reese, a true narcissist, said "I just thought you might want to." Ok, so I wanted to fight her. For reasons that would hold no merit among my higher circle of women. Friendship aborted.

Camille and I shared a more profound friendship. We had a similar drive about life and we connected on that level. Although she had an accent like Blanche from the Golden Girls and crazy romantic notions about the South, they were harmless, I thought. She had other Black friends and she didn't tolerate any level of prejudice.

Intoxicated from wine and St. Patrick's Day shenanigans, she was in the kitchen on the phone talking about a guy she was seeing—a white guy. I was in the den, but she was loud and clear. "That nigger said this. ..." One. "That nigger did that. ..." Two. "If that nigger thinks. ..." Three. When Camille entered the den, I had my purse on my shoulder and I was standing, fuming. Barely noticing, she continued her rant, however, minus the n-word. "Camille, are you out of your mind?" Puzzled, she says, "What are you talking about? Why are you leaving? What happened?" Her lack of judgment was isolating and infuriating.

I left, remembering something a Black mother told me as a fifth grader at the time after we observed a situation with a Black girl and white girl at my elementary school, "White people will turn on you." As a seasoned adult, I've learned that any person can turn on you, regardless of color. But something about the "white" and the "will" in that sentence resonates in the undertow.

I thought our friendship was over in the two weeks we didn't speak—was I a character in her chase of antebellum sentiment? Was it fair for me to have different rules for her than I do my Black friends who use the word? Should I consider the fact the she wasn't even talking about a Black person? What was it about her that I liked so much that I would consider her friendship again? I appreciated when Camille called apologizing but not excuse-full; she said it's been too long and she missed talking to me. I missed her too, but my stance was clear. We talked it out until the core of what made us friends found its way to the surface. Friendship restored.

Alice Walker and Gloria Steinem are longtime friends with common bonds. Solidifying the sisterhood, Gloria is the godmother to Alice's daughter. I often wonder, what was the impetus of the shift when Alice Walker (1983) coined the term "womanist" in her collection of essays, *In Search of Our Mother's Garden: Womanist Prose*. Moved or inspired to forge a perfect path validating feminism for Black women, what happened behind closed doors? Did it cause friction? As friends and leaders, making strides toward common, massively beneficial goals in the feminist movement, why the divide? Here is something I know for sure: When a certain kind of woman finds herself and her kind ignored by the thing that engages her most, she creates something else. Ms. Walker, through her Goddess work, sparked a movement.

Womanism fit Black women like a pair of silk stockings. Personally, it was a big sigh of relief. Alice Walker's definition does not forfeit feminism but includes that which is natural to the journey and the souls of Black women-folk. She gave us the freedom to feel valued as feminists and as Black women:

Womanist

1. From womanish. (Opposite of "girlish," i.e., frivolous, irresponsible, not serious.) A Black feminist or feminist of color. From the Black folk expression of mothers to female children, "You acting woman-ish," that is, like a woman. Usually referring to outrageous, audacious, courageous or willful behavior. Wanting to know more and in greater depth than is considered "good" for one. Interested in grown-up doings. Acting grown-up. Being grown-up. Interchangeable with another Black folk expression: "You trying to be grown." Responsible. In charge. Serious.

2. A woman who loves other women, sexually and/or nonsexually. Appreciates and prefers women's culture, women's emotional flexibility (values tears as natural counterbalance of laughter) and women's strength. Sometimes loves individual men, sexually and/or nonsexually. Committed to survival and wholeness of entire people, male and female. Not a separatist, except periodically, for health. Traditionally a universalist.

3. Loves music. Loves dance. Loves the moon. Loves the Spirit. Loves love and food and roundness. Loves struggle. Loves the Folk. Loves herself. Regardless.

4. Womanist is to feminist as purple is to lavender.

Or as filmmaker Erika Conner (2011) once said, "We're different type of girls." Meaning we come from a space where we walk, talk, and think in a rhythm that matters spiritually and connects Black girls. This is the very thing that makes many white women feel intimidated. It's impossible to have a real friendship when something so natural in a woman attacks another woman's sense of self. Our color purple is not against your color lavender, but we are bold, beautiful, and present. Quite frankly, we're hard to miss.

I had a conversation with my friend Ayana Byrd, an author of Black girl history books on beauty—*Hair Story: Untangling the Roots of Black Hair in America* (2002) and *Naked: Black Women Bare All About Their Skin, Hips, Lips and Other Parts* (2005). Living in Europe for many years and going to Barnard College, she's acquired true girlfriends, interesting women who are white. I asked her, in an effort to open my heart to all women, "Ayana, how are you friends with so many white girls?" Thinking for a brief moment, she answered, "We have to be able to talk about anything, including race. If we can't talk about race, we can't be friends." And there's the rub.

Friendships are a matter of chemistry, a complex mixture of unforced energies that make bonds viable, stimulating, and full of discoverable matter. Our history must be considered. Our reality must addressed. Remaining open is the key to relationships between women. True friendship—black and white, purple and lavender—should allow for any conversation that elevates the other.

References

Byrd, A., & Soloman, A. (2005). *Naked: Black women bare all about their skin, hair, hips, lips, and other parts.* New York, NY: Perigee Trade.

Byrd, A., & Tharps, L. (2002). *Hair story: Untangling the roots of Black hair in America.* New York, NY: St. Martin's Griffin.

Conner, E. (2011). Interview with Norell Giancana. 3-minute documentary trailer for *How to Make a Magazine.* Dingle, J. (Director). Los Angeles, CA: DaM Girls Media.

Walker, A. (1983). *In search of our mother's garden: Womanist prose.* San Diego, CA: Harcourt Brace Jovanovich.

· 2 ·

IT'S ALL ABOUT THE RHYTHM

Birthing Sisterhood

Stacey Gibson and Jessica Havens

A conversation between sister friends

In this conversation we hope to explore the ever-evolving dynamics of our own interracial friendship and how we arrived at this point. What we have included is a transcribed conversation, following in the footsteps of antiracist feminists who have come before us. Women have always made story and talked into, with, within, and through each other. In a world saturated with posts, tweets, updates, and downloads, it is the warm, rich vibrations that can only be felt when we speak to each other across a table that eclipses the digital dissonance. It allows each of us to retain our individual voice and authorship of the written piece, while allowing for complexity and disagreement.

Conversation Jump-Off: How Have Your Friendships With Women of Other Races and Ethnicities Evolved or Devolved Over Time?

Stacey: My relationships and friendships with women of different races have evolved as my standards and expectations around relationships have evolved. The number of cross-racial friendships has decreased exponentially over the years, but the authenticity and integrity of those new and remaining friendships are more lush, more dynamic, and more affirming. In past years what may have been identified as a "friendship" was quite often something else altogether. Those relationships were seemingly "friendly" enough, but because there was no acknowledgment of the ways race infiltrated our interactions, in hindsight, it is difficult to call that a friendship. I have experienced quite a few women, especially white ones, who were curious and seemed interested in forming a possible friendship, but their interest dissipated after they heard some of my personal politics, especially about white identities. Truth be told, many women of color also lost interest once they realized my politics. The challenge now is for me to not look askance at those earlier interactions and relationships, but to keep them in high regard because they reveal how my standards have shifted. I believe it is important to note that relationships across racial difference where the woman is a person of color is quite different for me than a cross-racial relationship with a white woman.

I have a general distrust of white women. Often I have encountered a frenzied eagerness from many white women where they have the latest lingo on their tongue. They seem ready to kiss me with their sound bite. In the past I misread the sound bite as marker of racial awareness and healthy racial consciousness. I quickly learned that anyone can colonize rhetoric and sound "aware." That frustration led me to push many women away because that behavior seemed like a form of fetishizing. As I recognized the patterns more, I felt less obligated to govern that space. Instead, I opted to practice healthy boundaries and check in with myself about what was going on with me in the moment … make sure I'm not longing for or bending toward white recognition as a way to see and feel my own sense of legitimacy.

Jessica: I think my relationships with women across race have evolved as I have evolved. … As a white kid growing up in communities of color, I was always searching for a sense of "belonging"; it was clear as early as second grade that I was white and that marked me as different. I naturally gravitated toward the other non-Black kids in my school, since we were in the racial minority, even though I felt boxed in by that group as well. As I got older, though, I found it harder to connect with many white people who didn't have the same cultural history as me. I often gravitated toward women of color because I made an assumption that there would be a commonality of consciousness. But I often found that I didn't always feel at home with women of color either, that there was still a disconnect and distance.

There was a time in my life where I embodied that eagerness for affirmation from women of color that you spoke of, that desire to "kiss you with my sound bite" (*cringe*). In my overly persistent attempts to connect with women of color, I experienced a lot of rejection. When I was younger I took that rejection very personally, and even allowed a kind of resentment toward women of color, and Black women in particular, to brew. I SO desired to connect and to be seen for the multicultural and complex woman that I was, but felt like Black women couldn't see beyond my whiteness. At the time, I didn't have the systemic analysis to understand how our interactions were a product of something larger. I think some of those women had already too many negative experiences with white women, so there was just not enough emotional psychic space to feel me in that way; there was a kind of protective shield they had to put up with white women. I also didn't fully understand how my own white privilege informed a lot of those interactions and the disconnect I felt. Living in a damn white supremacist society limits relationships and creates distance! Ugh. There was also the chance that this person might just have a different personality than mine, or had been having a bad day. I think I just had to accept that there were going to be women of color, and white women for that matter, whom I met in my life who did not want to get to know me or make space for me and I didn't need to always take it personally.

So, as I've worked to make peace with myself as a complex and multicultural white woman, and developed a more critical racial consciousness, I've become less concerned with seeking that constant approval or affirmation from women of color. In turn, my current relationships with both white women and women of color feel healthier and more grounded.

Stacey: But there is something real and live about women of color and white women. There is a shadow narrative about affirmation there. I have had relationships with white women where we have openly talked about "vouching for each other" and so this idea of legitimacy is still tied to whether or not this white girl will vouch for me. Those patterns and dynamics come into play more than people might be willing to acknowledge.

Jessica: Hmmm, vouching. Yes, and I think you and I have spoken about this dynamic, and even how the two of us are read by others when we walk into a space. I think that the vouching carries different weight for each of us though. In the cultural and political spaces we move in, I think that you have more at stake in vouching for me, a white woman, as your girl. I feel the weight of this risk, the knowledge that my behavior and words and energy in Black spaces reflect back upon you.

Stacey: Yeah it does. Over the years I have been increasingly aware of how all folks carry racialized trauma, whether individually or as a collective. I can also see and hear the deep fatigue all people have as they consciously or unconsciously navigate and wear their racial identities. I choose spaces and people who are bold about moving toward freedoms. The vast majority of these shape shifters are Black people. You are one of a few whom I would invite into some of those spaces, and so, yes, I would make sure to speak you up and vouch for you. First, I love heaping praise onto all my friends, and second, I have Black friends with staggering, irrecoverable racialized wounds. They don't know you. I do. Here's what I've seen and experienced more times that I care to recount: A white woman brings a Black woman into white or POC spaces where no other Black women are present and there erupts what I will unceremoniously dub "the Edgy Other Syndrome." EOS occurs when the white woman who brings the Black woman into white/mixed race spaces accrues some sort of cachet, for being in proximity to or for being in relationship with this Black woman. Yes, I know there are times when the other white people in the room may throw tsunami levels of shade, but far more often I have observed behaviors where the other white people in the setting are barely able to contain themselves as they shimmy closer to the "Black Woman Visiting" and ask a lot of bloody questions they have no business asking. I'm not sure how much of that is about vouching or fetishizing or if I'm just *that* compelling, but what I do know is that almost all of these white folks query hard around the origin and existence of our friendship. It comes off as a peculiar curiosity because I doubt highly those white folks question other white folks about their friendships with such ferocity.

When I was younger I briefly rolled with that whole narrative of "… as a person of color, I can teach them and help them to understand." I still hear that dull, worn narrative of "… these are teachable moments! if you stick in there and teach that white person, then they won't do it again. …" That refrain is a truncated pseudo-narrative because:

1. Most of the people hollering to use "teachable moments" are unconscious themselves, though they would lambaste anyone who told them so … and

2. In gaps of consciousness, many white people repeatedly commit those same acts of unconscious oppression because of their lack of self-investment around unpacking white racial identity.

In essence, the master/slave narrative erupts into this relationship where a person of color trades their labor, intellect, experience, and insight hoping for the betterment of a white individual. I did that a few times. In some ways I felt if I was willing to stay in an underwhelming surface relationship where I was supposed to "teach her something," I could convince this white woman of … what? I don't even remember. Fortunately internalized narratives of inferiority are far quieter for me now. I always have to check in to make sure I'm not over-functioning, because over-functioning is a glaring symptom of broken interracial relationships. At the heart of many of these relationships is the expectation that bodies of color hyperfunction and I've done a lot of work to stop myself from replicating those types of harmful patterns!

Jessica: And what helped you transition surface relationships into meaningful relationships?

Stacey: Observation. I wait and see how much they are revealing of themselves and if I want to be involved in that emotional investment. There are plenty of white women who show up all the time and think they want to be in relationship with me and I will test them. Can they acknowledge the complexities? Can they articulate their own path, identity, and levels of realization and not necessarily so that it matches with what I'm thinking? Are they conscious? Will they reflect and be both reasonable and responsible?

Take you for instance. When I think about how you showed up with a sense of steadiness and intensity and humility. All of that was authentically Jess. No airs and you radiated a willingness to be free while doing your own work. I am drawn to intense folks because I am as well. I take flight from the race zealot and I didn't see you as a curated white woman who was playing the race stage. (Hell … if Black and Brown folks play the race card, white folks can play the hell out of a race stage.) I don't think many white women have any clue about how predictable they are and how limited they are when they show up around issues of race. It's very easy for me to spot that kind of homogenized, fetishizing, limited, white woman and I didn't get any of that energy from you.

Jessica: In terms of our relationship from my side I think it's complicated. I'm trying to own the fact that I know that white privilege affects me in my life and how I move through the world, but there is a part of me that feels conflicted culturally about who I connect with and not. Being raised in white, Black, and Latino spaces, I want to feel like I can bring all of myself to the table without being perceived as pretending to be something I'm not. I feel like sometimes it can be trepidatious in relationships across difference to allow that type of vulnerability and trust to grow. Because I find myself often in multiracial and POC-majority spaces, I also experience a lot of that "testing" that you speak of. Or, on the other hand, POC who want nothing to do with me altogether, uninterested in gauging my consciousness. I am still learning how to flow with these interactions and not let it affect my self-esteem.

Every once in awhile though, there are these special moments in time where we are able to connect in spite of the ignorance/pain/trauma/loss that surrounds us and pours through our veins. Those moments are rare, but they do exist. Perhaps the only way for Black and white women to deeply connect is after a certain amount of personal critical work on both sides that allows us a space to meet in the in-between? So with us, there was just that kind of ease from the get-go. I felt your openness and acceptance very early on with me at least, maybe not with other people. And I think we were able to connect on a level of consciousness.

Stacey: And it seemed to be a level of consciousness that did not fight for stage time or get mired in expectations. I often observe how POC feel like they must show how well versed they are in white behaviors, theories, or white standards. I met you at a time when I no longer felt obligated to center white behaviors and standards for my own personal practice of self. Because my own agency was present I was able to worry less about performing race (which is what I think almost all people are trained to do) and instead just be the evolving me that keeps demanding ear/air time. For those white folks, though, who rolled up and assumed I was going to perform the language and dance of the oppressed while they "staged up" and wielded that oppressive whiteness … not happening. It was in the presence of that kind of white person—one who has no idea how committed they are to performing oppressive narratives of dominance—when you saw me be far less welcoming. I am always grateful I was able to be open and easy with the energy we shared. And I'm always glad we could find a dance floor even though it has been forever since we took to one together.

Jessica: Ok, focus (*giggles*), focus. And what if white people needed to be acculturated in POC cultures to survive? I feel like it is precisely because I was raised among Black and Latino people, and the cultural education I received in those communities, that I'm able to connect with people of color in the way that I do. This doesn't change the fact that I continue to be privileged because of my whiteness. But because you and I have these cultural connections even as people from different races, there are things that connect us beyond just a consciousness about race, that there is a familiarity and a comfortableness there 'cause we don't have to translate everything. We share house tracks and YouTube videos, or "girl can you believe …" stories of racist shenanigans at work or … maybe we just eat chocolate together cause these menstrual cramps are *no joke.*

Stacey: *True talk*! Remember how many times we watched the YouTube video about feeding our pelvises chocolate!! When we met, we were both like "what is this excessively white institution that we're in?!" Everybody misread both of us and we immediately read each other on a very different wave pattern. We decided "we're all good. Ya'll stay over there and misread us."

I'm thinking about the way that these experiences, landscapes, and the culture in the landscape informed our relationship. We were able to immediately find historical rhythms. "Damn girl, you went to the Promontory last week and back in the day you were at Red Dog and Mad Bar too?! … I remember when the movie theater over there closed down?!" (both cracking up here). So the land, the landscape, the architecture, the rhythms of the city … we knew all the spots, we were dancing at the same clubs. Dancing was a catalyst and a salve.

Jessica: Ooh, that's a sexy line—dancing was a catalyst and a salve … indeed. Our mutual love for house music and dancing was definitely another level of connection. For me, house music is this cultural glue that connects me to a whole rainbow crew of freedom loving, Southside-descended, urban hippy, soulful boogiers, feeling like we're at church on a Friday night. "Not everyone understands house music, it's a spiritual thing, a body thing, a soul thing. …"

There's like this ebb and flow into zooming in and zooming out in terms of thinking about consciousness; that delicate dance between two people for whom race is everything, an obsession even. So if I were to think about our relationship and the ways that we navigate that, there's just this different level of conversation, where we don't need to constantly prove ourselves to each other around consciousness; there's a certain level of understanding already. It allows space to create intimacy, safety, the ability to talk about commonality without feeling like it's masking our differences. This idea of being able to transcend boundaries without it requiring us to be the same. And, I mean, who doesn't like dark chocolate. ... (*laughter*). ...

I have all of these cultural markers that have been with me since childhood—from dancing and music to code-switching and common histories. And so I can relate with a lot of those cultural markers with other folks of color from the South Side. That has always existed for me. It's been coming into consciousness about the way that white privilege in particular plays out in my life that's allowed me to have a different level of relationship and community with folks of color, and allowed me to step back a bit and see how it's part of a larger system. I think that's been instrumental in my relationships with people of color and across difference. *Acknowledge*.

Stacey: And your acknowledgment of white privilege. I remember meeting you and waiting to see if you were going to responsibly acknowledge your white privilege. I have watched lots of white folks declare their white privilege and then believe that declaration is both a simultaneous beginning and an end to racially responsible behavior and somehow all kinds of race-based retribution and redemption has taken place in that short amount of time. I guess it's important for a white person to acknowledge privilege, but, so what?! Such recognition is a first step. My hope for white folks, especially white women, is that they can interrogate themselves about white privilege and recognize:

1. that acknowledgment is not going to be as transcendent for others as it might be for them;
2. understand that acknowledgment of white privilege is an unwavering invitation to interrogate the white imagination and the white sense of existence. And to do that interrogation is not a bad thing. In fact, it's probably one of the healthiest, most important gifts a white person can give to herself: a careful interrogation of this thing called whiteness without the expectation for me to hold their hand.

Upon meeting you it was just so clear that you had done that crucial self-check without letting white shame, white guilt, and the embarrassment snatch the transformative moment. It was clear that you were not looking for me to exonerate you from your whiteness. That's another ever lurking shadow narrative where the person of color makes a white person "cool" by being that "friend of color"; meanwhile all kinds of deeply racialized dynamics are tumbling about them. I have seen that occur in many, many interracial friendships.

Jessica: I think I go through white guilt, shame, all those things. I've felt all those feelings before, but I've just learned how to move through them in different ways. I'm not so hung up on it, it doesn't feel debilitating like something that I allow very much space. ...

I think it's a really natural part of the process, so I'm not "anti" those things. I just think that when white folks start to dissect all of the ways that their life and their circumstances have nothing to do with their effort, not nothing, but much less than we're taught, that if they are sitting with enormity and violence of white supremacy that is perpetuated and grasping that they are somehow connected to us, it can be a really devastating realization for someone who is trying to be a thoughtful, reflective person in the world. So I think that guilt/shame is a natural reaction ... .

My cultural lens of the world has allowed me to process some white racial stuff very differently than I think white folks who are acculturated in all white spaces do. It's a different type of shock. But I think it can be debilitating when people focus on that. I know that for a lot of folks of color this whole white guilt or white fragility stuff produces frustration and anger, or even from other white people who are saying there's no space for that guilt. ... I disagree. White people need to be able to do it in their own antiracist affinity groups, versus relying on folks of color to hold and support them in that process. I don't think the guilt is avoidable and I don't want to poo-poo people's emotions. It's part of this identity thing and it's why white supremacy is horrible and so damaging to everybody. It's a matrix, it's everything that's around us, it is literally the air that we breathe. Asking people to step outside of the matrix and visualize/articulate it can be a life-changing experience for both the privileged and oppressed. There are so few spaces, besides the classroom space, where you do that. I'm also continually honored to call you my friend and imagine this sisterhood together, cause our world makes relationships like ours damn near impossible.

Stacey: And raised glass to you too, sis. Our kind of activism is always ablaze with complexity. That's why I always appreciate you knowing we need to dance big, cause none of this is small to us, or on us. I regret missing the dancing opportunities with you. It's cool though. Summer's coming. Find me a sweet DJ with a deep beat and let's go birth some more of these freedoms.

· 3 ·

"WHEN YOU DO IT TO ME, IT'S RACISM"

Robin DiAngelo

I am having lunch with my dear friend Deborah. We are catching up on various recent events when Deborah says, "Robin, I need to give you some feedback." My chest tightens slightly, but I try to stay open. "Okay, what's up?" I tentatively respond. "You are always talking over me. That is your racism." She replies. I am shocked.

> What? Wait a minute! I know it's a bad habit, but it has nothing to do with racism. I talk over everybody! I come from a big Italian family, and if you didn't interrupt people at the dinner table, you wouldn't get heard. It's just a cultural style! How can it be racism if I do it to everybody?
>
> Robin, when you do it to me the impact is racism. My whole life I have been interrupted and silenced by white people. You put me yet again in the position to have to fight for visibility. You not noticing or attending to that is part of what it means to be white.

I am a white woman. This chapter is based on a cross-racial friendship I have had with a Black woman—Deborah Terry-Hays—for over 20 years. I met Deborah when I was hired for a position as a diversity trainer. The position consisted of cofacilitating a series of mandatory trainings for State workers in the early 1990s. For several years Deborah and I were paired together. Over time, we became close friends. Using several transformative moments for me over the course of our friendship, I want to challenge the ideology of individualism and share a key learning: our identities are not separate from the white supremacist society in which we are raised. Thus, our patterns of cross-racial engagement are not merely a function of our unique personalities and must be challenged. The following three vignettes illustrate three key concepts connected to this point that I came to understand through my relationship with Deborah: how individualism functions to deny racism; why carefulness around people of color reinforces racism; and why relying on people of color alone to educate ourselves about racism is a form of colonialism.

Individualism

When Deborah told me over lunch that my talking over her was racist, I was taken aback. While I saw myself as sensitive to racism and understood that we are all socialized into racist patterns, I didn't understand how something that I did with everyone could be racist. Wasn't racism insensitive acts that white people did specifically to people of color? So I insisted that it was just my personality and because I do it to everyone, it couldn't be racism. She patiently explained to me that when I talk over a person of color, the impact of that behavior is different because we bring the racial history of our groups with us. While white people tend to see ourselves as individuals outside of race, people of color tend to see us as white people. Thus the meaning of cutting off or talking over a person of color is very different. In effect, I was saying to her, "I will not adapt to you or this context, I will continue to act the way I always act and you will have to adapt to me."

As I struggled to understand Deborah's feedback I came up against a deep feeling of unfairness. Why couldn't I be myself with Deborah? Wasn't acting differently around people of color racist? Did I actually have to watch everything I said and did? What did people of color want from us? Would they ever be satisfied? What was I supposed to do if Deborah was going to see racism everywhere!? Looking back, the irony is that it was me that was looking through a universal lens—the lens of Individualism.

What I came to understand through Deborah's feedback is that I was denying that we are products of our social and historical environment and that the past bears upon the present and the current conditions we find ourselves in. I was positioning myself as outside of culture and history, as if my interactions occurred in a sociohistorical vacuum. Yet to be able to think critically about the phenomenon of racism, we must be able to think sociohistorically about it. Insisting that our cross-racial behaviors are simply a function of our unique personalities falsely positions us outside of society. As a white person, my psychosocial development was inculcated in a white supremacist culture in which I am in the valued group. I was raised in a society that taught me that there was no loss in the absence of people of color; that in fact their absence was a good and desirable thing that should be sought and maintained. This has shaped every aspect of my identity and what I think of as my "self" or personality: my interests and investments, what I care about or don't care about, what I see or don't see, what I am drawn to and what I am repelled by, what I can take for granted, where I can go, how I think about myself and how others think about and respond to me, and what I can ignore.

I may be told by my parents that everyone is equal. I may have friends of color. I may never tell a racist joke. Yet I am still impacted by the forces of racism as a member of the society; I will still be seen as white, treated as white, and experience life as a white person. My identity, personality, interests, and investments will develop from a white perspective. In a society in which race clearly matters, our race profoundly shapes us, and if we want to challenge it, we have to make an honest accounting of how it manifests in our own lives and in the society around us. Although racism does of course occur in individual acts, *these acts are part of a larger system of interacting and interlocking dynamics*. The focus on myself as solely an individual prevented the personal, interpersonal, cultural, historical, and structural analysis necessary in order to challenge this larger system. Yes, this means I have to pay attention to how I am interacting with people of color.

Carefulness

Another example was brought home to me during a planning session for a workshop I would be cofacilitating with Deborah. One of the exercises we would be leading the group in was designed to illustrate the unavoidable internalization of stereotypes. In this exercise, participants are paired up, they choose a racial group that neither of them belongs to, and together they explore their stereotypes about the group.

In discussing this exercise with her, I shared my fear of accidently saying something racist. I told her I thought the goal was to be careful not to expose these stereotypes, thus surfacing them in this exercise seemed dangerous to me. What if loosening them up made it more likely I would blurt them out? Wasn't it better to be careful about the racist ideas in my head? For me and other whites who see ourselves as racially progressive, this was our worst fear—that we would accidently "say the wrong thing" and be perceived as racist. Thus, being careful to me meant being racially sensitive, which was my goal. She paused and looked at me for several moments and then said, "Robin … do you think we can't tell when you are being careful?" Chagrined, I had another fish-out-of-water moment. I suddenly felt uncovered as a white person. I realized that I expected my friend to see me as I saw myself—outside of race. I also had a sudden realization of what it must look like for people of color when whites are being careful around them. We look stiff, uncomfortable, uptight, and reserved. As I pictured myself being careful around people of color in this way, I also saw why they experienced that as racism. I certainly wasn't warm, relaxed, sincere, or open when I was being careful. If they watched me with my white friends, wherein I was relaxed and open, the contrast would be painful.

For me, this was a great example of my own unaware and unintended racism and made clear why people of color so often shared that whites were reserved and cold around them and how awful that felt. This behavior is rooted in racism in that we are acting differently around people of color. This difference in behavior can be attributed to factors such as segregation, fear of people of color, and not valuing our relationships with people of color enough to build comfort with them. My friend's question caused me to realize that while I needed to be thoughtful about what I said and not just spill forth every racist thought in my head, carefulness was not useful. I have come to realize that people of color expect us to make mistakes and are less concerned about that than about how we respond when these mistakes are pointed out, what we are willing to do to "clean them up," and what we learn from our mistakes and do differently in the future. This willingness to repair is what makes for authentic cross-racial relationships between women.

Racism is a very complex, multilevel system. There are no easy and concise answers or solutions to it. While we need to develop strategies for challenging racism, no single strategy will work in every situation, and some strategies, if taken to the extreme, can become nonconstructive. For example, thoughtfulness is an important strategy. Thoughtfulness can include being cognizant of the history we bring to racial encounters, being considerate about the language we use, being sensitive to group dynamics, and being attentive to our patterns and blind spots. But thoughtfulness taken to an extreme can become carefulness, in which we are so cautious about making a mistake or offending that we end up engaging disingenuously.

Colonialism

Deborah was involved in an organization committed to critical self-awareness. While this organization is primarily white, heterosexual, and middle class, they work hard to educate themselves on various aspects of oppression and their role in them. Deborah was a member in one of the organization's weekly study groups. She was the only person of color in the group of twelve. At some point, the group's facilitator, a white male, informed her that for the next week they would be studying racism and asked her if she would teach that session. She told him she needed to think about it, and then she called me, very distressed. She was torn: on the one hand she wanted to give them this information because they desperately needed it; on the other hand, to be the only person of color in the group and have to explain to them how racism manifested—both in general and in the group—was terrifying. In so doing, she risked experiencing many common white patterns: minimization, defensiveness, anger, objectification, invalidation, and white guilt. She decided that she would share her experience as a person of color if I would come with her and speak to the group—specifically as a white person—about white patterns of racism, since whites are generally more receptive to hearing about racism from other whites. My presence would also ensure that she had a trusted ally at her side. I agreed.

As the days passed and she prepared her presentation, she called me many times to vent her fear and anxiety. This request to teach an all-white group about racism took a tremendous toll on her. In addition to the emotional work she was doing, she spent hours preparing her presentation so that it was clear in a way that could be understood by white people, and was as indisputable as possible so it could not be negated. Being in front of an all-white group also triggered her internalized oppression—as a Black woman she had a lifetime of messages from schools, white teachers, and society at large that she was unintelligent and had no knowledge of intrinsic value.

Finally the evening came. The group listened thoughtfully and then asked questions and made comments. One member of the group stated—in a way somewhat critical of the organization—"I am so glad this organization is finally teaching us about racism. I have been waiting for them to do that." This statement triggered in me another fish-out-of-water moment in which I could see a cross-racial dynamic I had not seen before. I had watched the tremendous amount of emotional and intellectual work Deborah had done in order to make this presentation. Now, watching this group sitting comfortably on their chairs and effortlessly receiving Deborah's presentation, I saw a metaphor for colonialist relations (one more powerful group occupies the land of another and exploits and profits from the resources and work of the people of that land).

Sherene Razack (1998), writing about whiteness and the pattern of studying those who are seen as "different," states that, "The cultural differences approach reinforces an important ... cornerstone of imperialism: the colonized possess a series of knowable characteristics that can be studied, known, and managed accordingly by the colonizers whose own complicity remains masked" (p. 10). Using this metaphor, the group was in essence saying,

> We will observe you and seek to understand you. In doing so, we will relax while you work. You will provide us with the fruits of your labor. We will receive these fruits and consider them; we will decide what to keep and what to reject—what we deem worthy of consideration and what we don't. We thank the organization for bringing you to us, for we have desired your knowledge. But if you were not brought before us, we would not (as we have not up until now) expend any effort in seeking it for ourselves.

Further, this group member positioned this as a shortcoming of the organization rather than of himself, so that he also managed to elevate his own moral standing. Still, his credit went to the organization, not to Deborah. While I am quite sure that this is not what the person meant to say or do, I do think that his response illustrates the dynamics of internalized colonialism (or internalized dominance).

And what role did I play in all of this? This is the question I haven't wanted to ask myself. While I could clearly see the racial dynamics in the group's behavior, I wasn't asking what aspects of my own racism were reinforced for me. But looking back I realize that while it was painful for Deborah, I found it to be an "interesting" learning experience, one in which I was the "good" white person, there for my friend of color. I came away from that incident feeling proud of myself and how I had supported Deborah, and been equipped with new insights on how *other white people's* racism worked. And I had accrued this racial capital at Deborah's expense, for no matter how painful that experience was for her and what difference it might have made to her that I was there, I still received resources at the expense of her pain. I got to be the white savior, enacting my own form of colonialism.

I understand that Deborah asked me to support her in that particular way, and for me not doing so was not an option. But that does not put me outside of racism. And as I write this I realize that I never checked myself and my own racial arrogance in that situation. What might it have looked like if I had? I could have challenged the white superiority I felt as I watched the group interact with Deborah. I could have owned what was happening for me in that exchange. I could have checked in with Deborah afterward about how she perceived my engagement. But I did not do any of those things. Instead, on our ride home, I assumed *for myself* that she felt supported by me, and instead of asking, I proceeding to point out everything I noticed about what the white people in the group were doing. This had the effect of both reinforcing the racism for Deborah (in case she had missed any nuance of it I was making sure she noticed it all) while positioning me as the "smartest white person in the room"; the white person who "got it." I didn't give her much room to express any pain or disappointment she may have felt about aspects of my own enactments of racism.

In Conclusion

Perhaps the most powerful interruption of white supremacy is building authentic cross-racial relationships. As I hope is illustrated by these examples, that will never mean that your relationship is free of racism. So what does an authentic cross-racial relationship look like? It is long term, equal, and based on trust and commitment. The white person will not give up when things get hard. In other words, these relationships are not temporary, contextual (I have a coworker of color I hang out with at work), superficial (we don't talk about sensitive issues such as race), or easily dissolved when a conflict arises. I may be friendly with a coworker, but if they never come to my home, sit at my kitchen table, and break bread with me, as do my other friends, it is only a superficial friendship.

Authentic relationships cannot happen between people of unequal status—for example, between an employer and an employee. I have heard many white people refer to their housekeepers, nannies, and other employees of color as friends or "family." While great feelings of fondness and affection may exist in these relationships, they are not equal, due to the differential in power between employer and employee. This power differential is both implicit across race and explicit across status in that, as their boss, you have the power to dictate the rules and fire them at will. This power differential does not allow for full honesty or trust to develop; when someone depends upon you for their livelihood they are likely to be careful about what they say and do, and that limits the authenticity in your relationship.

Most white people are not socialized in ways that would make the building of authentic cross-racial relationships easy—I certainly wasn't. Segregation in schools and neighborhoods makes it unlikely for us to meet or form relationships with many people of color. Dynamics of internalized superiority—reinforced by the relentless racist messages in the culture around us—and the sense that cross-racial relationships are not valuable make it unlikely that we will seek them out. Whites rarely venture outside of their social circles in ways that would make cross-racial friendships more likely. When white people do have cross-racial relationships, they are often the result of a person of color entering their existing social circle. We may also notice that these friends tend to be of the same race—in other words primarily Asian or primarily Black. While this gives us some cross-racial exposure we might not otherwise have, it isn't the result of our doing anything to seek out these relationships; we aren't challenging any of the dynamics that keep us separate.

Building authentic cross-racial relationships usually requires that white people go beyond merely hoping that these relationships will happen. We have to interrupt the status quo of our daily lives and interactions. This will require getting out of our comfort zones, taking risks, challenging our racial apathy, and our sense of entitlement to racial comfort. But most importantly, developing authentic cross-racial relationships from an antiracist perspective includes developing the skills and perspectives that enable us to engage constructively with issues of race and racism. One of the most critical and intimate of these skills is the willingness to remain in the relationship when racial tensions arise (and if the relationship is authentic, racial tensions will occasionally arise). Over and over I have seen or heard of whites who give up at the first sign of racial tension, who walk away and blame the person of color: they were too sensitive; they overreacted; they have a personal problem. And over and over I have heard people of color talk about how painful it is when whites give up and walk away, using the privilege of individualism and universalism to insist the issue isn't about race.

In my early days doing this work, I dreaded getting feedback from Deborah on my racist patterns and assumptions. But now I welcome this feedback and I actually worry if I am not receiving it. Perhaps the most powerful lesson I have learned in building cross-racial relationships is that this feedback is a positive sign in the relationship. Of course, the feedback seldom feels good—I occasionally feel embarrassed or defensive. But I also understand that there isn't any way for me to avoid enacting problematic patterns, so if Deborah trusts me enough to take the risk and tell me, I am doing well overall. Further,

her feedback helps me see dynamics that are difficult to see on my own, and thereby I can continually grow; this is a gift. Many people of color have shared with me that they don't bother giving feedback to white people that they don't think can hear it; they either endure the microaggressions or drift away from the relationship. But they do not feel close to white people to whom they can't speak openly and honestly about racism, and these relationships always have a degree of distance and inauthenticity.

"Getting it," when it comes to race and racism, challenges our very identities as good white people. It's an ongoing and often painful process of seeking to uncover our socialization at its very roots. It asks us to rebuild this identity in new and often uncomfortable ways. But I can testify that it is also the most exciting, powerful, intellectually stimulating, and emotionally fulfilling journey I have ever undertaken. It has impacted every aspect of my life—personal and professional. I have a much deeper and more complex understanding of how society works, I am able to challenge much more racism in my daily life, and I have developed cherished and fulfilling cross-racial friendships I did not have before. Of course there are many nights when I go to bed feeling hopeless. But in a society that is infused with racism, even hope is political. If I give up because it's too hard or too big or because I believe it will never end, it still serves me as a white person; the impact of my hopelessness is not the same as that of a person of color's. White hopelessness ultimately protects racism if it keeps us from challenging it.

Reference

Razack, S. (1998). *Looking white people in the eye: Gender, race, and culture in courtrooms and classrooms.* Toronto: University of Toronto Press.

· 4 ·

FILIATION

Nelle Mills

To my Mother, who refuses to see (and maybe all white mothers raising black or brown children):

Mom, You don't see me. I can't pinpoint the exact moment, but at some-time along the way, I stopped becoming real to you, three dimensional. I wonder if you ever really saw me. After all, you always said I was so much like my dad you felt like you were fighting with him. I want you to see me, and I want to see you, more clearly than I do now. I don't know if it's because you fail to see me and my siblings as Black or because you refuse to recognize your own privilege as a white woman. Whatever the reason, I am becoming unrecognizable to you. Like a transition shot in a student film, every time you see me, I become more and more blurry.

I have to write to you because words between us are like dynamite. I don't know how many more fights I can recover from. How quickly words between us turn to rockets launched with no direction. Quiet is not possible with you. I have tried biting my tongue until I taste only copper and hate. I love you, but I love me more and that is why I can't allow you to say and do things I would never tolerate from any other person, particularly any other white person. You have made me feel hopeless and in the process became a symbol. If you, you who have five Black children, who have fallen in love with Black men, aren't fighting for Black lives and even worse, are the antagonist, then who does care. You make me feel as if it is impossible for a white person to be completely antiracist. The suspicion of white people, particularly those that would name themselves antiracist or allies comes from you. How is it so easy for them? What is their investment? Are they lying? Am I missing something huge and glaring? Somehow, if I just found the right Tim Wise article to send you or gift you that one bell hooks book for Christmas, you would come around. But you haven't come around. I wonder if that's even a possibility.

Mom, you would probably be surprised to hear this, but you're on my mind a lot. Some days, when sadness grips me while my alarm beeps, I make the decision to stay in bed and call in sick. I choose to spend the day reading or writing or crying or watching Netflix or sleeping or reading my tarot. I realize that you never had that choice. You could not just decide to call off work, stay in bed, and get to know yourself a little better. You never had the chance to sit quietly with yourself. You never had that stillness. By the time you were my age, you had four Black girls, three jobs and a largely unsupportive family. Your life was no longer a mystery. You were so young; I don't know that it ever was.

Thank you. I think you're a fucking warrior for continuing to choose what you wanted to do, when everybody else in your life—your father, our father was telling you that you couldn't handle *another* (Black) child. You made that choice five times knowing the brutal struggle, the sleepless nights, the bouncing checks and familial isolation this would cost. You made that choice. And I think you're a warrior not because "it was the right thing to do," but because I cannot imagine my life void of my siblings. Without them, I would be hopelessly lost.

The resentment is expected. Natural, even. Before I was eight, I realized the inevitable resentment you carried for us. The regret, "what if" questions you must have asked yourself. Sometimes you would tell us to our face, paint a picture of what your life could look like if we weren't in it—as if we were mistakes to be edited out in the next draft. And I'm sorry. Sorry you never had the chance to decide to leave, move somewhere else, travel somewhere else or try somewhere else. You never had the option of flight like I have.

It makes sense you decided to return home after you realized my father was good for little more than giving you children. I understand the need for safety, comfort, security—and can only imagine the heightened need for those things when you have four little girls and a no-good man, who will inevitably leave. Is that why you kept us in Youngsville for so long? In that small small town?

Your comfort, unfortunately, meant our otherness. Our lives as shipwrecked aliens who were captured and put on display, with no warning. Every day felt like a blinding sea of whiteness. I know you were working, rarely home. Do you have any idea the battles that we had to fight? That getting on the school bus felt like walking between active gunfire. I know we told you. All the times we were called nigger on the school bus, in the lunch line, during Sunday school. I know we told you about the times we were followed home, high beams flashing, making every turn we did until we cut through a neighbor's yard. I know we told you about the mean old babysitters who rubbed our noses in their dirty, pissy carpet if we had an accident while taking a nap, like we were puppies to be trained. I know we told you how everybody else at the party got hats and cake, except us. And I don't know if the older we got, the feelings became harder to describe or if they just became more normal, no longer news. At some point though, we stopped telling you.

I don't know if this ever happens to you, but when I try and explain Youngsville, people can't believe such a place still exists. People think I'm lying when I say that we were the only people of color for several counties. People shake their heads when I say it was an everyday occurrence to see an Amish on horse and buggy, but if a Black person came to town, everybody would turn and look and whisper and question their motives. Today, when you talk about our childhood you describe a very idyllic, bucolic little town. You refuse to hear us, challenge our stories even. You demand receipts, tell us we are exaggerating and gaslight us into thinking we are making it all up. It's a good thing I have diligently kept a journal since I was eight years old. It's a good thing I still have every single one of them, in a stack nearing three feet. My past is not malleable and my journals guarantee I have a record untainted by memory and time.

October 13, 1998: Youngsville, PA, age 8. Something is wrong with me. Cody asked me why I was brown but my mom is white. I don't know why either. I am supposed to be halfwhite but I don't see white anywhere except my feet and hands.

February 12, 2000: Youngsville, PA, age 11. I fucking hate slavery. I hate learning about it in school. I hate watching those stupid movies. I hate when the teacher uses me as an example. I hate being Black. Everybody looks at me. Jake said today that picking cotton didn't look so hard to him. I wanted to punch him. I was sitting right next to him but I acted like I didn't hear him. The next time he says something, I'm going to hit him.

Imagine it, Mom, your whole life you not seeing anybody who looks like you, except your sisters. Imagine being given this visible mark, visible difference with no explanation at all. Yet, you are the sole representative. For the majority of my life, my Blackness felt like this impossible puzzle I was tasked to solve with only a few hints here and there. Why did you provide us with so few hints? Why did you never talk about it? I felt wrong 100% of the time. Whether I was in school, at dance class, in the grocery store, even at home, I felt wrong.

Even when the smell of magnolias lured you to South Carolina the summer I turned thirteen, that feeling of wrongness transformed but never disappeared. You brought us down South with very little warning. I had no idea what to expect. After living my whole life in a town whose population was less than 1,000 people, Florence, with a population around 40,000, felt massive. It might as well have been New York. And I'll be honest, Mom, I was drowning. I was breathing in water and you didn't even notice. You were busy with work and your new boyfriend.

Moving South changed us all radically, that is undeniable. I am so grateful you made the choice to leave Youngsville before I entered high school, before I was swallowed up whole by insecure white teenagers, ready to use my identity for batting practice. The year that we moved to the South, is maybe when I can pinpoint the moment I started to become blurry and out of focus to you. When we stopped speaking to each other tenderly and only mumbled or yelled. Looking back now, I think you were drowning too, learning too. If that is true, I'm sorry I didn't recognize that.

I did recognize other things. You started celebrating my sister's and my light skin, our longer hair, "proper speech." You worked hard to make sure we were set apart from the other Black girls. That we knew we were better. Even though we lived in the same trailer park, took the same classes and stood in the same "free lunch" line, we were better. You did everything you could to remind people that we were half white. I remember getting written up for one thing or another in the eighth grade. I brought it home for you to sign and you were more outraged that they put Black on the write-up slip than whatever infraction was listed. You demanded that they change my race to white. Even at thirteen, I saw that for what it was: a shallow attempt for them to see me as white. To see me different from the other Black girls. If I was Black, I deserved the write-up. If I was white, there would be leniency, phone calls instead of write-ups. You were attempting to transfer your white privilege to me. Attempting to erase any trace of Blackness that betrayed you. Do you remember what I told you then? *The teachers don't see me as white, so it doesn't matter what the paper says.*

That's when we begin to fight. Physically. You did not like who I was becoming and I did not like you. Ironic that in public, at school, you demanded we be classified as white, yet when we argued, you had no problem reminding me what I am. What I already knew to be true: I'm nothing more than a nigger.

I'm not going to ask you, because you have no idea how that feels. Do you know that a white person saying that word literally elicits a physical reaction from me? That when said with hatred and aimed like a loaded gun at a person, I feel electrocuted. I feel shocked. I feel like my body is filled with the rage of an angry bull watching a matador practice behind a closed gate. It fills me with a killing rage toward whoever has delivered that verbal blow. Do you know how it feels to feel that toward your own mother? Sometimes I wonder if I am absurd for continuing to love you, to passively forgive you. There is no other white person in the world whom I would have forgiven.

Chosen family will ask me, how could I forgive you? How could I still see you after that? And my answer is always the same: My little brother is ten. If I stop talking to her, I stop talking to him too.

And I guess, this is the reason I am writing you this letter in the first place: Joshua. When you told us you were pregnant, we were furious. All we could think about was ourselves. How this was disrupting our lives. Hadn't we lived fifteen years, just us? Then he was born and we all dropped our weapons, took off the armor and banded together around our baby brother. He was our little peace offering to one another, he brought us all together in our collective need to protect and care for him. But he's not a child anymore. He's nearly ten. When he was younger, my sisters and I protected him, raised him. Now, we are all grown and he is alone.

I see you, pushing him toward whiteness, becoming angry if he calls himself Black and not biracial. I can only hope your fights do not escalate to the levels that ours did. You cannot protect him from white supremacy. Have you seen the news? I'm sure you've seen the images of his body, splayed on the ground by now. I'm sure you've seen his picture, plastered all over the news, the papers—there is no escaping that a boy was lynched in America today. I know you've seen it, because here in Mexico City, I've seen it. His face is on the front page of papers here. American coverage playing over quick commentary on the 13-inch TV in the corner store by my house. Students at UNAM are talking about it. The friends I've made, asking me in slow Spanish so that I can understand, "Vi las noticias. Estas bien?" and my reply needs no translation: No.

I'm not okay. I feel sick. I feel like I want to get on the next plane out of here, run straight from the tarmac to your house and run up straight up the stairs to Josh's room and just hold him in my arms and keep him safe and never let him go.

Did you know that every 28 hours a Black person is killed in this country by police, security guards, or another vigilante? Every 28 hours. And you can teach Joshua that he's mixed, refuse to cut his curly hair and force him into soccer and Boyscouts all that you want to. You can demand he wear a sign around his neck that says, "I AM A HALF WHITE," and still the world will see him as Black. Because the thing is, people already have their mind made up as to who Joshua is, who Trayvon was, before they even open their mouths. You can teach him all the right things to say, but what happens when they shoot him before he gets a word out?

You're probably rolling your eyes right now, if you're even still reading this. I know you're sick of hearing me by now. I know you dread when I come home and the topic veers toward politics, race, or police. I know because I dread them too. I dread when words catch fire and cause physical pain. When you turn into a defensive frat boy at a bar who just said something racist or touched my hair. For a long time I projected my feelings toward you onto all white people. You became a symbol for me. If I couldn't even make you care about the liberation of Black people, I sure as hell couldn't make other white people. I put in work. I bought you books, wrote you letters, choked down my rage and listened to you say things like, "it's only a word. You've called me a bitch after all." And years pass and every victory I celebrate with you is quickly snatched. To be honest, I feel pretty hopeless right now. When I realized that my mother, who raised five Black children, couldn't even care, there's no way in hell those other random white folks do.

You remain one of the most difficult puzzles in my life. You make me wonder if it's even possible to love through white supremacy. I am unapologetically Black and that is not going to change. That is fixed, not malleable. My ancestors saw that for me before you did. I love you, Mom, and I don't want to leave you behind, but I will continue to fight for Black lives, for my life until I can't anymore. I will not stop until liberation, and I will fight anybody who stands in the way of that. Even you. This was my last attempt, I hope you've seen me.

Love, your daughter Nelle.

· 5 ·

THE SUPPORT I NEED

Liza A. Talusan

As a professional who works in diversity, equity, and inclusion education, my daily work calls me to be both provocative yet hospitable, risk-taking yet careful, patient yet outspoken. As you can imagine, balancing and navigating this world and work creates a great deal of tension. There are days when my emotional and intellectual pendulum swing so far left and right that I lose sight of center. And, at the center of this emotional journey is my own complicated experiences of identity as a woman of color, as an Asian American, and as a product of a predominantly white environment.

Over my lifetime, I have traveled a twisted road toward embracing my racial and ethnic identity. I was born in the United States to immigrant parents, two young doctors from the Philippines who moved across the globe to begin a new life filled with hopes of opportunity and promise. Though they landed in Boston and spent the first few years in a predominantly Black neighborhood and community, my parents were socialized to believe that the suburbs were the ideal place to raise a family. Within four years of their arrival in the United States, after working double shifts and alternating work schedules, my parents moved my sisters and me from our racially diverse apartment building to a predominantly white suburb twenty-two miles outside of Boston. Though I spent the first formative years of my life living among people who looked like my family, I spent tumultuous adolescent years in the suburbs trying to fit in.

See, for most of my life, I wanted to be white. I hated my brown skin, my almond-shaped eyes, and my straight black hair. Instead of embracing my identity, I spent my developmental years perfecting the spiral perm and crimped hairstyle of the late 1980s. I experimented with fake tanning lotion, not because I needed to darken my already brown skin but because all of my white friends were saving up their babysitting earnings on beauty products to make themselves look darker. I borrowed my friend's green mascara. I arched blue eyeshadow over my lids. And, in the summer, I used a hair bleaching product—one that came in a white spray bottle with a picture of the happiest blond woman I had ever seen—that made my friend's hair the color of sunshine but turned my black hair into a Halloween-like shade of orange. I dated white boys. I fell in love with white movie stars. I taped pictures of beautiful white women next to my mirror so I could imitate their makeup tricks. I joked along with my peers who made fun of the nerdy foreign exchange Asian character in our favorite movies, the one who never got the girl and was only invited to the party so others could poke fun of him.

I was always trying to get on their level; I was always trying to be one of them. I never thought about racial diversity growing up in my Irish and Italian suburb. I never had to. My goal was simple—try to be white.

But, college was different. College was an awakening. On move-in day, my family helped to shuffle my suitcase, computer, and desk supplies from our 1989 Chevy van into my basement dorm room. My parents and I took turns carrying bedding and desk supplies from the parking lot to my new room. Whenever my dad, who is best described as a man of few words, and I were alone, he blurted out different gems of advice like, "Always walk with a friend" or "Don't go out late at night" or "You are here to study, not to have fun." I waited until he left before I opened up my beer-filled backpack and arranged the cans neatly in my mini-fridge.

When my parents left, I was alone. After living nearly eighteen years with five brothers and sisters, being alone was something I had never truly experienced. I needed to find a friend, someone to talk to or meet.

Soon enough, I heard someone walking down the hallway toward my room. I hopped off of my regulation-sized twin bed, peeked my head outside of the door, and was surprised by the woman standing across from me. She had long, black curly hair that fell halfway down her back; dark brown skin; and a book bag so overstuffed with binders that the top zipper was praying to make it through the day. "Oh, hi," she said. "I'm Seema. I live next door." From that moment on, Seema and I were inseparable.

With Seema, I talked about race every day. We stayed up late at night, dipping salty, curly french fries into disposable paper cups filled with ketchup. We talked about our romantic relationships and bonded over common things people said to us in high school about "being good at math" or "about being so American." Seema introduced me to Ericka, her roommate, an African American woman from Hartford. And, Ericka introduced me to a dozen other Black women who hung out in our residence hall.

Within a week of moving into college, my entire friend group was women of color. I craved their company, our conversations, and the ease with which we connected with one another. I knew that despite our different ethnic and racial backgrounds, I felt supported and guided by this group.

While my in-dorm group of friends was all women of color, most of my friends outside of dorm life were white. I took classes with mostly (all) white students, sang in an acapella group with mostly (all) white students, and served on student government with mostly (all) white students. These spaces were familiar to me. In many ways, they felt like home. But, as I dove into my identity as a woman of color, I began to feel less connected to the culture of whiteness and began to resent the absence of people of color in my school environment.

Around my senior year of college, I learned, on my own, more about communities of color, my own people, and my Asian American identity. I read and reread Ronald Takaki's *Strangers from a Different Shore* (1998) and Howard Zinn's *A People's History of the United States* (1990) until their bindings began to break. I read fiction by Asian American writers and nonfiction works like *Yell-Oh Girls!* by Vickie Nam (2001). I threw myself into literature that showed me how white supremacy kept me from learning about other communities of color. And, I got angry.

By the end of college, I grew angry with white culture. I felt angry at whiteness and systems that kept whiteness in place. I began to feel cheated out of a curriculum and an education that never taught me about my cultural heritage. I began to resent that I had such a strong desire to be white for so many years. I was angry that no one in that circle of whiteness had told me it was okay to be me—to be Asian American-me. I was angry that I had, for so long, missed out on learning about Asian Americans who shaped our communities while I was so busy laughing at the nerdy foreign-exchange student character in the movies.

As an act of self-preservation, I decided that I would only surround myself with people of color. I found it protective, affirming, and necessary. I avoided spaces, as best I could, where I would have to socialize with white people and kept my relationships mostly superficial. I chose a graduate school in New York City where I knew I would interact with a diverse group of people, and that many of those people would be people of color. But, then, I met Missy.

I didn't want to like Missy. Missy reminded me of my childhood. She reminded me of the white girl I always wanted to be: liked by everyone, visible in every space she entered, and heard by everyone. And, yes, she was blond.

I kept Missy at arm's length, even though we were in the same graduate school classes and socialized with a similar group of people. I wasn't ready to be friends with her; I wasn't ready to be friends with her because she was white. But I grew to learn that Missy was fierce.

I soon noticed that Missy stood out wherever she went because, frankly, she was the only white woman in a sea of Black and Brown friends. I began to notice that the majority of her friends were people of color, and she had immersed herself in predominantly Black spaces. She led workshops on race and racism, and she deeply engaged in conversations about injustice.

But, most meaningful to me was that Missy was the first person I met who was aware of her whiteness. She named her whiteness. She knew she was white, and she knew what it meant to benefit from whiteness.

Despite all of this, I was slow to get to know her. Could I trust her as a white woman? *Could I trust her to have conversations with me that were genuine about race? Could I trust that she wouldn't say, "You sound so American" or "Could you help me with these statistics?" Could I trust that she'd understand that my own identity was complicated?* I could. And, I did.

As the years went by, Missy and I explored issues of social justice, leadership, and intergroup dialogue together. We sought out professional opportunities that opened doors in these fields, and we also supported each other through our own personal growth. After graduate school, Missy and I traveled separate paths. Over the next few years, Missy's career continued to soar. She sent me books that she had published—all of them about race, identity, and empowerment. She collaborated with strong women, many of whom were women of color and scholars of color, who intellectually pushed the boundaries of education, race, and gender.

Missy was the first person I knew who acted on being an ally to people of color. I identified her as an ally to me. Through Missy, I began to trust that there were white people who were committed to social justice. I began to trust white scholars invested in racial equity. I allowed myself to see white people who were willing to do the work around dismantling race and racism. Of course, as with any generalization, sometimes I was disappointed. Sometimes I thought an individual was down for the cause, only to hear microaggressive comments or a denial of systemic oppression.

Though Missy and I were no longer in daily, weekly, monthly, or even yearly communication, I still held others—people who are white—to a standard that Missy had shown me was possible. Our friendship highlighted what I needed: I needed people who are white to understand race; I needed people who are white to talk openly about race, to acknowledge that race informs a real experience; I needed people to listen to understand, and not hear to argue; I needed people who understood that whiteness meant something in our country, and that there are benefits that are given to those who are white; I needed people who were white to understand that I had spent much of my life trying to be like them, trying to benefit from skin that looked like theirs, and trying to pretend that my own race was not an issue.

My relationship with Missy allowed me to be open to the idea that I could trust women who are white. But she also set a high bar for what kind of vulnerability I was willing to share. While our friendship opened my heart to develop close friendships with white women, that same bar also kept me from developing meaningful relationships with white women. And, as our society continued to grapple with the tension of race and racial tensions, I grew even more protective of my identity as a woman of color. Patricia came into my life at the height of this distrust.

My relationship with Patricia never indicated that we would be friends. As the director of a multicultural affairs office, I was charged with supporting our on-campus Gender Equity center. Patricia was a prominent professor and scholar in gender studies. Knowing Patricia's scholarly work, I had emailed her for support. I heard nothing. I reached out to invite her for advice. No response. I asked around about her, and others responded that she was very into her scholarship and didn't get involved much in campus life.

My distrust of white women allowed me to easily categorize her as "the white woman who will do gender-related scholarship about white women but who didn't participate in intersectional feminism." Basically, I figured she was a white feminist for white feminists. So, I moved on.

Over the years, I developed our college's first Safe Zone training, an educational and interactive workshop to raise the level of understanding about the broad experiences of the LGBTQ community. In order to receive one of the Safe Zone cards, one had to attend a campus workshop and talk about what it meant to be a safe-space community. The workshop came and went, and I had never heard from Patricia.

On November 17, 2010, the night before my bilateral mastectomy, a major operation that would keep me out of work for almost two months but that would save my life from cancer, I received an email from Patricia. She was not happy. My first introduction to her would be this email. She chastised me, though we had never met, about not being truly inclusive in my approaches to safe spaces. Actually, her email said much worse things, but that was the basic understanding. I tried to respond as best I could, but my anxiety was building as my surgery was just a few hours away. "Serves me right for checking work email," I kept thinking.

Three days later, when I finally emerged from the morphine fog of my newly removed and newly reconstructed chest, I saw an email from Patricia. I assumed it was a continuation of how divisive I was being.

Instead, it was an apology. It was filled with words of humility, of regret for her behavior, of her embarrassment, and her reassurance that she was here if I needed her and available for anything. It was an acknowledgment of privilege, of power, and of misstep. And, I began to let her into my world.

A few months later, Patricia invited me on her radio show where we talked about feminism and Spring Break safety. Soon after that, she released (another) book and I posted a picture of my daughter carrying it. As the posts on Facebook progressed, we began sharing how much we admired each other. We exchanged words of encouragement. Just five months after our first Facebook posts to each other, she wrote, "Liza Talusan, I was telling my husband last night at dinner that you are one of my very favorite people on the planet ... that you are as courageous and alive as a person can be ... We all have hard days, sometimes too many, feel what you feel, be kind to yourself and enjoy all there is to enjoy. Your prodded gal-pal! Xo" We began to share posts about music, about our favorite authors, and our families.

Then, we started to share posts about race. I had a moment. I had a moment where I thought, "Oh, no. Is this it? Is this where we will have to stop being friends? Will we have to tiptoe around the race issue?" No.

We began to exchange posts and conversations about racialized feminism. As a white woman, Patricia really dove deep into intersectionality and constantly critiqued her own privilege. She not only talked about it, but she wrote about it. She willingly put herself out there into spaces that are not always friendly to women of color. She allied. She was an advocate. She was my friend.

In the midst of my doctoral program, when I was struggling to make sense of my methodology and my theoretical framework, Patricia sent me books (ones she coauthored or authored, of course) and made time and space for me to ask questions, to work through concepts, and to make progress. When I was contemplating a serious move, Patricia sat and listened to me, quietly and carefully. And, when my decision ran contrary to her opinion, she supported me. She asked about my identity as a woman, as a mother, as a partner, and as a woman of color. She intentionally opened up dialogues about race and about the impact of race.

Both Missy and Patricia are two of many people with whom I can have honest conversations about race. But they are two of only a small number of white women with whom I am willing to have honest conversations about race. I know that they hold my racial identity, racism, and my complicated experiences in a world that wasn't built for me in their hearts. They have consistently privileged my identity (identities) even when white supremacy has taught them that they don't have to consider me. They have worked on their whiteness and have not given up on that journey. And, most importantly to me, they ask how they can support me. They ask how they, as white allies, can support what I identify as a need. They follow my lead. They listen. They are present.

I wish I could say that my heart is open to all friendships, to all relationships, and to all humanity. But that would be a lie. My heart has been broken in the past. My trust has been stolen. And, my willingness to put myself out there has diminished. I don't blame the many white women who have come and gone into and out of my life. I know that white supremacy has played a major role in those relationships. I'm well aware of how systemic racism has shaped our interactions, our shared spaces, and our abilities to work and live together. Some days, I can convince myself to be bigger than the chasm that white supremacy has created; other days, I simply submit to it.

Recently, I had the opportunity to work in community with a racially diverse group of social justice educators. The group was predominantly white people with a few people of color. We had come together to explore the school-to-prison pipeline and the criminal injustices that communities of color disproportionately faced. I felt myself fall into old habits of judging the intentions of white people in this space. In this large group, some affirmed those old feelings of anger; but yet others affirmed that my heart was safe with my fellow group mates.

One night, during some down time, I realized I was the only person of color in a group of white educators. They were talking about white fragility and the impact on people of color. I wasn't sure, at that time, if I wanted to be invisible or if I wanted to dive into the conversation. I could feel those old, tense feelings of trust and mistrust surface.

That's when I heard her voice. A white woman whom I had kept at arm's length, leaned over and whispered, "How can I be of support right now?" I simply looked over and smiled. I didn't speak a word, but I felt myself warm to a new opportunity to open my heart.

References

Nam, V. (2001). *Yell-oh girls!: Emerging voices explore culture, identity, and growing up Asian American*. New York, NY: Harper Perennial

Takaki, R. T. (1998). *Strangers from a different shore: A history of Asian Americans*. Boston, MA: Little, Brown.

Zinn, H. (1990). *A people's history of the United States*. New York, NY: Harper & Row.

· 6 ·

MARGINAL FRIENDSHIP

An Exploration of Culture, Privilege, and Sisterhood

Jodi Van Der Horn-Gibson and Christina Marín

And of course I am afraid, because the transformation of silence into language and action is an act of self-revelation, and that always seems fraught with danger. But ... tell them about how you're never really a whole person if you remain silent, because there's always that one little piece inside you that wants to be spoken out. ...

    —Audre Lorde, from *Sister, Outsider: Essays & Speeches*

Mise-en-Scène

The sounds of a restaurant are heard— people talking, dishes clanging, and soft music.

Two women, one Latina and one white, sit at a table at IHOP. They prepare to eat the food just given to them.

JODI
(shaking her head)
I can't do this anymore. I just can't do this.

Christina reaches across the table for the syrup.

CHRISTINA

Can't do what?

JODI

I don't think I can do this research, Christina. It's so awful. It's so heavy.

> *Christina pauses, then covers her*
> *pancakes in maple syrup.*

CHRISTINA

What do you mean?

> *Christina takes a bite of her pancakes.*

JODI

My research. I find myself sifting through these images just crying. I have these auction catalogs with stuff from the turn of the century—this racist kitsch is appalling, Tia. I'm looking at framed pictures and postcards of lynchings, little children used as alligator bait, and the most hideous racist figurines. Who collects this stuff? I mean, people hold auctions for this stuff online.

> *Christina almost chokes on her pancakes and*
> *quickly reaches for her iced coffee. She takes a long swig.*

CHRISTINA

Now that's ironic!

JODI

I'm serious! It's so awful. I sit at the computer and just cry.
(she groans)
Can't I do something easier?

> *Christina takes another bite of her pancakes.*

CHRISTINA

No.

JODI
(laughs)

Ok. Thanks.

Pause.
Jodi takes a drink of her coffee.

JODI

I'm serious.

CHRISTINA

So am I. But I'm curious about what you mean by easier. Like how I thought grad school at ASU was going to be easier?

JODI

What do you mean?

CHRISTINA

When I was researching universities I made a point to look into the percentage of Latinos at each one. I was really excited that ASU had over 12%—being in double digits is a big deal for us. But then I got here and realized that 12% of over 50,000 is only 6,000 … 6,000 students spread out across departments and programs. So basically it feels just as white as my undergrad in the Midwest. It's not easy sitting in classes and not having someone to turn to that I can identify with. And let's face it, no one in this program really wants to talk about race.

Silence as they eat their food.

JODI

Honestly though. As a white chick, should I be writing about this … should I even be talking about race? Aren't people going to resent me?

CHRISTINA

Probably … some will. Both white people and people of color. You have to be okay with that.

Jodi sighs and stirs her coffee.
Pause.

CHRISTINA (CONT.)

I mean, sure. You could do something easier; but then you'd be just like all those other white people who refuse to engage in truly critical dialogue because it's too "uncomfortable." What I love about our conversations is that we talk about the uncomfortable; and we challenge each other to look deeper. When I came here I thought I would find more people who looked like me. This place is *la frontera*! I figured there'd be others who could speak to what I was discovering about my own identity. I never guessed it would be a white girl.

They laugh.
Pause.

JODI

So I just have to get comfortable being uncomfortable.

CHRISTINA

Welcome to my world.

JODI

Right.

CHRISTINA

But seriously … close your eyes.

Jodi complies.
Christina reaches into her bag and pulls out
her worn-out copy of This Bridge Called My Back *(Anzaldúa, 1983).*

Keep them closed and just listen: "No nos podemos quedar paradas con los brazos cruzados en medio del puente. ..."

Christina notices Jodi peeking through
one eye half open.

JODI

Um ... I don't speak Spanish, remember?

Christina gives her a scolding look.

CHRISTINA

M'ija! Cierra tus ojos! Just listen to the words of Gloria Anzaldúa.

Jodi shuts her eyes.
Christina continues.

CHRISTINA (CONT.)

"We can't afford to stop in the middle of the bridge with arms crossed. ... We are beginning to realize that we are not wholly at the mercy of circumstance, nor are our lives completely out of our hands. That if we posture as victims we *will* be victims, that hopelessness is suicide, that self-attacks stop us in our tracks. We are slowly moving past the resistance within, leaving behind the defeated images. We have come to realize that we are not alone in our struggles nor autonomous but that we—white black straight queer female male—are connected and interdependent. We are each accountable for what is happening down the street, south of the border or across the sea. And those of us who have more of anything: brains, physical strength, political power, spiritual energies, are learning to share them with those that don't have. We are learning to depend more and more on our own sources for survival, learning not to let the weight of this burden, the bridge, break our backs" (pp. iv–v).

Jodi opens her eyes. They sit in silence.
Christina takes another bite of her pancakes
as Jodi continues to stir her coffee.

JODI

That's good stuff.

Christina smiles.

Discomfort Is Revelatory: Cross-Cultural Relationships

At a presidential rally on February 6, 2016, former Secretary of State Madeleine Albright remarked that "there is a special place in hell for women who don't support other women" (Rappeport, 2016). While the intent of her comment was meant to encourage women to support Hillary Clinton's run for the presidency in the 2016 election, Madam Albright hits on a very real issue—the general narrative is that women have a difficult time supporting and, as this volume will unpack, befriending other women. Adding onto this the reality that women come in all colors, shapes, and sizes increases the probability that relationships with other females can be a challenge.

As we came together to write this chapter, we reflected on the beginning of our friendship and how far we've come together. Looking back on this conversation in IHOP—and oh, the irony of it taking place at the *International House of Pancakes* is not lost on us—we were reminded not only how we have helped each other grow as artists, teachers, and scholars, but how we have also supported each other as sisters, even as we faced challenges. Sitting at that table with Christina was a truly crystallizing moment for me because in speaking with her, I was able to voice my frustration, fear, and anxiety about being a white voice in a conversation about color. And as I looked across the table at Jodi, I realized it didn't matter that she wasn't a woman of color looking at the world from a similar perspective, because she opened up a whole different point of view for me that enriched my understanding of identity. She challenged my perception about how white people talk and think about race and privilege. Christina directly challenged my white guilt, not allowing me to put my head in the sands of white privilege which so often grant people an escape from engaging in dialogues about race. As Peggy McIntosh (1989) reminds us:

> To redesign social systems, we need to first acknowledge their colossal unseen dimensions. The silences and denials surrounding privilege are the key political tool here. They keep the thinking about equality or equity incomplete, protecting unearned advantage and conferred dominance by making these taboo subjects. (p. 4)

While the moment may not seem as revelatory as other intercultural experiences, it was sitting at IHOP in Tempe, Arizona, where I was faced with a fork in the road: do I continue? Or do I look away toward what would be more comfortable? What would be "easier?" Christina listened to me, loved me, and pushed back, not letting me off the hook for one second; my emotional response couldn't be the reality in which I stayed. To be able to do something or to say something, the reality of the legacy of racism I stared at couldn't be about how it made *me* feel. The focus had to be on saying something about it that didn't center on my emotional response to it but rather to the injustice itself.

Long before that one afternoon at IHOP—and believe me there were many—Jodi had awakened in me a sense of solidarity that I hadn't felt in our doctoral program until then. She wasn't afraid to ask difficult questions, she didn't shy away from conversations that engaged in critical race theory, she led discussions that unpacked the cultural hegemonic discourse and imagined a world which was turned on its head; she inspired me at every turn to dig deeper, think harder, and question even the best intentions. I admit, there were times when I may have looked for a hidden camera or two over my shoulder, as this white woman spoke so eloquently about race and class structures, often explaining to me the intricacies of some of the dense theory we were reading in class (until I read Gloria Anzaldúa, of course, and the veil was lifted from my eyes and I could see things through this new lens I could call my own). Until I met Jodi, all of those white European theorists seemed to be talking in circles and saying much the same thing. And then we were introduced to Paulo Freire, bell hooks, Anzaldúa, Audre Lorde, Gayatri Spivak, and so many more we were to discover along the way.

The fact of the matter is that graduate school is often a place where we find ourselves competing against one another for the next scholarship, the next publication opportunity in a journal, or the next conference paper acceptance. It is no wonder that, while some friendships developed in high school or college withstand decades of separation, relationships that form in the pressure cooker of graduate school don't often survive the tests of time and distance. In the present moment, while studying for comprehensive exams or sharing articles and resources for classes, the strong network of support in graduate school can mean the difference between successfully completing the degree and/or losing your mind. However, the final looming arena of competition known as the job market makes it nearly impossible to graduate with your best friend. Layer onto all of this the issues of difference, inclusion and diversity initiatives, affirmative action, and limited seats, graduate school can often be seen as *The Hunger Games* for adults.

But we found a strong alliance almost immediately in graduate school and took to writing together in order to unpack and process some of the pedagogical encounters we were having. In 2004, our first coauthored article was published in *STAGE of the Art*, a journal published by the American Alliance for Theatre & Education. "Toward a Collaborative Praxis: Our ArtsBridge Experience" was written in direct response to questions that we raised after an eye-opening experience we shared. The piece opens:

> As a university level educator, how do you facilitate a conversation when a student comments: "I know that racism used to be a problem, but ever since that thing during the 60s, it hasn't been a problem anymore" in a *theatre for social change* class. Is it possibly too late to foster a change of attitude, a transformation of perceptions in our already socialized college-aged learners? (Marín & Gibson, 2004, p. 9)

If each of us had gone off to our respective computers and tried to write an article about this moment alone, we would have missed out on the rich collaborative praxis that often helps us navigate problematic moments in our practice that just don't seem to make sense. As we write together we seem to finish each other's sentences and ask the questions the other might be afraid to ask. We give one another permission to make mistakes and push each other to challenge the assumptions other people make about us as individuals. While neither one of us can remember the precise moment our solidarity took root, we realized that we could complement each other rather than feeding into the competitive nature of grad school. We discovered an intercultural, dialogic point of view, and planted the seeds for the fruitful academic/artistic partnership we have been nurturing for over a decade. We believe one reason we have been able to avert the challenges of most interracial friendships stems from our acceptance that our individual versions of the world are incomplete without the reflection the other reveals.

Perhaps it's not surprising that this friendship sprang up and flourished in Anzaldúa's (1999) *Borderlands*. The intertextual nature of the theoretical frameworks we unpacked together paid homage to the *mestiza* consciousness: "the confluence of two or more genetic streams, with chromosomes constantly 'crossing over,' this mixture of races, rather than resulting in an inferior being, provides hybrid progeny, a mutable, more malleable species with a rich gene pool" (Anzaldúa, 1999, p. 99). This was the consciousness that informed every one of our conversations. How could it not? This was the blood that flowed in Christina's veins; this was the blood that flowed through Jodi's children's veins. In a constant state of becoming, we are the living, breathing proof of José Vasconcelos's *razacosmica* (Anzaldúa, 1999, p. 99). But at every turn, we seemed to be confronted by the challenges of race and gender politics; who gets to tell whose stories; and the never ending litany of "Why do you care? You're not black" (insert Mexican, homeless, queer, disabled, or any other identity perceived as "inferior"). Our collective response is, "How can you not care?" As theatre artists, our work revolves around the empathic act of storytelling; we consciously step in and out of different roles to effectively tell those stories.

"Don't Call Me a Racist"—Critical Consciousness and Hegemonic Ideology

One of the issues we believe stalls effective conversations about race is the defensiveness which seems to come along with them; the manner in which the subject is broached is so much of the problem. The conversations become rather static, really, as whites continue to make racism about them—that they've been discriminated against too; or that they've personally never done the discriminating. But they need to button their fly—their privilege is showing.

In the U.S. American national dialogue, privilege is located in this wide, wide (read white, white) world, but is in fact far more complex an issue than that. Dominant narratives suggest that privilege is a white, upper-middle-class experience where white folks are more concerned with Starbucks and BMWs than with systemic racism and white supremacy. But as our sisterhood developed and as we started sharing more and more of our personal experiences, we began to realize how Jodi's racial privilege as a white woman trumped Christina's position as a Latina from a biracial family, while Christina's upper-middle-class privilege trumped Jodi's status coming from a working-class family with a disabled Vietnam Veteran head of household. As Aída Hurtado (1999) reminds us, "Women's condition is so similar because of their gender that many other barriers will melt away as a result of this unconditional listening to one another's experiences" (p. 125). The fact that we came from such different worlds began to inform both of our perspectives on where privilege lives and how we talk about it. We shared the experience of standing on the margin, but it was the difference in our locations that helped the other gain a deeper understanding of that subject positioning.

And this is why the feminists of color facilitated our dialogues; because unlike the rigid, white, European, mostly male theorists we read in our graduate classes, these women opened up spaces of inclusivity and intersectionality. We began to realize that we were often more enlightened by our late-night phone conversations, after Jodi put her little ones to bed, than we were in any of our classes. It seemed like professors assigned readings to make you feel less intelligent, while the literature we were sharing with one another for our respective dissertation studies drew us in and empowered us to see the world through a whole new set of lenses. And yet there was one white guy who caught our attention in the midst of all these powerful women of color. Paulo Freire did more than just introduce us to the theories of emancipatory pedagogy; he liberated us and helped us recognize that each of us, as well as our developing friendship, was in a constant state of evolution.

We began to see every dialogue as an opportunity to inform our research. Playing off of the format embraced by Paulo Freire in the "talking books" he wrote with educational theorists from around the world including Donaldo Macedo, Myles Horton, Antonio Faundez, and Ira Shor, we spoke often, and about everything. Freire suggests that "through dialogue, reflecting together on what we know and don't know, we can then act critically to transform reality" (Shor & Freire, 1987, p. 99). This uncommon bond of ours serves as a safe haven to explore those places of the unknown to arrive at new destinations of understanding. "Dialogue is a moment where humans meet to reflect on their reality as they make and remake it" (p. 98).

Intersectionality and Privilege: Subverting the Dominant Paradigm

What do you see first when you look at me? My race or my gender? Pamela Barnett (2003) discusses how individual experience depends on a confluence of social identities (p. 33) and that the ones most impactful for an individual may not be the ones most apparent. In 1851, Sojourner Truth famously asked the assembly of suffragists to recognize her identity as both descendent of the African people brought to the United States as slaves and a woman forced into subjugation by capitalist patriarchy. Even then the impact of intersectionality of privilege was being troubled. What am I first? What impacts my worldview the strongest? Am I Colombian-American first, then a woman, then from an upper-middle-class background? Am I white first, then a woman, then from a working-class background? Barnett's (2003) article echoes what we have been saying to each other for years with regard to privilege; particular identities accrue particular privileges, but "other intersecting identities may either compound or counteract them" (p. 33).

Growing up the notion of "privilege" was something that belonged to people who stood in different circles than me: the people with the nice clothes, the new cars, and the big homes. I grew up in a rural, agricultural part of the country where my perspectives on privilege were based not on the fact that I was white but on socioeconomics and religion. While my family was among many who were working class, I had friends in my social circle whose families were economically privileged. Because the area was predominantly white, the concept of racial privilege wasn't something I dealt with until I went into college and found myself gravitating to people who thought like me, but looked very different than I did. I remember vividly one conversation when a friend of mine challenged me to consider my ideological positioning when he said that as a female, I should be as upset about oppression and exclusion as he was, as an African-American male. Perhaps what makes me feel a kinship with people who have been racially oppressed are my experiences growing up economically disadvantaged and in a religious minority. Peggy McIntosh (2010) describes this as acknowledging "many different kinds of privilege systems" (p. 6). What my friend said gave voice to things I had been thinking about, but didn't have a name for. Oppression is something that affects different populations systemically.

And while Jodi was not reminded on a daily basis of her whiteness, being biracial meant that I couldn't wipe the brown off me. But I could straighten the curl out of my hair in an attempt to fit in and look less ethnic. My father was an immigrant from Latin America, but he did not come to this country in search of a job because there were none in his country, he came to do a specialization in obstetrics and gynecology at a U.S. hospital. My mother is white and studied to be a nurse, but when she married my father she chose to stay at home and raise her children, a privilege not always afforded to Latino families in this country. But we were anything but a "typical Latino family." My friends were almost exclusively white from elementary, through junior high, and into high school. After grad school, I reconnected with a friend from high school when we both found ourselves working as professors in Boston. Ironically, we somehow made the connection that we were both Latinos and started speaking in Spanish. Across the table, both of our jaws dropped. It seemed easier for us to pass as white back in high school and not draw attention to ourselves. We had each allowed people to assume things about us rather than represent our heritage with pride. In each of the binary systems, whether we are talking about people of color and white people, or working class and upper middle class, McIntosh (2010) refers to the privileged as the "upside" and the oppressed or discriminated against as the "downside" (p. 6). At first glance, someone might look at Jodi and assume that she experienced the upside in terms of class, while Christina occupied the downside as a person of color. But along racial and class lines, we were the yin to the other's yang, albeit in ways that challenged other people's preconceived notions of "societal norms." This balance has fed our friendship and nourished our collaborative partnership.

In school we often laughed about getting different T-shirts with theoretical "jokes" on them. We both utilize postcolonialist ideas in our work and so "POCO" was one idea; "POMO" was another, referring to postmodernist thinking. But by far, our favorite idea was a shirt displaying: "Subvert the dominant paradigm." Indeed, this was even a call to arms that Christina would whisper into Jodi's pregnant belly as she carried her second daughter, proving once again that women can pursue doctoral studies while raising a family—not either one or the other.

The beauty of our interracial relationship is that we have never had conflict between us stemming from our differences. We have always been united and our differences influence our thinking, our perspectives, and experiences, but not how we interact with one another. On the other hand, they have definitely fueled the fires in how we've interacted with the outside world. Our shared perspective on racism and privilege trumped any differences that the color of our skin and our economic upbringing may have imposed. We operate from within a "'borderlands' feminism," one which, according to Chéla Sandoval (1998),

> calls up a syncretic form of consciousness made up of transversions and crossings; its recognition makes possible another kind of critical apparatus and political operation in which *mestiza* feminism comes to function as a working chiasmus (a mobile crossing) between races, genders, sexes, cultures, languages, and nations. Thus conceived, *La conciencia de la mestiza* makes visible the operation of another *metaform* of consciousness that insists upon polymodal forms of poetics, ethics, identities, and politics not only for Chicanas/os but for any constituency resisting the old and new hierarchies of the coming millennium. (p. 352)

More often than not, it was our solidarity within this *mestiza* feminism that helped us negotiate some of our career-defining moments when racist comments were hurled by our colleagues or university administrators. When it seemed we had nowhere else to turn, it was usually a phone call starting with "You are never going to believe what just happened to me today …" that reminded us there was always someone who understood what we were going through.

Epistemes, Paradigms, and Pink Elephants: Intersectional Sisterhood

So graduate school was where we met, but since then it has been our work interrogating the notion of privilege in and outside the classroom that prompted our coauthored scholarship, our creative collaborations, and this enduring friendship. The fundamental aspect of our sisterhood is built on the vast difference of our histories conflated with the shared struggle of marginalization. In 2008, we coauthored the chapter "The Pink Elephant Is Going to Ruin My Sofa: Theatre as Pedagogy Addressing Racism and Social Change" in the text *Teaching Race in Social Science and Humanities Higher Education*. In the Introduction we recognize what unlikely bedfellows we make:

> If the two of us had ever encountered each other in the typical high-school cafeteria, one might argue that we would have walked right past one another to sit in our respective camps with friends who we identified with based on the color of our skin. But neither one of us walked a color line back then. In fact, our "breakfast clubs" were each defined more along the lines of religious affiliations, economic status, and educational aptitude. Perhaps the one facet of our formative years that would have found us in the same circle after school was our propensity for drama. (p. 187)

Our solidarity stems from our wanting to dismantle the racialized structures of the places within which we have both worked, while "the powers that be" insist on keeping them intact, or maybe just repainting the outside. Audre Lorde (1984) writes of the ineffectiveness of using the master's tools to take apart a racist patriarchy, and how new tools need to be fashioned to effectively take the structure down. She writes that "only within [the] interdependency of different strengths, acknowledged and equal, can the power to seek new ways of being in the world generate [change], as well as the courage and sustenance to act where there are no charters" (pp. 110–111). In *The Color of Privilege*, Aida Hurtado (1999) remarks that examining difference between women is the only way an authentic coalition—authentic friendship—can be built.

Feminists of Color offer an inclusive paradigm but one that does not deny differences and does not deny anyone's history. Incorporating history into a multicultural feminism, however, entails confronting both "emancipation and shame" (Caraway, 1991, pp. 166–167). History has to be taken into account, both for its transformative potential as well as for its recognition of shame—acknowledging the structural and social apartheid that still exists between different groups of women. (p. 43)

Authentic friendship comes from not just *seeing* the differences in our backgrounds, but *examining* those locations to better identify points of intersection, whereas Hurtado suggests transformative, intercultural friendship can grow.

Mise-en-Scène: Part Deux

Jodi looks up from her coffee.

JODI

So about that research project on Shakespeare with kids ...

Christina laughs.

CHRISTINA

Please ... I'm eating.

They eat in silence for a minute.

JODI

I've been thinking about my theoretical framework ... I'd really like to look at Chéla Sandoval's ideas in *Methodology of the Oppressed*. And I love Patricia Hill Collins's writing about intersectional paradigms in *Black Feminist Thought*.

CHRISTINA

Cool. While you're at it, you should check out Aida Hurtado's *The Color of Privilege: Three Blasphemies on Race and Feminism*.

JODI

Do you think that's ok?

CHRISTINA

Why wouldn't it be?

Pause.

JODI

'Cause I'm not a woman of color.

CHRISTINA

Nope. You're sure not. ¿Y qué?

She eats her pancakes.
Pause.

JODI
(smiling)

I see what you did there.

CHRISTINA

You just have to accurately position yourself in your "stance of the researcher"; address it with an authentic sense of transparency. In my dissertation I own the fact that I am a Latina who comes from a world of privilege working with young people who live a very marginalized existence. The reality is you have a foot in two worlds. Scratch that. You have a foot in many worlds.

JODI

Wait, how many feet do you think I have?

They laugh.
Jodi takes a bite of Christina's pancakes.

CHRISTINA

So how do those authors support your framework?

Jodi drinks her coffee.

JODI

Lots of reasons actually. Sandoval addresses Fanon's black skin/white mask ideology as transformative code; that it can be looked at as moving structures of meaning into new categories.

CHRISTINA

Very Freirian.

JODI

Yes, and Audre Lordeian ... they both speak about "distorted mirrors" and making new tools to dismantle racist structures. So the idea I'm writing on, about imposed racial identification—

CHRISTINA

I love Audre Lorde.

JODI

I know! So do I! But they all unpack the idea of "performed self" as defined by dominant ideologies—"

CHRISTINA

Those pesky ideologies ...

The two women laugh and spiritedly continue their
conversation all the while enjoying their breakfast. The sounds
of the restaurant can be heard in the background:
voices, clanging dishes, and soft music.
Al fin.

References

Anzaldúa, G. (1983). Foreword to the second edition. In C. Moraga and G. Anzaldúa (Eds.), *This bridge called my back: Writings by radical women of color* (pp. iv–v). New York, NY: Kitchen Table: Women of Color Press.

Anzaldúa, G. (1999). *Borderlands/La Frontera: The new mestiza* (2nd ed.). San Francisco, CA: Aunt Lute Books.

Barnett, P. A. (2003). Social identity and privilege in higher education. *Liberal Education, 99*(3), 30–37.

Caraway, N. (1991). *Segregated sisterhood: Racism and the politics of American feminism*. Knoxville, TN: University of Tennessee Press.

Collins, P. H (2000). *Black feminist thought: Knowledge, consciousness, and the politics of empowerment*. New York, NY: Routledge.

Hurtado, A. (1999). *The color of privilege: Three blasphemies on race and feminism*. Ann Arbor, MI: University of Michigan Press.

Lorde, A. (1984). *Sister outsider: Essays & speeches*. Freedom, CA: The Crossing Press.

Marín, C., & Gibson, J. (2004). Toward a collaborative praxis: Our ArtsBridge experience. *STAGE of the Art, 16*(3), 9–12.

McIntosh, P. (1989/2010). White privilege: Unpacking the invisible knapsack & Some notes for facilitators on presenting my white privilege papers. *The National Seed Project*. Retrieved June 5, 2016 from http://nationalseedproject.org/white-privilege-unpacking-the-invisible-knapsack

Rappeport, A. (2016, February 7). Gloria Steinem and Madeleine Albright Rebuke Young Women Backing Bernie Sanders. *The New York Times*, p. A1.

Sandoval, C. (1998). Mestizaje as method: Feminists of color challenge the canon. In C. Trujillo (Ed.), *Living Chicana theory* (pp. 352–370). Berkeley, CA: Third Woman Press.

Shor, I., & Freire, P. (1987). *A pedagogy for liberation: Dialogues on transforming education*. New York, NY: Bergin & Garvey.

Van Der Horn-Gibson, J., & Marín, C. (2008). The pink elephant is going to ruin my sofa: Theatre as pedagogy addressing racism and social change. In E. Horowitz (Ed.), *Teaching race in social science and humanities higher education* (pp. 213–231). Birmingham, AL: University of Birmingham.

· 7 ·

FRIENDS IN REAL LIFE

Thembisa S. Mshaka

I am not just Black. I am blackity Black. Not easily pegged for being 'hood, street, bougie or militant, but all of the above in any given moment. On top of and inside all this blackity Blackness is serious smarty smartness. Not a rocket scientist by any means, but a highly educated lover of words who became a razor-sharp critical thinker. More on that educational path later.

I was told I was intelligent from birth it seems. My late mother had a favorite story about how I corrected her mother-in-law on the pronunciation of a word. "It's not lie-barry, Grandma, it's lie-brary." If I wasn't worried about backlash from correcting my own very stern grandmother as a kid, I'm not going to be too concerned with holding my tongue around anyone else. I can be intimidating.

And yet, I make friends easily. I am a true Sagittarian, so I love celebrating, I am the most fun as a travel partner, I live for adventure and am the life of the party. I am also a gift-a-holic. I love the whole gifting thing, no matter what side of it I'm on. I'm not high maintenance. I don't need to call or be called several times a day, don't' sweat invites to stuff. We could not talk for weeks or months and I won't take it personally. I have two kids and three jobs. I'm busy. I get it. And when you do call, or when you finally return my call, we can pick up right where we left off. Love is love.

But I am very exacting in my friendships. My friendship doesn't come easily. I am needy in one place—and that's intellectually. See, friendships are a choice, and therein, should never require the justification of my existence. Because I don't have to be here, in this space called "friendship." Looking back over the points where my most valued and enduring friendships across race lines were born—high school, college, and my early days in hip-hop journalism, I can't recall laying some set of ground rules down. I just made it clear that if someone wanted to be my friend, they needed to, in the words of Brand Nubian, "either love me or leave me alone."

I attended a very small elite girls school from eighth grade through to my graduation. My senior class had 44 young women in it. I was the sole Black girl. Now remember: I am blackity Black. I am also a Muslim covering her hair daily. I have Dorothy Dandridge, Malcolm X, and Michael Jackson keeping a watchful eye from the walls of my locker. I brought all their fiery determination and fierce creativity to all my friendships with my white counterparts, sans apology. Only a few could handle that up close.

Jenny Bradbury was among them. I was 12 in the eighth grade. Had zero understanding of intersections. I just knew racism was real, and that despite being in abundantly diverse Los Angeles County, I felt isolated in school. I don't remember how we met, but I asked her, and she and I agreed from deductive reminiscing that it had to be in Glee Club. She and I were both in the Alto I section. However it was, we clicked instantly. Everything about Jenny radiated happiness. Big blue eyes, wide generous smile. And when I tell you that we laughed making up the silliest catchphrases and song-jokes ... we were *always* laughing. Doubled over cry-snot laughing. Over everything. Over nothing.

We each have gone on to marry, have children, and relocate from tony Pasadena, California. I moved to New York to go deeper into entertainment, she to Oklahoma, where her husband's career took their family. I have since gone on to the road to divorce, with kids aged 16 and 5. She went on to have four children, now ranging in age from 10 to 18, including two adopted Chinese daughters. One of them, Katie, is a cancer survivor. In all our conversations as kids in school, unless we were studying race and racism, neither ever came up. And not by virtue of some uncomfortable inciting incident that muted us. And while I am the last one to be all kumbaya about race, it just never came up between us; it never needed to. Maybe because Jenny's parents raised her better than what people of color perceive to be the entitled, mannerless attitude often displayed by people with privilege. Maybe because

I was so relaxed in our friendship, I just never brought it up. Who knows what would have happened had Jenny not been able to understand the philosophies of Malcolm X? I'm confident that we would have had a nuanced conversation about the subject. That's how open our line of communication was. The confirmation of this has actually shown up decades later via social media. In my comment threads about intersectional politics, race, racism and certain areas of endeavor like entertainment or sports, Jenny's awareness comes through like a champ. Never defending white privilege. She reminds me it is important to view white people outside the limiting lens of oppression, and its tendency to negate human connection in its pure forms. To see difference and acknowledge difference, without racializing every interaction. Right when the temptation to lump all of those I call "members of the dominant group" into the crazy/clueless/careless boxes, the fact that Jenny Bradbury, who couldn't be more different from me down to her love of Laura Ashley florals, just let me be me. Gave me that space to laugh for no reason. She never questioned the Blackness. She loved me for it, not in spite of it—and still does, thirty-three years later.

It takes a mature white person to be friends with someone whose differences are many and vast. It requires an openness and a level of security of self that white privilege by definition seeks to deem its members exempt. Being Jenny's friend busted up a few stereotypes I had of white people too. And that allowed me to be open to even having friendships with people who were white.

Fast forward to my college days. I enrolled in a private, predominantly white women's college. I arrive on campus in August of 1988. I was sixteen. The antiapartheid movement and its protests in support of a free South Africa were taking place on campuses nationwide. You could not go anywhere without discussing race or racism. Divestment from companies that supported South Africa's government was the mantra as American students fought for racial parity among faculty and staff along with an end to a Eurocentric academic curriculum at home.

In this setting, I was constantly fighting to be seen as equal, visible, valuable on campus. Not everyone on campus was on board with a free South Africa, or an ethnically balanced and historically accurate curriculum. The intersection of race and gender in college was the opposite of my comparatively race-neutral high school experience. Not to say that in high school I was some beneficiary of colorblindness. I just think we were young and underequipped for the conversation in real-life contexts. But in college, political rock and rap combined with the issues of police terror, the "war on drugs," and apartheid served as the backdrop for a new education.

My blackity Black identity became my weapon of choice for survival. I was hit with a barrage of questions about being Black and being Muslim. And indictments for loving rap music given how misogynistic some of its lyrics were. Why was our hair that way? Why did we talk the way we did? Code switching was in full effect, but among groups of Black women, we went off duty and spoke freely. I know the white girls overheard and sought to negotiate their confusion.

Well, now, I'm offended. Why are you asking me? When did I become your blackity Black Ambassador? Is this condescending interrogation your way of making friends? Save it—and hit the library. Get familiar with Dewey and his decimal system. Do some research. It was like some of these women hadn't been in any real-life proximity to Black women. Perhaps this was the case.

But guess what? You're not in Kansas anymore, Dorothy.

The Black women on campus literally told the white ones that if they wanted answers, and wanted to fight white supremacy, they needed to do it on their own time, while educating themselves collectively.

And you know what? That's exactly what many of them did. These thirty or so women formed WWAR, which stood for White Women Against Racism. They took it upon themselves to check and dismantle their white privilege. The women of color on campus were hit with dual waves of shock and relief. We, Black, Chicana/Latina, Asian and Native/Indigenous women finally had a resource to point white women to when The Questions Borne of Ignorance Had Gone Far Enuf. The creation of WWAR showed me what allies in action look like; what human beings do when they want to be better and make living in our world better. These inquisitive, self-critical, determined and empathetic kinds of women were the caliber of friends I sought out going forward. This student organization actually set the tone for the kind of white woman I would consider befriending as an adult.

This was one of the more significant formative moments that made me the exacting and treasured friend I have become. It's probably also why I haven't made many new friends over the last couple of decades, with a few exceptions. But those new friends are so solid. So easy. There is so much depth. And so much fun. Because the foundation of mutual respect for difference is already there.

When it comes to my relationships with other women of color, the aforementioned dynamic has been the case without exception. I can't explain how

I never ended up with catty, backstabbing, shady girlfriends. Perhaps the Law of Attraction is at work; that's not how I operate as a friend, so I am a bit like Kryptonite to those types of women. I never understood when my friends who had women like that in their lives complained to me about their behavior. It is just foreign to me. I probably know these women, but they never come at me that way. My core circle of friends value and respect each other so much, betrayal is never on the table. Do we argue? Sure. Take a break or fall out of touch? Sure. But not because one of us tried to play the other one for a fool, or over some guy.

I do believe that the context for the development of my friendships with other Black, Latina, and Asian American women was decisive. I met most of them in all-women academic environments, where being supportive of other women was already baked in, so someone usually looked silly for being that stereotypical "mean girl." With respect to women of other ethnic backgrounds, I was always taught to connect from a place of authentic curiosity and develop a rapport before asking awkward cultural questions. And very often, my friend would have some questions of her own, that would spark dialogue and deepen our connection as the answers unfurled. It was my Chinese American friend that explained the differences between Mandarin and Cantonese language. It was my Korean American friend who helped me understand about North and South Korea beyond the pages of my International Relations class materials. It was my Mexican American–born and Mormon-raised friend who explained the dynamic between generations in her family, or between Latinos who did and did not speak Spanish. This information is the gold of human connection. But you have to risk getting your hands dirty, getting your world rocked as you mine for this gold. And because I've always been curious, I was always grateful for the education. But if I were just some stranger of a Black girl prying myself into their world? They would never have divulged these gems to me. Hell no. Why should they? They are reserved for friends by whom they are respected, and from whom they can expect reciprocity.

It is rare that a superficial encounter will generate this expansive and powerful a result. Friendship takes work, exploration, and it demands one take the risk of being schooled, in the same way it demands we take the risk of being hurt. But this process of vulnerability in the interest of being known and closely connected, with the goal of having others one can depend on, has taught me the difference between friends, acquaintances and associates. I'm not taking the same level of risk with people in the latter two categories. I don't need to befriend everyone I meet, nor do I need to alienate them. I can expend the energy of cultivation I deem necessary, and do so without apology. This allows me to preserve the gold for my *friends*. And this in turn makes me a superb, valuable, low-maintenance, but high-expectation-having friend.

I've worked in entertainment for a quarter century, mainly in the areas of Black music and popular media. While hip-hop taught me how to develop and maintain friendships with men, my women's education taught me how to do the same among women. This is something I don't take for granted. I don't have the need to feel jealous of another woman's success or beauty. I don't compete with women, because supporting women who support me is a much better use of my time and energy. I've always been my own best competition anyway. Now that I am in my mid-forties, I am deepening the friendships I've been blessed to cultivate while becoming the absolute best friend I can to them … and to myself.

· 8 ·

RACE IS A FACTOR, NOT A FOUNDATION

Amber Buggs

When I first started thinking about the topic posed by *UnCommon Bonds* it was a surprise to me that deep interracial friendships among adults are rare. I looked around at the photos on my apartment walls and thought about my friendships—feeling confident that there was clear diversity reflected in those closest to me. So, I popped open my laptop to have a look at my Facebook community. To see if their images would lean toward my diverse friend base, or reflect the scarcity of interracial friendships. What I found struck me: photo after photo of dinners, vacations, and parties filled with only Black, or only white, or only Asian people. There were some people of varying races peppered in from time to time, but overwhelming the people I saw on my computer screen—experiencing milestones together throughout the years— tended to look like the person whose Facebook profile I happened to be on. I started to wonder why are theirs like this but mine is not? Why are the people who look like me peppered into my diverse friendship base instead of the other way around?

I identify as a biracial Black and Mexican American woman from a multiracial family. My mother is Mexican and my father is Black; my parents divorced when I was almost three years old and both remarried, adding a white stepfather and Black stepmother to the mix. My brother and I share the same parents and my sister, brother, and I share the same mother. Racial diversity within my inner circle was a constant norm, leading me to believe it was standard, until I started interacting with people outside of home. At that point I began trying to understand what it means to be biracial in a society that tends to expect people to check one racial box. Growing up I tried to identify as both Black and Mexican—in a separate but equal kind of way. But there are so many variations to racial teachings and expression when a person is mixed. I am second-generation Mexican-American on my mother's side; however, I do not speak Spanish fluently and our family does not celebrate most traditional Mexican holidays. When it comes to my Black side, the amount of cultural and racial teachings I learned was limited due to the religious faith of my father's mother and siblings. As Jehovah's Witnesses, they did not celebrate holidays or birthdays, or closely associate with people who do not share their religious beliefs. So family gatherings were rare and I did not see family that extended beyond my father, stepmother, and her family often.

I share these background details because I believe my biracial identity, diverse family makeup, and cultural upbringing have profoundly influenced the friendships I have made (or not made) throughout my life. While the research motivating *UnCommon Bonds* suggests that adults do not typically have close friendships with people who are racially different from themselves, I do not believe this research adequately takes into account significant differences between the lived experience of monoracial people, as opposed to biracial and multiracial people—or even transracial adoptees. In order for a person to feel drawn to others who are racially like them, that person needs to know how they racially identify themselves, and needs to feel some level of community and acceptance from the racial group to which they feel they belong. I have observed that racial identification and acceptance by the identified community tends to be more seamless for people who are monoracial and are raised by family members who racially identify like them. These monoracial people have an opportunity to grow up seeing people in the home who look like them, go to family gatherings with people who share their same culture, and turn to people who look like them from an early age for community, strength, and support. I would imagine that once this foundation is set, it would be natural to gravitate to others outside of the home that reinforce these familiar feelings—thus making it more likely for monoracial people to make meaningful friendships with people who racially identify like them. From my experience, this is *not* the case for biracial people.

Being biracial, from a multiracial family, impacted how I grew up thinking about race and the level of acceptance from and comfort I have felt within both Black and Mexican communities. From a young age, I noticed that the color of my skin was different from everyone in my family except my brother, yet I felt unconditionally loved and accepted. When it came time to start school and to start making friends, I naturally gravitated toward a diverse array of classmates. Although these friendships felt natural to make, as I moved through educational levels I did become increasingly aware of a social hurdle that can come with being mixed. People seemed to need to racially classify me before we could move past surface-level interactions, and I started to notice that within the first few encounters with a person I would find myself verbally identifying as biracial. Surprisingly, the questions I got were from most people—not just those who did not present as Black or Mexican. Classmates, adults, and strangers alike would ask questions like:

> *"Were you adopted?"*
> *"But is she your real mom/sister/aunt/fill in the blank?"*
> *"Why is your skin that color?"*
> *"Is that your real hair?"*
> *"What are you mixed with?"*
> *"Why don't you speak Spanish?"*
> *"What are you?"*

You would think these questions upset me, but they didn't. At first they confused me, especially as they continued to come from people who looked Black or Mexican, but after a while they were so frequent that they became questions I expected to hear during at least the first few interactions with a new person. So much so, that if someone did not ask a question along these lines during my first few encounters with them, I would intentionally mention my biracialism so they would not be surprised later. I still catch myself doing this sometimes—and can see now that expecting and answering these questions again and again, fostered an internal sense of difference that made it viscerally uncomfortable for me to identity as *only* Black or *only* Mexican. I always identify as racially mixed, which means I am always aware of the fact that I can only be part of each community—not completely a part of it.

Claiming each race as part of my identity, but not my full racial identity, has never felt like an insurmountable obstacle to feeling embraced by the Chicano community. This may be in large part because although I racially identify as mixed, I culturally identify as Mexican American. My mother's side of the family is close and celebrates holidays, birthdays, etc. I grew up seeing my grandparents, aunts, uncles, and cousins on a bimonthly basis. The comfort I feel in the presence of others who embrace Mexican culture makes it relatively easy for me to make friends with them, provided we share some common interests. This is the closest feeling I can relate to, in terms of what it must be like for monoracial people who gravitate toward friendships with members of their racial community. For the most part, there very much is a sense of belonging that feels natural, familiar, and safe for me with people who are Chicano. We normally have similar upbringings, share knowledge of food, customs, language, and have a foundation of unwavering belief in and loyalty to family. However, despite my comfort in these spaces, as a biracial person there is still a border I am careful about crossing—particularly around Chicanos who do not know me. There have been times when I have had to qualify my statements by reminding people that I can make them because of my Mexican background. I have been quizzed about where my mom is from before the questioner believes I am "a real Mexican." Also, I have been told I am not "Mexican enough" because I do not speak Spanish fluently. While I do feel a deep sense of belonging to this community and have found it easy to make friends within it, I am still conscious of being an "other" because I am mixed. Yet despite these reminders of my "otherness" within the Chicano community, I have consistently felt more welcomed than not, and have many friends who identify as Chicano.

My relationship to my Black side and the Black community has been much more complicated. Close Black friends have been peppered into my diverse friendship base throughout my life; however, until college I had never sought Black friends for racial community, but was instead drawn to these friends by our common interests and personalities. If I am really honest with myself I have to acknowledge that I racially saw these friends in the same way that I saw all of my friends who were not Chicano. There was no extra layer of belonging because they were Black, because although I acknowledged my Black identity, I did not feel part of or particularly welcomed by the Black community. My evolving sense of self, general ignorance, and a lack of cultural teaching from my father's side contributed to this, but so did several first-hand experiences. Black women who were strangers or acquaintances would ask my mother if she was my nanny, or say that it was a shame that my father had married a Mexican instead of a Black woman to "keep the race strong and pass on our people's culture." Interactions like this made me feel like the

Black community was prejudice and unwelcoming of people who were racially mixed. So up until the end of high school, I did not feel inclined to seek out the Black community for kinship.

This always bothered me though. As someone who is exactly half and half, it felt wrong to favor one side so much more than the other. As I started to look toward college, I thought that would be the perfect time to expand my knowledge and to try to make friendships with people from that side of my racial identity, for the sake of building racial community. It was a new chapter—a time to explore and become whoever I wanted to be with people who knew nothing about me. So, I decided to push way outside of my comfort zone and request to be housed in the Black Scholars Hall my first year at University of California, Santa Barbara (UCSB). It was not my intention to *not* make friends with people of other races, but rather to challenge myself to step outside of my comfort zone, to occupy a space I never fully felt I belonged in; and if that led to cultivating friendships with more Black people my age—all the better. As I prepared to transition to college I was nervous, but when I was granted my housing choice I was also really excited. I moved in determined to cultivate friendships with my Black UCSB classmates—and at first it was great and full of genuine community. I of course had to answer the obligatory "what are you?" questions, but after that I felt welcomed. Welcomed and encouraged to attend Black Student Union (BSU) meetings, to go out, and just chat. I didn't get some of the jokes, understand all of the historical references, or know how to sing Stevie Wonder's version of "Happy Birthday"—but I did feel welcomed. I learned a lot about non-mainstream Black history and about how my Black peers felt about race in America. I came to respect the Black community's need for a safe space on an overwhelming white campus. We had a tight-knit group that I was included in—and appreciative of—but conflicted about.

Conflicted because while I learned a lot and felt more belonging than I ever had before, I still felt inherently like an outsider because I did not feel the way many of my classmates felt about race issues. Learning about a people is not the same as living that people's experience—and what I learned had not been my personal experience. Many of my hall-mates were either full Black or were African, and race seemed to be a salient identity for them. They knew who they were racially and it was important to them and impacted their belief system—so it became a sore subject for me to claim Blackness as part of my identity—but not my full identity. Several of my Black friends suggested that saying I was half Black was an indicator of internalized hatred, that I was ashamed, or that I was willfully refusing to embrace my community. I would try to explain that my behavior was impacted by my *not* only being Black, and that embracing my Blackness in such an overt way was new to me. After many of these conversations it became increasingly apparent that to get to the level of Black pride my new friends wanted me to be at, would require squashing my Mexican side—and even then I was convinced I would still not be "enough," since being mixed had already impacted what I could say in certain spaces in front of some people. Certain words or gestures were called out by some as offensive coming from me in the same way I had been called out by others in the Chicano community. The Black space was no different than the Chicano space in this way—both often reminded me that to be biracial is to be in and out simultaneously.

This push and pull between my identities, and the way it was perceived by the Black community, ultimately made it feel impossible to make anything but surface-level friendships with monoracially Black peers during my time at UCSB. There was too much pressure to embrace being Black above any other identity, and there were also too many instances in which I found myself in disagreement with the Black community's response to situations. The most significant instance of disagreement was during the second quarter of my first year at UCSB. Our BSU worked with University leadership to host an annual conference that rotated between University of California (UC) campuses for Black students to attend workshops, discuss important topics pertinent to the Black community, and build cross-campus solidarity. I attended this conference and enjoyed it and the people I interacted with throughout—it was informative, fun, and uplifting. I walked into the next BSU meeting after the conference feeling like we should be proud of ourselves, sure that there was going to be some really productive discussion about what we had learned and how we could implement some of the takeaways. Instead I found that our BSU leadership was livid—one of our sister campuses had brought allies to the conference and according to our leadership this was completely unacceptable and insulting.

I had already been struggling with the strict policy that only Black students could attend BSU meetings, but I could recognize the need for safe spaces to have conversations that are charged. As a woman, I can easily understand that it is necessary and appropriate for women to have some discussions without self-identified men in the room. But to have a large conference that educates people on topics relevant to the Black community and explores ways to empower Blacks at micro and macro levels, and to actively try to ban allies

was very upsetting to me. All I could think about was my younger sister. My
sister who is half white and half Mexican but whose only siblings are Black
and Mexican, not being allowed to come to a conference to learn how to
advocate for her brother and sister. The thought of her being pushed out and
met with the hostility I saw in our BSU leadership that day was the last straw
in a pile of mental straws that had stacked too high for me to tolerate. So I said
my piece about the situation and excused myself from BSU membership. This
only further reinforced how I was viewed in the tight-knit Black community
on campus and stunted any hope I had of cultivating deep friendships with
most of my monoracially Black peers. I felt that I could not talk about racial
topics with this group without censoring myself or feeling defensive because
of their insistence that I did not agree with them because I was anti-Black/
internally biased against Black people. Did disagreeing with them really mean
I harbored internalized hatred? How could I be anti-Black as someone who
identifies as half-Black? I didn't know what to think about these accusations.
What I did know was I was tired of trying to understand. So I threw up an
emotional wall against most of the Black community in response and spent
the rest of my time at UCSB returning to my friendship comfort zone: seeking friends based solely on common interests, personalities, etc.—not race.
With these friends I did not feel like I had to be careful about how I phrased
opinions or how I looked—or whether I felt the impact of racial history on my
experience at the moment. I could just be myself—all of myself—and it was
such a relief.

As I reflect on my experience trying to fit in with the Black community,
I realize that this experience had a tremendous impact on me for years afterward. Not feeling like I belonged but never truly trying before college felt less
hurtful than trying hard and feeling like I failed. In the years that followed I
made friends with women from diverse racial backgrounds, a few of which I am
blessed to say are some of those friends whose photos hang on my apartment
walls. And as those friendships continued to grow, my desire to try to seek
friendships within the Black community lessened even more. Especially while
living in New York City, where I encountered the most blatant discrimination I have experienced, almost exclusively from dark-skinned Black women.
I had store employees throw my credit card back at me or lie about services,
saying they could not help me before turning to someone else to help them
with that same issue. I have had dark-skinned Black women outright lie about
something I said in professional settings and others cuss me out because their
boyfriend or husband looked in my direction. I don't share these examples to

imply that all dark-skinned Black women act like this toward me, because that is definitely not the case. But I do bring up these instances to explain why the emotional wall I built after my experience at UCSB stayed standing strong for so many years, and to highlight how colorism further complicated my sense of belonging within Black spaces.

At the time, I still felt a general lack of acceptance from the Black community, so the hostility I encountered in NYC reinforced that and reminded me of various comments my hall-mates had made about color and beauty. There had been many frustrated exchanges with my Black Scholars Hall roommate, who was frequently angered by Black representation in the media. She was Nigerian and had dark skin, and was regularly offended by light-skinned Black women with long curly hair on television and film. She argued that these women were not what "we all look like" and that they were the only "type of Black" that Hollywood viewed as beautiful. At the time I was offended. The women whom my roommate railed against looked like me. It was not until I grew older that I really started to understand the privilege that has come with being light-skinned and that there exist varying degrees of systematic hardship that is based not just on race but on color. While I have become much more aware of colorism, it is still a concept I continue to grapple with and seek to understand. The existence of skin-lightening creams, research studies that show children pointing to dark-skinned Black dolls as "bad" or "ugly" and the light-skinned dolls as "good" and "pretty," and numerous scholarly articles and books written about how particularly darker skinned Black people disproportionately face systematic discrimination and violence, all point to the fact that colorism is very real and impacts individuals and communities around the world on a daily basis (Clark and Clark, 1939).

As I have become more mindful of the impact and implications of colorism on communities of color, and as I have grown older and more politically aware, I have slowly removed bricks from my emotional wall and have started to feel much more inclined to seek friendships within the Black community again. While I do not always feel comfortable having race-based discussions because I worry I may lack the right language, after George Zimmerman gunned down Trayvon Martin in 2012 and was not convicted for it, I felt compelled to be much more active about educating myself and speaking about racial injustice in the United States. This was an interesting shift for me. One of the many reasons why it has felt more natural for me to have friends of diverse racial backgrounds is that it requires nothing of me but to be myself. I don't have to worry about being Black enough or Mexican enough—being half and half is just fine. That being said, as I've started to feel moved to have conversations about race-based issues, I have become increasingly aware of the fact that most of my close friends are not Black. So when I have these racially charged conversations with my friends, I find that I am just as careful speaking with them about it as I used to be speaking with members of the Black community at UCSB. I am much more cautious and strategic than I typically am in my conversations about women's issues or my own personal dramas. There is a pressure to use unbiased language and to be factual instead of emotional in explaining how I feel about racial issues, in order to not offend my white friends or sound like what anyone might deem as "an angry Black woman." This pressure is also felt because I recognize that for some of my friends I am the only Black or Mexican friend they have, and I don't want to let my people down in these discussions. Mexican culture in particular believes very strongly in "we." Since childhood I have been told that I represent the family, and that regardless of whether I do something well or terrible—what I do is a reflection on the "we." I represent Black people to some, Chicano to others—that is a responsibility and I do not forget it when having race-based conversations with friends who are not of color. This doesn't undermine our ability to maintain deep friendships though. Perhaps that would be different if I had started talking about race before our foundation was set, but I would like to think it would not have stunted our growth—since my friends are open minded and willing to challenge themselves to grow.

I am blessed to have an incredible base of smart, loyal, and loving friends and am grateful for their diversity and the way they embrace me for who I am. That being said, I sometimes feel like I'm the authority on what racism is in my friendship circles devoid of Black women, so it would be nice to have others who are able to educate me on the topic—but in an understanding way that assumes good intentions. As I mentioned previously, learning about a people is not the same as living the experience of those people. There are some conversations and topics that I now recognize are much more comfortable to have with Black women. So I find myself trying to cultivate these friendships again but with fresh eyes and a new sense of self that does not require that I feel compelled to be "Black enough." Through accepting that being biracial is to be an "other" whose lived experience is separate from a monoracial person who fits in with their racial community, I am able to feel like I have much less to prove and more of a willingness to be vulnerable in Black spaces. While this realization may upset some because it puts some distance between my claiming either community in their entirety, it frees me from trying to feel like

I *need* to be, think, and speak a certain way. It allows me the freedom I need to embrace being an "other" without guilt or the need to feel like I am "enough" for either race. I can now reenter Black spaces as unapologetically me.

As a twenty-eight-year-old I recognize that my current understanding of what it means to be biracial will undoubtedly continue to evolve. But for now, this is where I need to be in order to continue moving forward and cultivating friendships—whether with my Black side, Mexican American side, or anyone else. Being biracial is a separate racial category that makes it easier for me to make deeply meaningful friendships with people from various racial backgrounds in a way that may be challenging for monoracial people. That being said, as I reflect upon this writing experience I also realize that while I crave racial difference in my friendships, it has always also been important for me to have monoracially Black people in my circle too—I just didn't see it. In my determination to fit into a racial box I forgot to apply the same openness to the Black community as I do with others—a critical mistake that I now own and acknowledge. As a biracial person, race is not a strong enough foundation for me to form my friendships off of alone. It can only ever be one of the various factors that influence the friendships I make and strengthen the ones I have cultivated throughout my life. This is a liberating conclusion to draw—it makes me feel like any space is a space where deeply meaningful bonds can form and that these bonds can be limitless *both* because of and in spite of race.

Reference

Clark, K., & Clark, M. (1939). The development of consciousness of self and the emergence of racial identification in Negro preschool children. *Journal of Social Psychology* (10): 591–599.

· 9 ·

ACROSS THE ABYSS

Millicent R. Jackson

"Bad news. Unfortunately, I won't be at your writing group next Thursday," my friend Susan said.

"Why not?" I asked.

"I'm not allowed to participate." She sighed into the telephone.

"What are you talking about? You asked Shayla right?" I asked referring to our mutual friend who facilitated the group designed for an upcoming performance at a university.

"Of course I did. Shayla said the workshop is a space for women of color exclusively."

"Yes, she's right. I'm sorry I didn't think about that when we discussed it." I wondered why this fact hadn't crossed my mind in a previous conversation with Susan. This particular workshop had been this way since its inception, which was the beauty of it.

"I told Shayla I would put dark makeup on my face and sit in the back of the room if that meant I could participate and now she is not speaking to me. She said something to me about blackface and my being racist. I am not racist. You know me. *She knows me.*"

I held the telephone. My mind temporarily went blank. "Wait a minute, what?"

Susan was quiet. I heard crying in the background. "I know, I am really disappointed Shayla would say that to me. I know the pain of racism. I would never say anything like that. Let alone think it. Shayla and I have been friends for over thirty years. I thought we were sisters. I feel like the song 'If You Don't Know Me by Now.'"

I held the telephone for a moment to allow the words to sink in. The words slowly resonated one by one. She couldn't, she didn't. Susan couldn't have meant it in that way. Not our fellow writing partner and good friend Susan. While I had been the recipient of blatant racism and primarily numerous microaggressions from other white women I had no emotional connection with throughout various times in my life, I never expected that any white woman I allowed myself to be vulnerable with or called a friend would ever think of me in any way other than a woman. My twenty-four-year-old self had never experienced anything like this before. It was arduous for me to believe she had said something like this because Susan in my mind, despite our difference in race and thirty-year age difference, was the "*real deal.*" Susan attended nothing but Baptist churches, her close-knit social circle was comprised mainly of African American and Latina women. Her twenty-year relationship had been with a man of color, she championed my writing endeavors which included issues surrounding race and African American women, nursed my heartbreaks, and strongly hated the racial injustice that divided humankind. This was the Susan I knew and loved. What she said was significant of the racial injustice that has tainted the very fabric of America.

After pondering the issue, I realized that I knew Shayla (not as well as Susan) but I knew her well enough to know she wouldn't just cut someone off because of one incident. I also know there are two sides to every story and then there is the truth. I wanted to get to the truth behind this.

"How could Shayla think I possibly meant anything other than I really wanted to come participate in the group? That is all?" Susan asked.

Yet again, I remained silent. My mind was a swirling vortex of numerous thoughts. The first thought being had this been a woman of color she would have known that this was a problematic statement. Second, had she been someone who was conscious of the way the world worked, she would have not taken Shayla's reaction as a personal attack. A minute passed. Then another. Finally, I recalled saying, "Give it some time. Give it space. You and Shayla should let this sit and revisit the conversation later. That is my opinion. I just don't know what to say other than that." This is about all I could muster toward this.

"Okay," she said. "I hope you are right." I still heard her sobs in the background.

Immediately following our telephone conversation, I called my mother. My mother was the one person who I ran everything by. When I finished recounting Susan's side of the story to my mother she said, "I know Susan. I really don't believe she meant the comment in a malicious, racist way. She doesn't strike me in any way as that person; however, she needs to be mindful of what she is saying and its implications. She has to realize she can't say malicious things regardless of the intent and expect that they be received well."

When the opportunity presented itself for me to speak with Shayla I was able to get a different perspective. She said, "This is not the first time through the years I've had to call Susan out on her comments. I have been very clear with her on each occasion the problem with each remark, but this will be the last time." At this moment it was crystal clear there was history between these two women.

Later that week I shared my mother's feedback with Susan. Susan said that she understood and that she was so thankful for the mercy of my mother and for mine to know that she didn't mean anything hurtful by that comment. All she wanted to do was be included in this writing group.

In her profound book, *Citizen*, for which she won the national poetry award, Claudia Rankine (2014) writes about these "slights," these unintentional racially driven comments that persons who are not of color make; usually identified as "friend." While it is true that these comments to some degree may be unintentional they are still impactful. I didn't fully recognize it at the time, but this was one of those instances.

Anyone who truly knows me is aware that there are three things in this world that I take very seriously: family, friendships, and my writing. I don't use the word *friend* lightly. If I am your friend, you have a friend for life. The exception to that personal mantra is that you hurt someone in my family, betray my confidence, or break my heart with an outright lie or intentional hurtful action. There is where I draw the line and no longer consider you a friend.

I certainly understood everything Shayla said. I also understood that not every white person is racist. However, I acknowledge that all white people possess privilege. This is a privilege that my skin color does not afford me. I find that white privilege is the very thing that can murky the waters of an interracial friendship. The benefit of white privilege is that one can choose to fight racism one day, and ignore it the next. This situation with Susan felt like one of those times. I felt like Susan had never been told "you are privileged" and now she had to confront a reality that was all too common for Shayla and me.

More than nineteen years have marched on. A lot has transpired with Susan and me through the years: deaths of parents, murders of friends, dissolved romantic relationships, writings reached publication, homes have been relocated, jobs changed. Despite this journey we remain friends. One day my best friend Kim called me and told me about *UnCommon Bonds* and the possibility of a submission.

Immediately Susan comes to mind. I didn't give it a second thought. I asked her if she wouldn't mind editing a proposal for a possible essay submission. Of course she says sure. I let her know briefly what it is going to be about and that I would include her. She agreed. The very day I gave the proposal to Susan for her to review she called me immediately.

"What's up?" I asked.

"I didn't know this was going to say this," she said.

"What are you talking about? I don't understand. I told you."

"The incident with Shayla and I. I didn't know you were going to talk about *that*. I don't want that in there. Besides, that is between her and me. That is our story to tell. You weren't there."

"I understand I wasn't there, but you involved me by asking me what I thought. You told me and asked what I thought so you indirectly involved me."

"Honey, listen, if anyone was involved it was your mother and Shayla and I. Your mother extended her loving mercy upon me. I would never ever use the word blackface to come to a writing group. I know the hatred behind those words. I just wanted to come."

I took a deep breath. "Okay, Susan. You didn't use those exact words, but you said you would put on dark makeup and sit in the back of a room to be included in a group with all women of color. It's semantics. You lashed out because you felt rejected. You are used to never being an outsider and for once you were. That is the truth."

Susan began to cry. "Millicent, please don't put this in this writing. I am asking you as a friend not to. I am very hurt. This is bringing up all my hurt. I lost Shayla behind this."

I remained quiet doing my best to compose myself, reminded myself this is a friend. "Susan, my intention is not to hurt you. I love you, but you are focused on your hurt here. I realize you lost Shayla, but that is something you must own. This is not about you. This is about friendship and how we came together to overcome something that could have been very messy."

"I don't want it. I am hurt."

Suddenly anger swelled up in me from her constant repetition of her, she, her, and she. What about me? I wondered how this is about her. "Well, I am hurt too. Does that even matter to you? Black people hurt every day. We don't go around making a major ordeal out of it. We adjust and we continue on." The words had left my mouth and I didn't feel bad for them. "Susan, I'm sorry that you don't want this written, but it is important to me and I am going to write it. You gave me permission earlier when I asked and now I am going to do it. I didn't have to ask you to begin with, but I did. You agreed to it. You will not dictate what I write and how I write that. If that means our friendship is over, then so be it."

Our conversation was over. Susan asked me to come and get the proposal. She was sobbing. I was so mad I saw red. I was surprised by Susan's reaction because since she supposedly meant no harm by what had transpired then the sharing of that experience would be a teachable moment. Somehow what was supposed to be a story about sustaining our friendship through difficulty/ misunderstanding reverted to the victimization of Susan? It became about how *she* was hurt because she unintentionally slighted a woman of color. *She* was hurt because she lost her friendship with Shayla. It became that she didn't understand that a comment about putting on dark makeup and sitting in the back of a room is not supposed to be taken as it was said. Susan's white privilege allowed her for her entire life to never be accountable because she didn't have to. She could not relate to what has never been her experience of being excluded. It had been my experience that when things come up regarding race that are not understood or that a person doesn't want to be examined, it is easier for the said person to cry, shift blame, or use whatever tactic they deem fitting for their needs. The microaggressive behavior was a classic case of a micro-invalidation. These micro-invalidations are communications that exclude, negate, or nullify the psychological thoughts, feelings, or experiences of the other group. Susan chose to overlook the feelings and experiences of myself or Shayla and make this experience about her, not about the underlying micro-insult. The micro-insult being if I put dark makeup on my face and sit in the back of the room I can blend in like the rest of you Black folk.

As I drove a familiar route to Susan's home tears of frustration rolled down my cheeks. I wished I could call the one person who could talk me down, who could sort out all the emotional murkiness that I am consumed in: my mother.

Mom had died three years ago, and talking aloud to her in the sky was not going to cut it. I cried even harder at the reality. It is then that I called my best friend. I was so mad my hands are shaking on the steering wheel. If there is one thing I know, it is that she will give me the truth straight with no chaser. I gave her a play-by-play of everything that has happened. For a moment there is dead air on the phone.

Finally she said, "Mill, what did you expected Susan to do? What is so different about her response now than it was twenty years ago?"

I am confused, but then again I am not. "She actually wants me to not write this story. I mean not talk about it."

"Again, I'm asking you what is so different. She couldn't deal with this before and she still can't. You are making her the wrong person here and she can't let herself feel that. No one wants to be called racist or feel that."

I remained silent. I was at a loss for words. I am never at a loss for words.

"I don't know. I can't think right now. I am pissed. Just really pissed. I am so sick of the crying. All the damn crying to deflect what is really going on. Do you know how long Black people would be crying?" I said.

"Girl, she doesn't get it."

"Really? This is a retired teacher with her Master's degree, well-traveled and so called Christian."

"What do you want her to say? That she said something racist? What do you want her to do? Join racist rehab?"

"I don't have time for these jokes, Kim."

"But I'm not joking, nor am I excusing her behavior. I feel like nothing she will do in your mind can help you get past this."

Later when I got home and mustered up the energy to open the proposal I notice a large x through the part on the proposal about Susan and her black-face comment. I noticed in the margins her notations about speaking about our commonalities for the proposal would make it a stronger piece of writing (in her opinion). The anger that had quieted down resurfaced in a major way. Is she serious? That is far from the truth of my experience. Here comes her playing the "victim" role. Playing the victim allows the blinders to remain on. Playing the victim allows her to address racism if and when she feels like it. This proposal, this topic has called up everything that both she and I couldn't see from the original incident over nineteen years ago.

That night as I lay my head to rest, Kim's question was embedded in the forefront of my mind. Why now? What is so different about Susan's words and their impact now? I finally came to the painful conclusion that it is the culmination of many things. For starters it is age. It is life experience. It is what is allowed and what I cannot any longer tolerate. It is the combination of white people cutting in line in front of me at Whole Foods and saying they didn't see me. It is a supervisor labeling me hostile when I speak my mind, while my white female counterpart is considered assertive. It is the people on my job and their institutionalized racism that is never policed let alone acknowledged. It is a world where the lives of Treyvon Martin, Michael Brown, Sandra Bland, Eric Garner, Tamir Rice (among countless others) didn't and still don't matter, It is a world where levies drown poor brown people, leave children without parents and parents without children, and where celebrities like Beyoncé, Serena Williams, and Cam Newton are criticized because they own and love their Blackness. All of these things have reached a crescendo in my mind. If I hear and witness one more person inflicting another hurt stating that it was "unintentional" I will implode. It will be worse if that person claims to be a friend of mine.

I edited my proposal, submitted it, and then I decided what is meant to be will be. Susan and I didn't talk for weeks. Nevertheless, I was proud of my decision to write the proposal and I stand by it. I am at the stage in my life where I realize some relationships are seasonal and not meant for a lifetime. The reality of it stings in an uncomfortable way, but once you lose a parent, anything after that from my perspective never hurts as much.

A few weeks after the Susan incident, as the universe would have it my employer offered a mandatory workshop of Microaggressions in the Workplace, which I am grateful for, but doubt will make any lasting impact. The workshop is four hours of discomfort. Throughout the majority of the workshop my coworkers roll their eyes out loud, squirm in their seats, and refuse participation. Our facilitators are wonderful, insightful, and do their best to ease the unspoken discomfort. Despite the stressed environment I am grateful for the wealth of information. I am thankful for the suggested reading material and the various roleplays that I witnessed to combat this sensitive topic. I had always carried Susan in the back of my mind and wondered how to address what I would say to her one day when I ran into her as I believed it would happen. Despite my feelings of resentment I needed closure, but I knew that I would have to initiate the first step. I realized it is more about my overall growth and not who initiates the process. After all, that is the way of the universe.

That same evening after the workshop, I called out to Susan. She began the conversation stating she was so glad to hear from me and wondered if I was okay. I told her that I was fine and would like to have a conversation with her about the proposal and the difference in opinion that we had. She agreed.

I remembered my first words being, "I want to go back to what was brought up in our conversation about the proposal, and the comment about putting dark makeup on your face and sitting in the back of the room came. You minimized the impact these words had on me. You refused to try to understand that my hurt came from a long history of mistreatment of people of color, the devaluing of our bodies in the street, and the way that we are invisible to most of the world. I felt the focus on the hurt you were feeling trumped my feelings. Twenty years ago this pain was not as prevalent as it is today. While I understand your intention was not to be racist, that could be perceived as a racist remark. I feel like with more information and more awareness it would enable you to not state things in a way you didn't intend."

"I would never want to hurt you and I love you. I am truly sorry. I am ignorant and I hate that my ignorance causes so much pain. I really didn't know," she said, "but that is no excuse."

"I don't have a problem with your stating you are hurt, but it hurts me when you don't see that others hurt as well because the focus shifts exclusively to you. I think it may be helpful if you did some reading or we actively communicate on how misunderstandings like this can be prevented." I said.

"Can I say that I was hurt that I had hurt you?" replied Susan.

"I appreciate that. I appreciate your acknowledging my hurt."

"This is a challenging planet. I was so caught up in what I felt was my being wronged that I couldn't see how you felt. I apologize. I can't imagine what it is like to be ignored or treated poorly because of my skin color. I can't imagine how those parents feel who lost their children at the hatred of another. I know that this is not going to be an overnight thing, but I am thankful that we are at least talking. I am truly sorry and I never meant to hurt you in any sort of way. But it's good we are talking about this. This is what needs to be talked about."

"I agree and it needs to be an ongoing conversation in order for this relationship to work."

"I want to do more. Learn more. I think if we keep the lines of communication open, talk, pray to God and keep working in love we will be okay."

"I think that's a good first step," I said.

"Still friends?" she said.

"Baby steps." I said.

I held the telephone in my lap for the longest time after our conversation ended. I realized the words that had been exchanged were simply words because an unsettling feeling resided in my stomach. Despite her words, I realized I still questioned in the back of my mind her sincerity. True mending of this relationship (if I could truly allow it) would require time, and even then there was no guarantee. Only time would tell.

Reference

Rankine, C. (2014). *Citizen: An American lyric*. Minneapolis, MN: Graywolf Press.

· 1 0 ·

DEAR SIS/LOVE, SIS

Felice Belle and Anne Murphy

Context: As creative writers, and lovers of the lost art of letter writing, we decided to write a series of letters—exploring milestones in our friendship and why race seems to be the least discussed and, perhaps, least compelling part. We wanted to explore how we were able to move from a "surface friendship," or one in which there is little or no deep exploration of each person, to a friendship that is deeply meaningful.

Letters

(Anne 1)
Dear Sis,

Lately I wonder why we so rarely talk about race. Of all the subjects in the wheelhouse of our friendship—men, writing, work, "social media cutting," as you call it when one of us is eavesdropping on another's virtual life—how is it that I am white and you are Black so rarely arises in our conversations?

For almost twenty years you have been the person I talk to more often than anyone on earth. So often our friends and family have come to call us sisters. I loved how, during Christmas in the Bronx with your family, your brother hugged me and said, "Any best friend of my sister's is a sister of mine."

I felt like I belonged, though of course I was the only white person in the living room. It didn't matter.

Do you remember when we first started calling each other sister? We were poets. We did a reading somewhere downtown, in New York. Afterward, a Black woman came up to you, also a Black woman, and asked if you would read at her event, "Sisters Black Like Me." You said yes, of course. I stood there feeling white and happy for you. The woman then turned to me and said, "And would you like to read at the event with her?" I also said yes, of course. Later, with both of us enjoying great rounds of laughter, I rhetorically asked you if you thought the woman realized I was white? Immediately we began calling each other Sisters Black, and then just sister.

When did we drop that word? Black?

In my memory it was the year of our mutual friend James's death. When we began talking every day. When we lost a fellow friend, and poet. A man you loved, deeply. And who I loved for bringing us together. There we were, day after day, that horrible year that gave us this friendship. At the hospital. At the funeral. And eventually/always, back on stage. Was it loss that caused us to drop the moniker of race in what has become our cherished nickname?

I think for me it might have something to do with what I consider as foundational to my identity. Above all else, I identify myself as a writer. It is how I most want to be seen, and remembered. I also have a lot bound up by way of identity with being Irish, a woman, a private investigator, and from Bakersfield, which is the second worst place to live in the nation, according to numerous media reports.

But this identity also shifts depending on the context. For instance, when I walk down the street in Bed Stuy, I think: Here I am, a white woman walking down the block with Black families. Here are people planting flowers, talking, living their lives. And I feel like an intruder of sorts: a lanky white girl in a historically Black neighborhood. One afternoon, walking home from a coffee shop in my neighborhood, this homeless man on the street, who seemed by his mannerisms to be on drugs, screamed at me: "Hey you fucking cracker. Get the fuck out of Bed Stuy. You don't belong here, white bitch." I went home, feeling defeated, and called you immediately in tears. And you were so sorry that I had the experience.

Not long after, I was walking down the street near my house, and there was a group of young Black men standing outside a bodega. Pants slung low, hats backward, laughing and talking. And in my head I thought: "Cross the street, don't walk in their way." I noticed the thought and had a counterreaction, which was essentially that I had seen a group of young Black men standing on the corner and some part of me thought: "Danger." I thought it was problematic that I had this internal reaction, and decided to walk by them. As soon as I passed them they got quiet. Then one of them shouted at me, "Hey beautiful! You having a good day?" I laughed, and shouted that I was having a good day. "Great baby," the guy shouted back. "Welcome to the neighborhood!" For me, it was a victory. Everyone participating in a humorous exchange while still acknowledging that race and gentrification was in play.

(Felice 1)

Dear Sis,

I had a similar experience, when I lived in Crown Heights, circa 1999. The young, Black kids who lived next door and raised pit bulls in the backyard would some nights congregate on my stoop. New to the neighborhood, I'd had that internal flash of "danger." I also had to check myself. They're kids, I thought. And they were never anything other than respectful. I mention it, only to point to the insidious nature of racism. That even though these boys looked like me, I had also internalized every image that branded them a threat. And they were not.

I remember that night, with the woman. It immediately became our favorite joke. You're my sister ... Black like me! I searched my e-mail for the earliest occurrence, and you're right it is around the time of James's death. Although by that time we'd already shortened the e-mail signatures to "sister Black" and "sister white," respectively. Your grandmother passed around the same time that James did. It was a rough year. All that grief. I think our daily check-ins eased the transition to just sister. I also think, in mixed company, it was lot of backstory to explain: the woman, the reading, and so on. Sister was much simpler, to the point.

I was talking to Benny the other night and he said he was done with his brother, wanted nothing more to do with him. And I said, "You can't be done with family." Obviously, he can. But family, by my definition, is for life. And we were already in the process of developing that bond. Not without its own drama. As I recall, in the early days, we had a bad habit of wounding each other with our words. There were a lot of arguments, tears, hurt feelings. And multiple conversations about whether or not this was a friendship worth preserving. But the answer was always yes. At any point, we could have made another choice, but we chose to stay connected. It seems important to note that neither one of us has a biological sister. I don't know about you, but I always wanted one.

I remember calling you from "the most racist town on Fire Island." I had been so excited to spend the summer there, teaching poetry and playwriting workshops for kids. Only to be assaulted by the reality of white boys shouting nigger at me and the overprivileged preteens who told me I looked like their nanny. Like *all* of their nannies. It was like that Countee Cullen poem (2016). *All that I remember.* You and the ladies came out to visit for the weekend, and I could not have been happier to be held and taken care of, to connect with people who loved me and knew me as more than a type.

As you know my own upbringing was solidly middle class. I have an Ivy League degree. It is the type of privilege that is equated with race, but not the sole province of it. Both of my parents are from Guyana, they came to the United States to go to college. My brothers and I were the first generation born in the States. Growing up, my brothers called me "white" because of the way I spoke, the friends I had, the Johnny Depp poster on my wall. To my cousins, new to the States, I was a Yankee, who didn't want to eat rice unless it was Chinese takeout. My mother studied at Iowa State. She tells the story of being a recent immigrant, sitting in the school cafeteria, eating a piece of watermelon. One of her Black American classmates admonished her. What are you doing? You can't do that here! For my mother, it was a piece of fruit. For her classmate, it was the perpetuation of a dehumanizing stereotype, and in Civil Rights Era America, an affront to the movement.

On the flipside, in undergrad, I got flack from my fellow engineering major Jason, born and raised in Guyana, because I was a member of the Black Students Organization, but not a member of the Caribbean Students Association. To him, my choice was a denial of heritage. But there were so few students of color at our predominantly white institution, the distinction felt negligible. My thought was there is power in numbers. Which translates to how race is played out on a national scale. But I question what is lost. I was raised in America, so mine is a Black American experience, but my culture, my history, my blood is Caribbean. I find conversations about race often lack nuance.

Like you, I identify primarily as a writer, an artist, a lover of life. But I live in a world that will never mistake me for white. In this way, race is foundational to my identity; it is one of the first things a person would notice about me. It informs my daily experience in the world. And I take pride in it, the way I do all aspects of myself that I love. But it is not all that I am. Race becomes a substitute for actual knowing. You look like X, so you must be Y. It is a flawed equation. And most days I am exhausted by it.

On a micro level: my old hairdresser and I had an undying love for George Michael and Matchbox Twenty. We used to joke that we were going to start a club called "Black Girls Who Like White Music." That our musical tastes fell outside a culturally prescribed notion of Blackness was at once hilarious and a badge of honor.

On a macro level and historically speaking, race has been used as a tool of oppression, to deny the humanity of entire groups of people. This country's economic and political systems are built upon a construct that enforces, justifies, perpetuates manmade inequalities—that is, all men are created equal, except you. You're three fifths of a person.

There's this Toni Morrison quote that perhaps explains it, better than I can:

> The function, the very serious function of racism is distraction. It keeps you from doing your work. It keeps you explaining, over and over again, your reason for being. Somebody says you have no language and you spend twenty years proving that you do. Somebody says your head isn't shaped properly so you have scientists working on the fact that it is. Somebody says you have no art, so you dredge that up. Somebody says you have no kingdoms, so you dredge that up. None of this is necessary. There will always be one more thing. (Morrison, 1975)

So much of our friendship has to do with the limitless nature of this life—creation, art, beauty, truth, the contradictions of our own minds and actions. I'm interested in race as a lived experience, but I find race, as a construct, limiting. Mainly because it is a label I did not choose, that comes with conditions I don't subscribe to. I think there is an external expectation that race should mean more to our friendship than it does. I don't think there is conscious or unconscious deemphasis on our part. We talk about it as it comes up. Which is most often in the context of some direct or indirect aggression from the outside world. In contrast, I think of our friendship as a space where I can be about the real business of why I am here. Which is not about justifying my existence or convincing the populace I'm equal. It's a space where I get to explore the fullness of my humanity—which is enlivened by my racial identity, but not limited or defined solely by it.

(Anne 2)

I've never thought about longing for a biological sister, a point you raised, and logically so. I do feel the same as you: that we have moved into the realm of family. It seems the community has moved through this narrative with us, e.g., when your cousin Mary asked if we could adopt her, though we are neither gay, nor married, nor lovers. But sisters and prospective adoptive parents of a twenty-something woman in need of direction? Why of course.

I like Ms. Morrison's quote very much. When I was in graduate school in Chicago, I was obsessed with Edward Said. I believe he was teaching at the University of Chicago at the time, where I was a graduate student, though I could be mistaken on that note. In any case, I was reading a tremendous amount of cultural theory. Said had published *Orientalism* (1978), which had swiftly come to be recognized as one of the preeminent texts on postcolonial studies. Part of his argument was that the history of European and American imperialism (whiteness, the West) must be viewed in the context of the racialized "Other" (darkness, the east), and that to reach any understanding of race, power, colonialism, politics, and literature, one must cross not only national borders, but disciplinary borders. I fell in love with the theory that in order to understand history, in order to move it, reshape it, we have to swing for the fences, go broad. Look as critically at the narratives we are fed in the papers as we do at those on television, in music.

The University of Chicago as you likely know is located in Hyde Park and Kenwood, a largely African American community. I was often the only white person on the bus, the restaurant, jogging by Farrakhan's house. And I felt white in those contexts, which is to say I felt the privilege of whiteness bearing down on that geography. By privileged I mean largely that because I was white, it seemed people made certain assumptions about me: that I was a student, not a long-time member of the community (correct) that because I was white and a student, it reasoned that I must be rich or middle class (incorrect). As you know, I put myself through college and graduate school on scholarships. My father worked for a moving company. My mother, for a cattle auctioneer. But there was a richness I felt on the south side of Chicago in the sense that I was unafraid of what might happen to me on the streets because of my race: for example, if I saw a police officer, I generally felt safer, protected. I did not fear they would mistake me for a criminal, and I had Black friends at school who had a deep fear of the police.

You'll also like this: while in graduate school, I called myself a socialist, and in Chicago joined the International People's Democratic Uhuru Movement, founded by the African People's Socialist Party. The group is largely associated with Fred Hampton Jr. and works against police violence, alongside other issues. At those meetings, I was also one of the few white people in the room.

And eventually I came to believe I did not belong in that particular room. It was not for me. The members of the group tolerated my presence, yes. But I was not truly a part of that space. I felt the same way when you and I went to church together in Fort Greene a year or so ago. When the Black preacher started talking to the Black congregation about white people oppressing Blacks, I thought: This is a critical space, and a spiritual space, and this is not the place I will come to pray. This space is not for me. Here I am seen, because I am white, as the oppressor, the bad guy, the gentrifier. I'm not inside, I'm out.

When I moved to New York and began the little flare of my poetry "career" at the Nuyorican Poets Cafe where we met I also felt anxious about being white in the context of a largely Black, Puerto Rican, Caribbean crowd. And yet I felt I belonged and was accepted. And I was brought into the deep folds of that community. Race constructed, race deconstructed with the help, perhaps, of poetry. I think for all of us, art was how we transcended nation, class, race, gender, sexuality or at least tried to, with words on the page. Not by skating around the issues, but by writing them out, and having our stories heard and shared. After all, if art cannot transcend into the universal, it cannot survive. I feel the same way about our friendship. I don't think of you as my Black friend, or our bond under the moniker of "my interracial friendship." You are my friend, my sister. This is our friendship. To me, we transcend race. Not by denying it or failing to acknowledge it, but by going in our experiences together above and beyond its limits. That is how I think of our friendship at its foundation: as limitless.

I agree with you on the race-as-social-construct front. And I've experienced as much. Not only race, but nation. I'll never forget checking into a hotel in India, when a woman at the desk looked at my freckled face in horror and said, "Miss, can I ask what's wrong with your skin? The spots on your face?" I laughed. I wasn't offended. But she was horrified for me. She explained that her sister had a special cream to remove these unsightly spots, and she could call her if I wanted? I declined. I told her I was Irish, and in some parts of the world freckles are considered a mark of beauty. What I later came to understand through long conversations with various Indian women was that the hotel clerk thought I had vitiligo, the skin condition wherein white patches appear on otherwise beautiful brown skin. Whiteness in this context was a curse, a stigma, an affliction that translates into hardship in acquiring a job, and in prospects for a husband. It would be hard for me to stand in that same hotel lobby and suggest to the Indian woman that race is a construct, always shifting. For her, freckles meant curse.

Thinking about the subject more deeply, one of the things I appreciate most in our friendship is the fact that we seem to have, I hate to use the word, but *transcended* the construct of race. One of the Toni Morrison quotes I love most is the one wherein she discusses her refusal to be categorized and pigeon-holed as a writer, and pressurizes this notion of the universal:

> It is that business of being universal, a word hopelessly stripped of meaning for me. Faulkner wrote what I suppose could be called regional literature and had it published all over the world. That's what I wish to do. If I tried to write a universal novel, it would be water. Behind this question is the suggestion that to write for Black people is somehow to diminish the writing. From my perspective there are only Black people. When I say 'people,' that's what I mean. (Morrison, 1981)

(Felice 2)
Dear Sis,

To your point about Edward Said, I think the wonder of colonialism, the gift that keeps on giving, is that entire cultures of people believed/believe that they are inferior, that they should be someone else. I remember being on a students of color retreat, in undergrad, and a Filipino woman was talking about being the darkest member of her family. And I was amazed that was an issue for her. And then I thought, right. Your people were colonized too.

I think art can transcend, I question whether people do. In part, because I just read an article about dead, Black celebrities, by Lawrence Ross (2016), that problematized the idea of "transcending race" as if it were an admirable achievement. Ross made the point that Michael Jackson, Prince, Muhammed Ali didn't "transcend" anything, they were Black and proud. But because they reached the mainstream (read: white people liked them), it meant that they could now be seen as something more than Black. He went on to say the onus is not on anyone to transcend their race, gender, etc. It's on the hegemonic, white, patriarchy to transcend the psychological mindset that privileges whiteness over all other identities.

Which brings me to Rachel Dolezal. Remember her? The white woman who pretended to be Black. I found that whole news cycle fascinating, for a number of reasons. First, there was the unspoken assumption that given a choice, no one would ever choose to be Black. Second, there was the reality that no matter who you date or how you wear your hair, you will never be another race. But third, for me, there was the idea of what if? What if you could, regardless of how you look, "choose" your race? I get the ridiculousness of it, how there are systems in place to prevent the possibility. But as a creative, I deal in imagination. And I think much of being any type of "other" is an (over)identification with oppression. And again, I emphasize the struggle is real. But whiteness, as a construct, connotes power, privilege, freedom. What would it look like, feel like for every "other" to own that? Even if only on a metaphoric level.

When we first started this project, I suggested maybe we shouldn't talk as much, so that there'd be more to say in our letters. And I don't remember your response verbatim, but it was something to the effect of, "We are still going to talk every day." What's come up in conversation, that has yet to make onto the page, is that this exercise in race feels academic, inorganic, not at all like how we usually speak. It's been weeks since I've written you, in part because I was writing a play. And the night of the reading, you my dearest friend, skipped class to be there, and you had a cold!

As evidence of the depth of our friendship, I often tell the story of you walking from Cobble Hill to Crown Heights, during a transit strike, so that you could go with me to Peter's wake. How if I didn't already know, I knew then that you were a friend for the ages. And I know that crisis management is your specialty, by profession and personal trade. When times are hard, you show up with whatever I need most—love, Indian food, an open mind and ear. But truth is, I don't think it's the times of crisis that define our friendship. I think it is forged in the everyday conversations, about whatever matters most that minute—an hour on the phone about whether or not I should go out with Justin on Halloween, conflict resolution strategies for dealing with a bananas coworker, assorted heartbreaks.

I remember saying that I had written the play for you, that you were in fact my ideal reader/audience member for this one. I think there is a fullness and depth to the level of conversation we have with each other. I don't think most people talk to each other the way we do. It reminds me of the Adrienne Rich (1979) quote, about love being a process of refining the truths we tell each other. "Whatever it takes to get to the truth," as our friend Robin is fond of saying. When I am in any way lying to myself, you have a talent for asking questions, or sharing a parable, that helps me find my way to my truth.

And then there is the writing, the love of story and words and craft, that is at the foundation of our friendship. I am as invested in your writing life as I am my own. I want to see you win, as much as I want it for myself. And there are the small victories—the stories published, plays produced, but mostly there is the daily support of a sister-in-arms, dedicated to showing up at the page.

(Anne 3)

Dear Sis,

I was very touched by your letter, as I always am whenever you bring up our closeness and its accordant presence, the terrible day of Peter's wake. And yes, while we both love Frank O'Hara's (1996) poetic dictum: "In times of crisis, we must all decide again and again whom we love," you're right that the bond we have is deep, daily, and constant. It kicks into high gear whenever our friends get sick and die, which feels like often, and it kicks into high gear when you get hit by a car and roll over the hood and you relay this information over the phone with the emotionless tone of a war reporter. Or when I have another cancer scare and you go with me to Sloan Kettering. "This place is like a TV hospital. I'm making myself a hot chocolate." I'll never forget sitting in the waiting room listening to the machine froth out a warm beverage for my sister, who was enjoying the view, the orchids, the graham crackers. Another day in the life of Felice and Anne. Assorted heartbreaks, as you so beautifully put it.

Our friendship shows up at hospitals and it makes long distance phone calls from Paris and sends flowers when the occasion arises. It fact checks. It goes to the video. It goes to the overhead camera and tries to look down on the situation without judgment. The bird's eye view. The God's eye. By the way, you were the only person in my life who asked what I wanted for my fortieth birthday: espresso cups. And you were therefore the only person who gave them to me. I love them. They're sitting on the shelf in my kitchen.

I think our friendship is like a Johnny Cash song: steady like a train, sharp like a razor. When I'm knee deep in questionable behavior, I call you. When I have zero news, I call you. In a way, and while it sounds saccharine to say it, ours is the greatest love story of my life, if one is allowed to talk about love in the context of platonic friendship between women. One who is white, yes, and one who is Black. But it's the love, the truth, the friendship that transcends.

I think the year we became friends—the year of Peter and my grandmother's deaths, with the backdrop of the Nuyorican was the same year we dropped race from our moniker: from Sisters Black, to Sisters. We talk about race when it comes up in our own lives, and around issues more broadly, for example, police violence, gentrified neighborhoods, etc., but I don't think race is the key identifier for our friendship. I remember when I was dating Charles, who as you know was Black, race came up constantly. Because it was a romantic relationship, and involved the two of us interacting with two sets of parents, it was something we often talked about. Charles was frequently pulled aside

at airports because security guards thought he looked like a terrorist, essentially. When we broke up, I remember Monique's uncle saying, "We'll find you
another Spanish man." Charles was constantly being misidentified. It plagued
him, and it plagued our relationship. I remember at one point asking him,
because his father was a Black civil rights attorney married to a white woman,
"Do you think your father wishes you were dating a Black woman?" He didn't
hesitate when he said, "Yes." My parents never made me feel anything but
accepted and loved in my romantic choice. But Charles's father made it clear
that he didn't approve of his son dating a white woman. I remember warning
you when we met him that he wasn't a warm man, and not to be insulted if
he ignored you entirely. I was shocked, and a bit crushed, when he met you,
and fell head over heels in love and awe of you, as he rightly should have. But
I thought: Oh, wow. It's not that he's a cold person. He's cold toward me, his
Black son's white girlfriend. And he's warm to my best friend, my Black sister.
I remember we talked about that extensively. How race was undeniably at play
in that dynamic.

There have been many moments in my life where I feel breathlessly overwhelmed, and think: "I need to talk to my sister immediately." And I know
you feel the same. The calls from the bus stops, from the street corner, the
proverbial situation room. I remember being stuck in an unhappy, impossible
relationship, standing with you late one summer night in tears, and you said to
me, "Sis, you don't have to do this any more. I know you can get out of this."
I didn't know, but I believed you believed in me. And I trust you so completely
that it helped me breathe, and leave. And you carried me through that experience. When I was convinced I'd never find an apartment, you said: "This is
New York. Everybody finds the apartment. I think you should make a vision
of what you want, and then look for it." I wanted Brooklyn, old building, new
luxury, a view of the treetops, the side of the church, birdsong and owl hoots.
Impossible.

So much of what I have is thanks to you. Showing up for the hard stuff,
the boring stuff, the work and the play. In the world of hospitals and heartbreaks. And always always in the other, the magical world of words on the
page.

(Felice 3)

I don't think I realized how difficult that moment was for you, meeting
Charles's dad. He and I actually exchanged information, as if we might keep
in touch. I think because you guys had come to see my play, I thought maybe

he's just being nice. But I was also legitimately in awe of the life he'd lived. In high school, I attended the Ella Baker Summer Academy for Nonviolence Training. And he *knew* Ella Baker! I also couldn't believe that he'd take issue with his son dating a white woman, when he had married a white woman. But people are complex.

When Phife died, I wrote a tweet in my head, #rip #phifedawg #my youth. I didn't know him, but it hit me hard. The year 1993, I waited in line at Tower Records to get a copy of Midnight Marauders. I bought the tape, because I was convinced CDs wouldn't last. I got my Source magazine signed, A Tribe Called Quest was on the cover. End of an era, I thought. Two weeks later my friend Sharon's mom passed away. She had been ill for a while, which didn't make the loss any less brutal. And as much as I hate funerals, I went. Because she's been my girl since seventh grade, and as we've discussed, when friends are in need you show up.

Last week, I got a call that my college friend Sean died. Cause of death unknown. Friday he was alive. Monday afterschool his son found him, keeled over at his computer. This one hit hardest. Sean was pure love and light, the biggest of personalities. Freshman year he directed a campus production of For Colored Girls; I played lady in red. He told me, I want to do this play at the Apollo next year. It seemed preposterous that a college student could pull that off. But a year later, there we were on the Apollo stage in front of a sold-out crowd. That was the kind of man he was. The dream realized. All this death made me think of us, planning each other's funerals. Side note: At my service, I want to hear "Party Don't Cry" by Tony Toni Toné and "Seasons of Love" from RENT.

When we were on the phone the other day and I told you I'd been procrastinating on getting my application in for a teaching position I really wanted. I said I wanted to make a conscious effort to make decisions out of love and not obligation. And you said, either way it gets done, so why not love instead of fear. And I know you heard me, because you are a great listener, but I was struck that you said fear. It was only later that afternoon that it sunk in, I was terrified, because this position is something I really want. I'd applied to the same college five years ago. Six months after my second interview, I got a letter saying they had aborted the position, which I thought was terrible language for an academic institution to use. I felt like they burned me once before, but so did Justin and I took that ride again and again, so why not this? But mainly it was my fear of moving in the direction of my dream, getting closer to the life I desire most. Hearing you say what I could not helped me move past the monsters in my head. This is one of the things you do best. Like all great writers, you read for what's there and what's underneath it.

There's a lyric in "La Vie Boheme," another song from RENT: "The opposite of war isn't peace, it's creation." And what are we about if not the business of creation. It's the gift of this life, one of many.

References

Cullen, C. (2016, September 6). Incident. *Poemhunter.com*. Web.

Larson, J. (1990). *Rent*. S.l.: EMI.

Morrison, T. (1975, May 30). "A Humanist View." Black Studies Center Public Dialogue on the American Dream Theme Part 2 of 2. Portland, OR: Portland State University. Lecture.

Morrison, T. (1981, March 21). "The Language Must Not Sweat." Interview with Thomas Sinclair. *New Republic*. Retrieved September 12, 2016, from newrepublic.com/article/95923/the-language-must-not-sweat

O'Hara, F. (1996). To the film industry in crisis. In *Meditations in an Emergency*. New York, NY: Grove Press Reissue Edition.

Rich, A. (1979). *On lies, secrets, and silence: Selected prose, 1966–1978*. New York, NY: Norton.

Ross, L. (2016, June 6). Dear white people, Muhammad Ali didn't "transcend race." *The Root*. Retrieved September 6, 2016 from www.theroot.com/articles/culture/2016/06/dear-white-people-muhammad-ali-didnt-transcend-race/

Said, E. W. (1978). *Orientalism*. New York, NY: Pantheon Books.

A Tribe Called Quest (Musical group). (1993). *Midnight marauders*. New York, NY: Jive/Zomba/BMG Records.

· 1 1 ·

CHOOSING EACH OTHER

Love, Friendship, and Racism

Jennifer M. D. Matos and Gail E. Norskey

It's not obvious how we would come to be so close. We come from different places. Gail is a white (Polish and Italian), upper-middle-class, straight, Catholic, female, temporarily able-bodied person. Jen is a queer, disabled, middle-class, Catholic Latina. Gail was raised in a homogeneously white neighborhood in Gardner, Massachusetts, and Jen was raised in a predominantly people of color neighborhood in Jersey City, New Jersey. We couldn't look more different, but it's what you can't see that connects us.

We feel we are like the same person on the inside. What we mean by this is that we share similar values. We value loyalty and humor, family and authentic relationships, honesty and justice. We are connected and similar—when we are on the phone together, our respective spouses will say, "I know who is on the phone—I can tell by how you are laughing—you only laugh like that with each other." Our laughter is a powerful metaphor for our relationship. What our spouses understand when they hear us laugh is that we are completely free with each other. We can laugh like that because we don't fear being vulnerable. We trust each other deeply.

We came to truly know what was inside each of us because of some terrible things that we experienced together. The details of that particular story are for another essay, but simply put, we were working in the same office and we were confronted with a shared experience of racism. We each had a lot to lose by speaking up, but we both made the only choice that we could live with, and we faced the brutal consequences together. Throughout it all, we found a way to laugh, and we formed profoundly deep and abiding bonds. We discovered how amazing it is when another human being stands up for you with lots of love and courage.

In our mutual vocabulary, there is no word strong enough to encapsulate the essence of what we feel for each other. We don't share parents or siblings, but we are like family. We've worked together but, our relationship has never been about hierarchy and power. We have looked to each other for guidance and support and have learned so much from each other. We're not romantic partners, and yet, we have deep and intimate bonds of love that exist outside the traditional lexicon. So without defining words, we'll try to give you some insights, by sharing the following letters we have written to each other.

***

Dear Gail,

All my life, whether it was through what I learned at home about the consequences of racism or what I learned in my life, that racism was real and had the ability to crush me, I was taught that white people are not to be trusted. Our daughters (your Greek and Polish youngest daughter and my biologically white-raised Puerto Rican only child) both love the movie *Pocahontas*. In it, white colonizers arrive to steal land from Native Americans. In my life, I was taught that, like John Smith, white people want to steal what belongs to people of color and that they want to demean us, make us small, and in the worst cases, erase us altogether. I have seen racism in action.

In my elementary school I was laughed at and picked on in my predominantly white school for knowing Spanish. I was terribly bullied about my Spanish speaking skills. I remember going through our phonics workbook and coming across a picture of a pink slipper on a green background. The white teacher wanted us to name the items in each picture. I began to sweat as I desperately tried to grasp the English word for slipper. Suddenly my vocabulary was trapped in Spanish. As I struggled and sweated, I remember that I couldn't say the picture was a "chancleta." In this white world, it was a slipper. That was the exact moment where I rejected my culture and anything to do with the Spanish language. During my kindergarten graduation, the Puerto Rican kids were paraded on stage to sing "traditional Latin songs" and later, we wore the makeshift headdresses we made and danced around, "like Indians." The same kids that I was friends with told me that they weren't allowed to have Puerto Ricans in their houses, but that I was allowed in because I wasn't like "the other Puerto Ricans," I didn't fit their stereotype.

In high school, I remained best friends with Gina, whom I went to grammar school with. Her sister was older, and drove, so she would drive us to school. One morning Gina's sister, Lisa, told her mom where she had parked the car. Upon hearing the location of the family car, Gina's mom erupted at her saying *"You can't park the car in front of the Puerto Rican's house! It will get stolen!"* I felt the top of my head get tingly and cold and that feeling spread to my face into my red-hot cheeks. I was so embarrassed and felt like I could die right there, but what I noticed most was how invisible and small I felt. I stopped going to Gina's house after that and we were no longer best friends.

My high school years wouldn't be restricted to interpersonal racism. Before my night sweats, fatigue, hair loss, joint pain, and weight loss were officially diagnosed as lupus, white male doctors coerced me into taking pregnancy tests. I was tested for HIV and AIDS. It didn't matter that I was a good student and a virgin. What they saw was a Puerto Rican teenager with a single mom from a bad neighborhood. I know that if I had been a well-off white kid with two parents, I wouldn't have been stereotyped in such ways. It was also in high school that I met you. There were other white people in my life by this time who I saw as allies, though I wouldn't have had that vocabulary yet. They were nice and kind and generous with their time and believed in me. When I first saw you, you were smiling. And every time you saw the girls from the program, you were smiling. I don't remember ever talking to you, but I remember your smile. I've been smiled at by white people before when I have been in a group of kids of color. Then, the white people would smile at me like I was a caged animal who was given a day off from the zoo. Those smiles were painful and patronizing. When you smiled at me then, much like you smile at me now, it's as if to say, "I am happy you're here with me." You created a space for me that summer where, even in a world of racism, I could be a scholar, a scientist, a regular kid with friends who never cut me out or cut me up because of my color.

I thought my college years would be just the same as that summer. But the summer of 1990 was an anomaly. In college, classmates would tell me— without hesitation—that the only reason I "got in" was because the college wanted more diversity. And it was more that I was "let in" rather than earning my way into college. Other students would treat me like I worked for them when they handed me their dirty dishes as my work-study job in the kitchen. The institution would protect hate speech under the guise of free speech and I knew that I would never be safe in any school.

You hired me to work in the same summer program I was in as a student. As my supervisor, you trusted me. You never treated me like I was stupid or I lacked capital. You treated me like I was gifted, an asset, and you took me under your wing. There, I learned how to be a good supervisor, and there, I got to work with other young girls who came from similar places. I listened as you explained why activities in the program were free ("so no one feels left out because everyone might not have money") and I witnessed your ire and swift action when a student of color wasn't being fairly treated or cared for at the local hospital. Unlike the other white people I have met before who put on a show for my sake, I could tell yours was no act. I could tell by the way you really listened to and laughed with the parents of color when they came to visit. How you were thoughtful about making them as comfortable as the white parents, if not more, when they came to visit. You possessed an awareness about injustice and how you could use your privilege to make a difference.

If there was any doubt left, like dust left behind from a lifetime of racism about your intentions, it was wiped away when we got to work together many years later. You were going to retire and there were so many other people whose names you could have offered as your replacement. I was shocked when you said that you wanted to recommend me. You listed qualities about my work that no one ever mentioned, but I also saw as my personal strengths. When my promotion was not offered as we were told it would be, you could have left it alone. You could have walked away with your retirement package and left me with the college's new and less fair offer. You wouldn't have lost anything. But you committed a sin in the white world; you called the institution and your white peers out on racism. You questioned why no people of color had held your position before, and you made your claims very public. You were shamed, laughed at, disregarded. You had a taste of what it was like to live in my world when you became disadvantaged by association. I watched as you were tossed out, socially and professionally. I saw you, as the world around you started to shrink, the walls closing in on you with no place to hide. Just as white people couldn't hear me, the same white people tuned themselves out to you as well.

I could have left you, too. It would have been easy, to laugh at their jokes and call you names. It would have meant I could keep my job and support my wife and our new baby. The institutional oppression was first betting that you would turn you back on me, and then when that failed, they bet that I could be bought, and turn my back on you.

But how could I leave you? In that process when you were being exiled, you taught me what vulnerability looks like and shared that with me. When my precious daughter was born, you were among the first people she met. She met you even before she met her grandparents. It was fitting that you were there every day with us because you became a part of my family, too, during that time. It was, in large part, watching you with your beloved daughters that I learned how to parent. You offered advice, rest, good humor, and healing. Without you, I don't know how I would have—or could have—survived the racism we both endured. You did for me what no white person had ever done before. You risked yourself for me and for what was right. I did what I was never allowed to do for another white person before, either, and I was able to risk my job, for our friendship, for what was right.

Taking the risk was supposed to tear us apart. But it brought us closer together. We have become like women before us, risking themselves for friendship and connection. I know that you see my color, and I know that you appreciate it and value it. I know that I can trust you and that whether or not I am here, you will be standing up for the "other." I cannot tell you what our visits mean to me because it is beyond words. I get to be me when I am with you and I don't have to be afraid that you will hurt me because of it. I can face other white people because of you, and I know that I am worth something.

Our friendship was born through taking a huge risk. And I will be forever grateful that we did.

Love,

Jen

***

Dear Jen,

I just read your letter and I feel so moved, tears welling up as I write this. I am so touched by your honesty; I feel pain for your having to endure a world filled with judgment and hate. I am humbled by the trust that you have in me. I am intensely grateful for all that you have done for me, and I am happy because when I am with you, I get to be me too.

I've thought a lot about why we are so drawn to each other. Some of it's our personalities. We're both smart strong women. Professionally we are highly analytical, optimistic, and brutally honest. We love to work with committed visionary people to make the world better. We are happy to reward others for their good work and we especially don't like hierarchies or being micromanaged by others. Personally we are fiercely loyal to our families and friends, and romantic to a fault. We are also vulnerable, because we don't hide our feelings very well. We love to laugh—despite our serious and deeply held values, we find humor in the most absurd and sometimes inappropriate situations—when we find our stride in humor, it's hard to stop us and it's so much fun. When we were going through the worst of our experiences at work, you started sending me news releases that made sarcastic, irreverent fun of the hateful and unjust people who were attacking us—I still can barely read those and breathe, I am laughing so hard.

When I first met you over 25 years ago it was at the summer program for high school girls at a college in Massachusetts. The program was about giving girls a chance to explore their interests in science. I loved working on that program because it gave me a chance to do something that I really cared about. I cared about girls in science because I had personally experienced so much gender bias in science. I cared about giving girls a chance to attend college because I grew up with two grandmothers, smart talented women, who never were given a chance to go to school beyond 5th grade. I cared about giving girls financial aid and access to education because when I went to college my parents had fallen on tough times and I needed full financial aid. I cared about making this "elite college" a comfortable welcoming place because for me—despite my status as a white, middle-class woman with a Ph.D.—it continued to be a place that made me feel "less than." I knew I didn't have the pedigree of classmates and colleagues who for generations had attended such colleges. Knowing you helped me to finally believe that I am not "less than" the people I went to school with and worked with, but I am different than some of them. I am different because I have different values around what is right and what is fair.

Because of the values my grandmothers taught me, I have never felt "better than" anyone else, but that doesn't mean I am some profoundly aware person. When I first met you it was because the summer program had received a grant for girls of color from Philadelphia and New Jersey. At that time I had zero experience with urban schools and not much awareness around issues of race and privilege. In my hometown everyone was white. It wasn't until I attended college that I met people of color, and they were dramatically underrepresented there. It was working in the summer program that started to change my awareness around race and privilege. I became a firsthand witness to how institutional racism works. I met you and countless other girls of color who came from schools where you were being undereducated because your schools lacked resources. As a white insider I became highly critical of the college's admissions policies for economically disadvantaged girls of color, and that was probably the beginning of my speaking up about race and class, making some people I worked for very uncomfortable. Over time I became very intentional in my efforts to raise funds to support scholarships for girls of color to attend the summer program, to hire staff of color, to do outreach to parents and teachers, and to enlist allies within and outside of the college.

By the time we began working together in 2012, I felt confident about what I was doing professionally, but I didn't fully understand how much I was still working from a position of privilege—safe and secure, sitting at my desk as an administrator, a white person doing "good work." When I started making plans to retire and recommended you as my successor it made perfect sense to me. You are one of the best strategic thinkers I know and you would bring wonderful new energy to the work. I am shocked that you were surprised I would recommend you, another reminder of the privilege I felt and you didn't. When my white supervisor reversed her position and told me that she would likely not appoint you and that she hoped I hadn't raised your expectations about the position, I felt like I couldn't breathe. I was supposed to tell you that it had all been a misunderstanding. How could I do that to you? How could I live with myself if I lied to you? I was supposed to choose me over you. It was supposed to be okay because you would understand, you would stay in your place and behave. I have never for a moment regretted calling my boss out on her racist actions. It's the only time I ever really put myself at risk. You live with that risk every day.

When I told you what had happened, you didn't for a moment think about yourself. We were in it together. When everything at work was at its worst, I came to visit with you and your daughter in the hospital shortly after she was born—I was a mess, I cried and cried, and you took care of me. You say that knowing my daughters has taught you something about being a good parent, and I say that my daughters are so fortunate to know and love you. I have learned so much from you. More than anyone else in my life, you taught me to be true to myself, and not to be afraid. I know deep in my heart what it took to forge the bonds between us. Calling you my friend sounds so inadequate—I am so grateful to be a part of your life. What we have been through was terrible in so many ways, but I would do it all again to experience the awesomeness of truly knowing and loving you.

Love,

Gail

Jen and Gail

Ours is a relationship founded because of race that grew in depth and meaning, greatly impacting both of our lives, and forming an immutable bond between us that unites us far beyond the power of any differences that society defines for us. We truly love, trust, and respect each other, and we always will.

· 1 2 ·

BLACK, WHITE, AND BROWN

A Collaborative Autoethnography Analyzing the Race and Friendship of Three Women in Academia

S. Lenise Wallace, Eman Mosharafa, and Joni Schwartz

Introduction

Women's friendships can be empowering and establish bonds of sisterhood that are unique. Perhaps even more unique are women's *interracial* workplace friendships. This chapter addresses the friendship that has evolved between three women in academia, a Black Latina, a white, and an Egyptian whose relationship, as fellow faculty members, created deep bonds and the foundation for potentially long-lasting friendships. Researchers agree that women are more likely to see the advantages of workplace friendships and more likely than their male counterparts to describe workplace friendships as emotionally and socially beneficial (Morrison, 2009). Furthermore, Settles, Pratt-Hyatt, and Buchanan (2008) found that "Black and White women view womanhood as comprising many of the same broad components: gender-based mistreatment, perceived advantages, community and friendships, and caretaking" (p. 463). Employed at a college in the northeastern region of the United States, the women featured in this chapter formed a friendship that resulted in working on several projects professionally, celebrating personal milestones, and supporting each other through tragedies and disappointments. Additionally, the chapter focuses on their candid conversations around race and cultural barriers while establishing trust and sisterhood.

Utilizing autoethnography, each woman defined *race* and *friendship* and described how these constructs apply to their friendship. The autoethnographers and friends are: Shaunee who identifies as a Black Latina, Joni who identifies as white American of Czech descent, and Eman who identifies as Egyptian—Black, white, and Brown. Their ages range from late 30s to early 60s. The intersections of race, identity, culture, and age were also examined. Drawing from the language and conceptualization of Critical Race Theory (CRT) (Bell, 1995), each woman describes a counterstory of how they have navigated race within the friendship. Each also shares how the friendship is a counterspace within the professional environment. Four themes emerged from this research, *Therapeutic Counterspace*, *Racial Identity*, *Defining Race*, and *Interracial Friendships*. The chapter begins with background on the friendship's inception, an overview of the theory behind this autoethnography, and then explores the four themes that emerged.

Beginnings

It was approximately five years ago that I (Shaunee) was waiting patiently in my "interview suit" in the reception area of the office. My Costa Rican parents taught me to be polite to all people, in this case, particularly receptionists, because interviews always start with the receptionist. This was not my first interview for a college professor; however, it did come with the typical interview jitters. To distract those jitters, I exchanged small pleasantries with the receptionist, while occasionally glancing at the clock. At one point I noticed a blond woman (whose name I later learned was Joni) emerge from a back conference room area. We smiled and exchanged subtle greetings before she left. I thought to myself, "If I am called to that same area, we may be up for the same position." My assumption was correct. However, there were four positions available, and I later found out that Joni and I filled two of them.

Joni and I initially became close through a first-year seminar required for new faculty. During that year, we also befriended another colleague, Eman. Eman recently had moved to the United States to pursue a career in academia. Joni, Eman, and I along with another colleague created a proposal for a grant to do research at our college. To our surprise, we received the grant and through spending hours together on it, our friendship was organically born. In the five years since, we have experienced the highs and lows of our personal and professional lives—births, deaths, promotions, publications, traveling to conferences, and so on. Our unique interracial friendship also created safe spaces that we originally had not imagined. Those safe spaces provided the opportunity to discuss almost everything from romantic relationships to #BlackLivesMatter and Donald Trump. So as different as Joni, Eman, and I are racially and culturally which informs the way we see the world, we value the emotional and social benefits of our friendship and as women faculty at the same institution we are very often in accord professionally.

Critical Race Theory and Interracial Friendship

Critical Race Theory studies the nature of race and racism in all facets of the United States (Dixson, 2007). For the purposes of this chapter, CRT is instrumental in broaching how race is endemic to both individual and structural dynamics, friendship and specifically friendships formed in educational institutions (Closson, 2010; Ladson-Billings, 2005). Furthermore, CRT emphasizes the intersectionality of race, gender, and social class and acknowledges the interweaving roles that these three constructs play in institutions. Historical background upon which current prejudice, bias, and discrimination are based in America is also central to this framework (Byrd, 2012).

This chapter contends that race plays a central role for women of color in the academy (Jones, 2011) and that white women in the academy must work to examine and center both their "personal and work life in ways that are both sensitive and strategic" (Bergerson, 2003) to address racial dynamics. From the focus of this chapter, an individual friendship formed between three racially and culturally diverse female professors in an American college—CRT would maintain that race impacts not only the individual relationship but the institution in which that friendship grows.

Furthermore, CRT educators are committed to addressing educational inequity through hearing and telling of the *lived experiences* of people of color—*counterstorytelling* or *counternarratives*. Counterstories challenge pervading American narratives that inform majority opinions and perceptions about racial minorities (Solórzano, 1998). CRT also developed the term *counterspaces* which are corollaries of counterstorytelling (Schwartz, 2014). These counterspaces provide room for marginalized individuals often in white universities to counteract racial microaggressions (Solórzano, Ceja, & Yosso, 2000). Using these conceptualizations of CRT and borrowing its language—*colorblindness and white supremacy*, this chapter explores issues of identity, solidarity, interest convergence, and microaggressions in an interracial friendship. It is important to note that the authors view their friendship as a counterspace.

Therapeutic Counterspace

We first think of our friendship as what we call a *therapeutic counterspace*. Words like *bond* and *trust* are central, and we see it is a sacred entity shared between people that have deep-seated feelings for each other. All of us mentioned that there was a level of comfort, support, refuge, and safety within our interracial friendship. We discussed the importance of having the ability to be able to discuss race, culture, and gender without the feeling of being judged or ashamed. This freedom in the workplace was what made it not therapy but therapeutic.

Joni and I (Shaunee) share commonalities of spirituality, so when experiencing some very rough times during my tenure, I was able to confide in Joni, who was able to help me immensely through her personal counsel and spiritual guidance. We connected through being women of faith and relying on our love and trust of Jesus Christ to see us through trying times. In addition, I felt a sense of safety with her. She would pray for and with me which is always comforting.

Eman and I had a different bond. We are around the same age. Eman is one of the kindest and most thoughtful people I have ever met, I am intrigued by her. I often find myself enlightened by her worldview. It is enlightening to be close to someone who sees the world slightly different due to a different cultural background. We are learning many new things constantly while being friends, and I thoroughly enjoy that.

I (Joni) am the age of my colleagues' mothers. I see friendship longitudinally developing in different spaces and groups during one's lifetime. In my mind it is a continuum from acquaintance to deep life-altering friendship often connected to some stage, or time of life. By stage I mean, for example—childhood friends, college friends, friends at work, neighbors as friends, mother's groups, book club friends, church friends, partner friends, and mentoring friends. These friendships can be long term or short term, deeply emotional, spiritual or intellectual or superficial, and they can change over time.

I (Eman) define friendship from my Egyptian culture. An Arab's view on friendship is best depicted in a report by the (American) Defense Language Institute and the Foreign Language Center:

The Arab concept of friendship is one of duration and intensity. Maintenance of friendships takes priorities [sic] over most other needs of life … [including] work requirements and other duties. In the Middle East, it is not unusual to make a point of visiting a good friend every day, or at least several times a week. A true friend is someone you feel free to impose on at anytime, knowing that he will do his very best to help you, even if it means a personal sacrifice. Friendship in the Middle East is much more demanding than it is here [America], so that what we call friends they would consider merely acquaintances. (pp. 52–54)

I do believe that friendship is built on trust, honesty, support, and love. However, I rely on advice given to me by my family to be mindful as to who to call a friend. My mother and older sister would always say things like, "be careful to not call just anyone your friend." I took that advice to heart and as an adult, understand and value true friendship. Having someone tell you the truth and what is right rather than to tell you the popular answer is a friend.

Based on these definitions, we all feel the importance of safe counterspaces within the academic setting for faculty members and students alike. According to Su-Lin Yu, "Sisterhood has traditionally acted as a powerful emotional bond. In other words, sisterly relations have been a means for providing comfort, and, most importantly, empowerment in the practical realm of social relations" (Yu, 2006). Sisterhood as counterspaces are important because they afford AfricanAmericans space to vent their frustrations and to get to know others who share their experiences of microaggressions and/ or overt discrimination. From our own friendship we learned that this is not just the case for AfricanAmericans. The same can be said for other races, both homogeneous groups of race and interracial groups. Each of us discussed how important it is to have workplace colleagues that we can confide in.

Having been in the United States for only six years, I (Eman) found it very important to have a counterspace with two female colleagues to navigate American culture. Since I am in the United States on my own, in my relationship with Joni and Shaunee I find refuge from harsh city life. These are two people I can ask to explain aspects of American culture without feeling embarrassed. I feel comfortable debating with them sensitive issues on race, religion, and politics without judgment. I feel blessed to have this counterspace that offers me safety, comfort, and emotional support.

I (Joni) also agree with the comfort and safety that this interracial friendship provides. Furthermore, I realize that the term *counterspace* is a CRT concept reflecting safety for Black people in white spaces; I can ironically identify with the necessity (as a white faculty member) to have a safe space to engage race. Discussing race is sometimes not welcomed by some whites so I do feel our friendship is a counterspace—it is a comfortable "space" within a largely white faculty—it is a friendship where I can talk about race, my feelings, and feel safe. My experience is that whites are dismissive and less comfortable addressing race.

In addition, as a white female engaged in scholarship around race, I am frequently experiencing "reflexivities of discomfort" (Pillow, 2003), an ongoing grappling with how my position, my race, and my age influence in this case the friendship. This position of privilege requires that I question and monitor myself consistently. I understand that privilege demands responsibility. Whites benefit from interest convergence. I ask myself how do I benefit from writing and researching oppressed groups? I am frequently wary. Shaunee engages with me and has tried to comfort my unsettledness. I appreciate that but some unsettling is good. Yes, this friendship always helps me to be emotionally safe in my reflexivity.

We all agree that we have a genuine care and respect for one another related to our common career goals and intellectual curiosity. We behave in a professional and ethical manner toward each other seldom gossiping or backbiting. Since we are collaborating on projects and attending conferences together, much of our friendship is work related. But sometimes we move beyond the boundaries of work, sharing other parts of our lives; this is what has made the friendship therapeutic.

Perhaps the differences of our races make our friendship stronger. The space to discuss race as it relates to our friendship only deepens the communication. For example, during the writing of this chapter Eman made herself vulnerable as we talked candidly about race. On several occasions we (Shaunee and Joni) told Eman "That is a racist statement," in response to something she said, but Eman was gracious to listen and learn. I (Shaunee) acknowledge that if Eman's statements were said to other people, depending on who they were, some might either take offense or perhaps agree with her. Subsequently, a disagreement or argument would ensue or a discussion validating Eman's statements would. However, since Joni and I have vastly different backgrounds, educating Eman about her statements (particularly from our perspectives) was necessary because it was clear that she didn't realize the depth of the racist undertones within them (her statements). The place of our friendship is sound footing for grappling through America's racial quagmire.

I (Shaunee) believe that the depth of this type of interracial friendship at the workplace is rare, at least within my own lived experience. I cherish the friendships that I have with Joni and Eman because I know, as colleagues, we don't have to be as close. As colleagues, particularly working as faculty, we have very different schedules. For example, out of an entire three-month semester, I may only see them at monthly faculty meetings, if that. So, the bond that we all established was created and fostered. It may not have been an intentional bond, but it was genuine. In addition, I am not sure where I would have met either of these women outside of my place of employment. Neither of them attend my church, live near me, or went to college with me, so to form close friendship bonds with women outside of either of those spaces is something I don't take for granted.

We also do not take for granted our freedom to talk about race. In some settings, we may feel it inappropriate or embarrassing to ask certain questions to interracial friends, for fear of offending or saying something politically incorrect, that discomfort is not evident within our group. CRT framework explains that counterspaces are imperative for people, particularly for people of color, to express frustrations, shared experiences, and story-telling in a safe environment. The "Therapeutic Counterspace" theme that emerged from this group of interracial faculty women is a direct illustration of this.

Racial Identity

Our frank discussion on friendship led to another discussion on our racial identity. While these questions seemed straightforward for Joni and Shaunee, I (Eman), growing up in Egypt, struggled with them. Joni and Shaunee seem to define their racial identities with ease.

I (Joni) consider myself a white American of Czech descent. I came to recognize myself as white (within the social constructs that American culture sets up) about 15 or 20 years ago. This was a process, through both lived experience and education. Living in Brooklyn, NY, for nearly 30 years, I would estimate that 70% of my friends are people of color and 30% are white.

Although I grew up in a white world, almost every area of my adult life: work, home community, and church is in interracial settings; I am the minority. In friendship, I gravitate to people of color. I am more comfortable in interracial, or Black settings than in white settings because most of my adult life has been lived in interracial settings. Now I consider myself a white anti-racist scholar and activist.

I (Shaunee) am very clear about racially identifying as a Black Latina. *Black* because that is the clearest and closest to how I feel. It could be that as a woman born in the seventies that was what was associated with me. In the eighties when race activist Rev. Jessie Jackson suggested *Black* people adopt the term *African-American*, I wasn't on board. I completely understood as a woman of color that my roots were in Africa; however, I didn't feel that African-American represented my racial understanding. I also feel a connection to the Latino culture because my family is from Costa Rica. I know the values, culture, food, music, and all things Costa Rican. The majority of my friendships are women and men of color, not necessarily Black Latinas, however, people of color.

Conversely, I (Eman) was completely lost. Having no knowledge of my racial identity, I researched it. Even then I did not get a clear answer. Some sources state that Egyptians are Africans, while others call us Semitic. Adding to the confusion, the U.S. Census Bureau defines North Africans/Middle Eastern as white. In fact, the question of the phenotypical characteristics (skin color, facial features, and hair texture) and genetic affiliations of the ancient Egyptians is a point of controversy (Jablonski, 2012).

I try to explain my Egyptian perspective on race (or lack of) and how this perspective makes it hard for me to relate to questions on racial identity. Egyptian skin colors fill all the shades from white to black. The word Egyptians use to describe people of my complexion is *wheat*. Wheat symbolizes Egypt and the cultivating of wheat and eating bread and the word carries positive connotations.

To describe people of darker complexions, Egyptians use the word *burgundy* which also carries positive connotations. Burgundy is a color associated with wine, an appealing drink; *burgundy* also symbolizes a woman so beautiful that she drives people to lose their minds. These words describe appearances and have no racial associations.

In ancient Egypt, writings show that the people of that era were not occupied with race either, except that artists depicted outsiders from different regions distinctively. Depictions entailed variations in skin color, facial feature, hair, costume, and material culture—tools, weapons, other artificial products (University College London, 2003). View Figure 12.1 depicting from left: a Libyan, a Nubian, an Asiatic, and an Egyptian (Von Minutoli, 1820).

Figure 12.1. Tomb of Seti I.
Source: Von Minutoli, H. (1820). *Copy of a drawing by an unknown artist after a mural of the tomb of Seti I.* Retrieved from https://en.wikipedia.org/wiki/Black_Egyptian_hypothesis#/media/File:Egyptian_races.jpg

These depictions were symbolic; i.e., regardless of one's looks, a man will be depicted as in Figure 12.1 depending on where he comes from. Also see Figure 12.2 of Kemsit, the Nubian queen of the Egyptian King Mentuhotep II (2061–2010 B.C.), and her servants (Pinterest, n.d.).

It seems that centuries of occupation by whites pushed Egyptians to associate fair skin with royalty and princesses, hence with beauty. Yet it is important to note that while white skin might be related to definitions of beauty, this has never been an issue of race. Whether one is of light or dark skin, they are identified as Egyptian and the question of race is never thought of. It is for this reason that growing in Egypt, I never developed a racial identity. I never describe friendships from the Egyptian/Arab circle by race; we are not bound by race, but by language and culture.

Defining Race

The three of us have differing definitions of race and are at divergent stages in our understanding of race in America. We are willing to engage in

Figure 12.2. Kemsit.
Source: Pinterest (n.d.). Painting in tomb chamber wall of Nubian queen Kemsit; Metropolitan Museum of Art, New York; from Naville, The XI Dynasty Temples at Deir el-Bahri III (London: Egypt Exploration Fund, 1913). Retrieved from https://www.pinterest.com/pin/76209418670199804/

complex conversations around those definitions within the counterspace of our friendship.

I (Eman) define race as groups who share physical similarities, such as height, skin color, nose, eyes, or mouth; race appears to be a physical and biological construct viewed from an individual paradigm. From this perspective, I understand racism as personal acts of discrimination directed against a person of color based on the characteristics of color and physical attributes. Based on this individualistic perspective of race, I have not seen or experienced racism since coming to America six years ago.

I (Joni) define race differently than Eman. My understanding is that race is social construction. In America, because of our tragic history of slavery and continued institutionalized racism, the concept of race permeates our social interactions, institutions, power structures; race is a socially constructed concept that is with us on a daily basis. I do not disagree with Eman that racism often includes individual acts of discrimination directed at particular individuals, but I contend that the overriding definition of race and racism in America has to do with a social construction, not biology, which is institutionalized rather than solely being acts of individual bias. Therefore, in response to Eman's assertion that she has not witnessed racism, I argue that frequently, racism is invisible but ever present as it operates on a structural level more often than a personal one.

I (Shaunee) juxtapose Eman and Joni's perspectives. It is well known that race is a social construct. Society often provides the foundation of how people define race. However, how one personally defines race is all of one's perspective and subjective in nature. Race, in my perspective is a construct associated with a group of people within a culture or subculture often associated with skin pigmentation, hair texture, and vernacular. These elements are also a matter of personal and social perspective. I think my attitude on race in the United States is evolving.

In unpacking our definitions of race further, I (Eman) expressed that I really don't care what race a person is. I only pay attention to race if it helps me learn someone's ethnicity. I feel that ethnicity can give me some background on the person, such as culture, language, or religion, which could help me infer his or her way of thinking.

In response, I (Joni) believe we must care about a person's race and … we have to pay attention to race because it is present and often insidious in our everyday interactions. Our awareness of how race and racism operate in America is crucial to our ongoing efforts to dismantle institutional racism in educational settings, prison systems, housing markets, and employment cultures perhaps as well as in friendships.

In light of our conversations, we wonder if part of the reason why racial conversations seem frequently contentious is that the individuals speaking are operating out of differing definitions of race and speaking not only from variant cognitive schemata but contrasting paradigms of race and racism. Defining the terms within an interracial friendship seems to be an extraordinary way to begin, we three have certainly found this so. And in light of current racial rhetoric in our political and entertainment arenas, all three of us are still processing our understandings. This ability to engage these complex and frequently painful conversations is a great gift, and this is something that we all three agreed upon.

Race's Role in an Interracial Friendship

Does race play a role in our friendship? My answer is yes it does. Readers would be surprised to know that this yes is actually coming from me, Eman, the one who previously claimed that race is not a factor in her relationships. I explain that the writing of this chapter has been an eye opener for me, I am now paying attention to details that I never noticed before.

I remember one of my first encounters with Joni; we were at the program director's office. The director talked of an initiative to send faculty to teach in prisons and juvenile centers. I was stunned that I might voluntarily go to a prison to work with criminals but stunned again by Joni's reaction; she screamed enthusiastically, "I would love to do that." I was in disbelief, an elegant white lady interacting with dangerous criminals! They will eat her alive! She can't be serious! I dismissed her desire to serve prisoners as insincere. When I later discovered that Joni has an adopted daughter from Haiti, I realized she was not bluffing; this lady is genuine. This was a major step in our friendship, as I started to perceive her as a kind, caring, and giving person. Now I wonder if my first impression had something to do with her being white, because in mind I never associated white women working with the incarcerated.

My impression of Shaunee was positive from the start. She has what we call in Egypt a *Bashoosh* face, i.e., a friendly face that people like and feel comfortable with. But one particular incident made me appreciate her even more. At the beginning of each year, our school holds Opening Day sessions where faculty present their work and their research. The first time I presented research, Shaunee was in the audience—actually Joni too. After I finished my presentation, I turned off my slide show and started a Q and A session. As we were discussing the topic, the president of the college walked in. Shaunee complimented me on the slide show to let the president know that I had prepared a media presentation. This sweet gesture from Shaunee showed me that this is a colleague I can trust; this made me interested to become friends with her.

Although Shaunee and I have commonalities, being single ladies of the same age with similar interests, our friendship wasn't growing strong very fast. I (Eman) began to notice Shaunee saying that she grew up in a predominantly Black neighborhood, went to a predominantly Black college, and that her church serves mainly AfricanAmericans and Caribbean Americans. Also, I noticed that in my residence, I do not meet any Black neighbors. This made me realize that apart from work, we have separate social circles. Could that be what Joni meant when she said that institutionalized racism permeates not only our institutions and power structures, but also our social interactions? I wondered. I picked up the phone and called Shaunee to clarify. The beauty of our friendship allows me to do that. As soon as Shaunee said hello, I poured her with questions: where do you live? Why did you pick that location? What are the demographics of that location? How much do you pay for rent? Which gym do you go to? Where do you hang out? Where did you study for your bachelor's? What about your master's? And your Ph.D?. We talked for hours. As much as I was grateful for our friendship that permits me to ask all these questions, I was concerned if we could ever be really close friends, when she has to explain some basic knowledge that any Black person intuitively under-stands. So I asked her about that too! Luckily she didn't seem to mind.

From my perspective (Shaunee), speaking on how race plays a part in our friendship, I realized early on that Joni was an activist for equal and civil rights. I had not met many white people as determined to eradicate racial injustices as Joni. She was passionate about marginalized and oppressed Black men and women and had done extensive research and projects in this area. As a Black Latina who had experienced my share of racial discrimination from whites, particularly in former employment, I have a certain level of trust, respect, and comfort knowing that Joni has an interest and experience in being a champion for movements such as #BlackLivesMatter. She and I are on a college committee for a #BlackLivesMatter conference where other activists will speak. Both of us being onboard to raise awareness and establish opportunities for dialog on racial injustice makes our bond stronger. I realize as a Black Latina that this nation needs whites like Joni to work together along with other groups of people from other cultures and ethnicities in order to eliminate racism.

Summary and Discussion

Our friendship is a *Therapeutic Counterspace* that has allowed us to explore and talk about our *Racial Identity*, compare how we *Define Race* and examine the role of race in our friendship. In terms of racial identity, we (Joni and Shaunee) are clear on how we chose to racially identify as white and Black Latina, respectively—both being born and raised in the United States. The history of tense race relations in this country, among other factors could be why we have less doubt about our racial identity.

However, as stated earlier, I (Eman) had difficulty identifying by race because of not being born or growing up in the United States and the Egyptian perspective on colorism. Perhaps this suggests that the development of racial identity in America is a complicated process for international adolescents and adults coming to America and that interracial friendships are spaces wherein the understanding of America's racial paradigm can be understood in order for all immigrants, but particularly immigrants of color, to grapple with their own racial identity.

We believe our autoethnography also suggests that how individuals define race and racism matters. All three of us had somewhat differing understandings of those terms. It was important to "unpack" these concepts to have any intelligent and healthy race conversations. We suggest that shared definitions of complex concepts like race ought to be understood at the beginning of conversations making for a common language around race and that interracial friendships are ideal spaces for this.

Finally, we maintain that our friendship is not colorblind. Race was present in my (Joni) recognition of privilege as a white and yet assuming less privilege as a woman; it was present in my (Eman) grappling with my class, socioeconomic status, and the realities of how these intersect with race in America; and my (Shaunee) position as a Black female in a predominantly white program and department. These are just beginnings; our friendship is still evolving.

Next fall, we (Shaunee and Joni) will return to our college, but I (Eman) will move on to another academy. Will our friendship last? If so, how will it change? Will it evolve? We are uncertain, however, we do know that we have a great gift in our friendship at this stage for which we are all grateful.

References

Bell, D. (1995). *Who's afraid of critical race theory?* [Lecture Manuscript]. Retrieved from https://sph.umd.edu/sites/default/files/files/Bell_Whos%20Afraid%20of%20CRT_1995UIIlL-Rev893.pdf.

Bergerson, A. (2003). Critical race theory and white racism: Is there room for white scholars in fighting racism in education? *International Journal of Qualitative Studies in Education*, 16(1), 51–63.

Byrd, M. Y. (2012). Critical race theory: A framework for examining social identity diversity of black women in positions of leadership. In C. Scott & M. Byrd (Eds.), *Handbook of research on workforce diversity in a global society: Technologies and concepts* (pp. 426–439). Hershey, PA: Business Science Reference. doi:10.4018/978-1-4666-1812-1.ch025

Closson, R. (2010). Critical race theory and adult education. *Adult Education Quarterly, 60,* 261–283.

Defense Language Institute, Foreign Language Center (1997). *Cultures of the Arab world: Head-start/first semester middle east schools.* Monterey, CA.

Dixson, A. (2007). *What is critical race theory in education?* [PowerPoint slides]. Retrieved from http://steinhardt.nyu.edu/metrocenter.olde/programs/TACD/Summer%20Institute/

Jablonski, N. G. (2012). *Living color: The biological and social meaning of skin color* (pp. 104–105). Google E-Book.

Jones, V. (2011). Building bridges for women of color in the professoriate. In J. M. Gaetane & B. Lloyd-Jones (Eds.), *Women of color in higher education: Contemporary perspectives and changing directions* (pp. 261–280). Bingley, UK: Emerald Group Publishing.

Ladson-Billings, G. (2005). The evolving role of critical race theory in educational scholarship. *Race, Ethnicity and Education, 8,* 115–119.

Morrison, R. L. (2009). Are women tending and befriending in the workplace? Gender differences in the relationship between workplace friendships and organizational outcomes. *Sex Roles, 60*(1–2), 1–13. doi:http://dx.doi.org/10.1007/s11199-008-9513-4

Pillow, W. (2003). Confession, catharsis, or cure? Rethinking the uses of reflexivity as methodological power in qualitative research. *Qualitative Studies in Education, 16,* 175–196.

Pinterest (n.d.). *Painting in tomb chamber wall of Nubian queen Kemsit; Metropolitan Museum of Art, New York; from Naville, The XI Dynasty Temples at Deir el-Bahri III* (London: Egypt Exploration Fund, 1913). Retrieved from https://www.pinterest.com/pin/76209418670199804/

Schwartz, J. (2014). Classrooms of spatial Justice: Counter-spaces and young men of color in a GED program. *Adult Education Quarterly, 64*(2), 110–127.

Settles, I. H., Pratt-Hyatt, J. S., & Buchanan, N. T. (2008). Through the lens of race: Black and white women's perception of womanhood. *Psychology of Women Quarterly, 32*(4), 454–468.

Solórzano, D. (1998). Critical race theory, racial and gender microaggressions, and the experiences of Chicana and Chicano scholars. *International Journal of Qualitative Studies in Education, 11,* 121–136.

Solórzano, D., Ceja, M., & Yosso, T. (2000). Critical race theory, racial microaggressions, and campus racial climate: The experiences of African American college students. *Journal of Negro Education, 69,* 60–73.

University College London. (2003). *The question of race in ancient Egypt.* University College London. Retrieved from http://www.ucl.ac.uk/museums-static/digitalegypt/social/race.html

Von Minutoli, H. (1820). *Copy of a drawing by an unknown artist after a mural of the tomb of Seti I.* Retrieved from https://en.wikipedia.org/wiki/Black_Egyptian_hypothesis#/media/File:Egyptian_races.jpg

Yu, S. L. (2006). Sisterhood as cultural difference in Amy Tan's *The Hundred Secret Senses* and Cristina Garcia's *The Aguero Sisters Critique: Studies in Contemporary Fiction, 47*(4), 345–361.

· 1 3 ·

A JOYFUL DANCE BETWEEN FRIENDS

The Story of Our Hindu–Muslim, Jewish–Christian Friendship

Mira Sengupta and Samantha González-Block

Introduction

Living in a post-secular, post-9/11 world of increased religious diversity and conflict, where various cultures and races violently clash together on the global stage, it is more pressing than ever to find positive ways of interacting across boundaries and borders. In today's fraught world, Mahatma Gandhi's words feel especially relevant: "We must respect other religions, even as we respect our own. Mere tolerance thereof is not enough." If there is ever hope for significant positive change on a grand scale, it must begin first on the smallest scale—our communities, our own lives, our friends. This is why we want to share our story. Perhaps by shedding light on our journey of deep-seated friendship that flourished across racial, religious, and cultural difference, we can offer a slice of guidance and glimmer of hope that a more united, positive society is indeed at our fingertips.

We first crossed paths within the confines of a long, rectangular, faded bathroom mirror that was hanging above the sinks in our dormitory's yellow-tiled bathroom at Barnard College in New York City. Both of us were newly minted freshman, busy readying our faces for our very first college party. Our approaches couldn't have been more different. A meticulous Mira carefully outlined her dark almond eyes with black pencil, while Samantha zipped through every shade of eyeshadow in the box.

We giggled in unison as each of us caught sight of the other's contrary approach to primping for the big event. Despite our obvious differences, our shared laughter made us both hopeful and curious about the other. *Could this be a friend?*

Mira, in her white lacey top, was a soft-spoken, cautious, and studious girl of Bengali, Indian descent, who had spent years exploring and finally connecting deeply with her Hindu faith. She grew up on Long Island, New York, in a town where only a handful of South Asian families lived. As one of the only Indian girls in her town, Mira was used to being on the receiving end of wide-eyed stares. She remembers a blond-haired five-year-old girl pointing at her tan skin and long black hair, crying out in astonishment, "Pocahontas!" Now, in the yellow-tiled bathroom at Barnard College, Mira could see a young woman peering at her through the mirror, offering a warm smile.

Samantha, who sported a neon blue tube top, was a loud, bold, rambunctious "Jew-Rican"—the product of a Presbyterian Puerto Rican mother and Jewish father of Eastern European descent. She had grown up in Montclair, New Jersey, a town famous for its diversity and that largely accepted interfaith and intercultural families such as hers. That being said, Samantha had never come across anyone who had her same mix of backgrounds, nor the facial features that came along with it. With brown eyes, curly hair, an olive complexion, and a prominent nose, no one could ever seem to identify where she was from: "*Are you Iranian? Italian? Argentinian? people would ask. Puerto Rican?? You don't look Puerto Rican.*"

Despite our contrasting appearances, we had much in common. We were two freshmen peas in a college pod—living for the first time away from home, and beginning the most exciting, nerve-racking adventure of our lives. With the innocence of open-hearted youths, we were not fazed by our apparent racial differences. Needing and longing for connection, we shared the same hope—that in that mirror could be the reflection of a new friend.

In the days and semesters to come, our racial and religious differences did not feel like insurmountable roadblocks on our journey, but rather, time and again, contributed to the richness of our burgeoning connection. We took pride in introducing one another to the most coveted aspects of our separate traditions and rituals—from dance to spirituality—and invited each other to ask questions, participate, and embrace something new. Since we never knew many people who looked like us, we were accustomed to building friendships across differences. At the same time, our parents instilled in us great regard for our colorful cultures and traditions, and always welcomed neighbors of varying backgrounds to share in our family celebrations. We carried these experiences and this open-armed approach into our relationship.

In this chapter, we look forward to further exploring how our multireligious and racial identities as minorities have impacted our friendship, and how our embracing of one another's cultures, especially through movement, music, and spiritual practice, have challenged and motivated us to flourish into the women we are today. Moreover, we will use our narrative as a source of reflection for the ways in which our greater diverse society can rethink its approach to building relationships across difference.

Reflecting Through Mira's Eyes

Upon entering college, the first thing I thought I needed to do was get myself some Indian friends. Having grown up in a relatively small town on Long Island, I was the only Indian girl in my school, and had no other Indian friends my age. I wanted to connect with people who watched the same movies, listened to the same music, and traveled to the same places as I did. But after that fateful meeting in the yellow-tiled bathroom at Barnard College, I realized I had met someone who actually wanted to share these experiences with me, who was curious about the vibrant sights and sounds in Bollywood movies, who actually wanted to learn about Indian music and dance. Sam didn't see my Indian heritage as a challenge to overcome. She was actually excited by the prospect of learning about a culture so different from her own, and equally thrilled by the idea of inviting me—a shy, soft-spoken Indian girl—into the beautifully complex world of a "Jew-Rican."

She eventually became a lover of Bollywood movies, music, and dance, and I learned to keep up with Sam on the dance floor of Salsa clubs in New York City, swinging my hips and kicking my feet the way she showed me to. It wasn't long before Sam found herself barefoot and dressed in a *saree* for Columbia University's South Asian dance show. Amazingly, it was these cultural differences that actually brought us together. It was our way of bonding. We developed a relationship fueled by a mutual desire to share the best parts of our cultures with each other. This cross-cultural sharing helped us to develop a level of intimacy that can only thrive between people willing to open themselves up fearlessly to one another.

Of course, there were aspects of each other's cultures that we had difficulty understanding at first. It soon became apparent to me that Sam's home
life and relationship with her family was very different from my own. I realized this difference when attending one of Sam's famous family parties. These
events were always extravagant affairs that began with Sam's mother, literally
Salsa dancing her way through the kitchen to prepare tons of delicious Latin
dishes and finger-foods. The scent of *arroz con pollo*, *habichuelas*, and *sazón*
filled the air. The house would eventually be bursting at the seams with hundreds of guests, booming music, and, of course, the ceremonious Salsa dancing. I remember cramming into Sam's living room, the coffee table carefully
pushed aside, to make way for dozens of aunts, uncles, cousins, and neighbors
dancing in unison to the sounds of Celia Cruz and Gloria Estefan. When the
dancing subsided, the games would begin. And I don't mean just board games,
but *full-on relay races*. Guests would shuffle out into the backyard to partake in
three-legged races, potato sack races, hoola hoop races! There were musical
games, theater games, charades, and tug-of-war. And when things began to
wind down, someone, usually Sam, would hop on the piano and regale the
guests with Broadway show tunes. From my perspective, these events seemed
less like family gatherings and more like a day at the carnival.

Family parties in my own Bengali household consisted of a few close rel-
atives and friends, usually sitting in a circle in the candle-lit living room,
sipping *chai* while quietly listening to one of my aunts sing the music of
Rabindranath Tagore. So you can imagine my surprise when attending parties
at the González-Block house.

I also learned at these parties about the close, intimate dynamic between
Sam and the rest of her family. She was more free and open with them than
I could ever be with my own. At one party, I was surprised, even shocked,
to see Sam being affectionate with her boyfriend in front of her parents and
extended family. *What a scandal!* I thought. Coming from an Indian background, public displays of affection—especially in front of parents—are strictly
forbidden. As Sam held hands and cuddled with her boyfriend, I couldn't help
but wonder, *was this a bold act of rebellion?* But it didn't take long to notice that
Sam's behavior wasn't scandalous at all. In fact, her parents were not only
comfortable, but delighted to see their daughter so happy. When I questioned
Sam about these public displays after the party, she laughed and said, "In my
culture, my family would be concerned if my boyfriend and I *weren't* affectionate. They'd probably think we're in a fight!"

As surprised as I was by these stark cultural and familial differences, Sam was equally as shocked to learn that my parents didn't even know about my boyfriend at the time, a Muslim, Pakistani boy from Long Island. And of course, his parents didn't know about me. At the age of eighteen, I—like most Indian kids my age—knew better than to parade my significant other around my parents, especially a Muslim significant other. It wasn't uncommon at all, I explained to Sam, for Indian kids to keep their social lives and habits separate from their family life. It's not that dating was expressly forbidden—but I assumed it wasn't an appropriate topic of conversation in my household, since no one ever talked about it. I explained to Sam that my parents followed the "don't ask, don't tell" policy, in which they probably knew I was dating boys, but there was no need to expressly address the topic.

Sam explained how hurt her parents would be if she kept such secrets from them. What a different life she led! Sam's relationship with her parents was built on free and open discourse, while mine was built on privacy, or more accurately, secrecy. When Sam innocently asked, "What would happen if you told them about your boyfriend?" I honestly didn't know how to answer her. I assumed it would be a disaster. Would they cry? Beat their chests? Lock me in cellar? Or would they be understanding like Sam's parents? Grateful that I decided to open up to them?

I didn't actually get the courage to tell my mother about my boyfriend until he had already become an *ex*. On a weekend at home, I sat my mother down in my childhood bedroom, and explained that I had dated a Pakistani boy whom I met over the summer before college, that we had dated a few months, and then broke it off. When my mother asked me why I hadn't told her before, I said that I thought she would be upset that I was dating a Muslim. After a brief, very pregnant moment of silence—she burst out laughing and said, "Why would I care that he's Muslim?"

I realized, then, that I had learned something very important not just from my mother, but from Sam, who encouraged me to be more open with my family. After taking the time to thoughtfully compare Sam's cultural habits with my own, I realized that many of the restrictions that I thought came from my parents and their culture actually came from none other than myself. I had assumed that secrecy and privacy were essential to maintaining a good relationship with my parents, and that such restrictions were just a part of the unspoken social codes of Indian culture. But if so many of these codes are *unspoken*, how are we to know how our families actually feel about them?

It turns out, my parents were happy to know about my boyfriends, and even happier to meet them going forward. Of course, public displays of affection were still forbidden. Even today, I refrain from holding my husband's hand in front of my parents—an aspect of my culture that still puzzles Sam.

The surprising cultural exchanges Sam and I experienced helped me understand my culture, my family, and myself a little better. And it was these exchanges that eventually became the building blocks of our friendship. Throughout college and beyond, we became increasingly more interested in these private, intimate aspects of not only our cultures, but also our respective religions. In fact, though of different faiths, Sam and I would eventually help each other through the various personal and intellectual challenges posed by our religions.

One late night in a study lounge, I noticed that Sam wore both a cross and Star of David around her neck. Curious about this seeming contradiction, I asked her, "Are you Christian or Jewish?" She paused before saying,

"I think I'm both."
"How does that work?" I inquired.
"I'm not sure, but it works for me."

Born to a Presbyterian mother and Jewish father, Samantha was the product of an interfaith household, something that fascinated me immensely. I told Sam that Gandhi identified as a Hindu, a Muslim, a Christian, and a Jew—and that in the book The Life of Pi, the protagonist also practices Hinduism, Islam, and Christianity simultaneously. "Are you very religious?" Sam asked me. I leaned over, and pulled out from under my shirt the crystal idol of Ganesh I wore on a chain around my neck. I considered myself a devout Hindu, and explained that Hindu philosophy embraces the notion that multiple paths can lead us to God. I told her that my grandmother had shared with me once, long ago, her belief that religions are like rivers all leading to the same ocean. Perhaps one path isn't always enough. "I think I'd make a good Hindu, too!" Samantha exclaimed. I told Sam that I love that she adheres to more than just one form of faith—not knowing then that she would eventually inspire me to embrace two religions myself.

Sam, even as a first-year in college, was the kind of person to challenge conventional ways of thinking and being. From my perspective, it was almost as if she were a living contradiction. At the time, I could easily process the idea of someone simply having a Christian mother and Jewish father. But what intrigued and fascinated me about Sam was that she actually believed, as strongly and intensely as I did in my own Hindu faith, in the tenets of both Christianity and Judaism—two religions that, while both Abrahamic in origin, espouse vastly antithetical positions about the nature and identity of God. She was one of few eighteen-year-olds who had already integrated a pluralistic worldview into her life, because she had grown up in a home where an entire family thrived on difference.

I remember a cold winter day, sitting next to Samantha's Jewish father, while watching Sam, her mother, and her sister all perform in the Christmas play production for the neighborhood church. I realized then that Sam wasn't a product of a household that kept their two religions separate and distinct, but one whose family made a concerted effort to integrate them. And that day, I myself was integrated into this interfaith world. I couldn't help but privately notice the irony of the situation. There I was, a Hindu, sitting next to a Jewish man in a Presbyterian Church, laughing out loud to Sam's mother, dressed like an old lady in a wheelchair, cracking jokes about Christmas. Many people, especially in recent times, have spoken of the divisiveness of religion, but my experience in that church was just the opposite. Sam's Presbyterian church was bringing people of various faiths together in a single space, where they could all be included in its message of love, laughter, and kindness. There was something about the warmth in that church that made me feel like I was connected to something bigger. That day, I got a glimpse of what it was like to be a part of Sam's joyful interfaith household. I didn't learn until years later, however, the kind of courage it takes to actually be an interfaith person.

Four years after graduating from Barnard, my longtime boyfriend proposed to me. Though a Bangladeshi immigrant, he had much in common with me. We were both Bengali, we spoke the same language, and we were familiar with each other's cultural customs. In many ways, we were a perfect match—except for one important difference: he was Muslim and I was Hindu. In order to marry into a Muslim family, I would have to convert to Islam. Converting was something I never thought I could do. So while I happily accepted the marriage proposal, I wasn't entirely sure whether converting would be right for me. My fiancée tried to make my decision easy, telling me it didn't matter to him whether I converted or not. But I knew that remaining Hindu would make it difficult for his family to accept the marriage, and potentially strain his relationship with them. Many of my own family members and friends advised me, with the best of intentions, not to give up my religion, and some seemed surprised that I was even considering it. "Why should you be the one to convert?" they asked me. "He's not even very religious. You're more religious than he is. Why should you sacrifice yourself?" In the midst of these conflicting and confusing voices, Sam offered her support and guidance.

Sam asked me what my exact fears were about conversion. I told her I considered my religion an integral part to my identity. If I weren't Hindu, I didn't think I could be me. How could I sacrifice such a huge part of myself? Sam then asked me, "Why do you think you have to sacrifice it at all?" Sam, one of the only people I knew who managed to balance two distinct religions, challenged me to do the same. I began then to reorient my thinking: instead of conceiving of conversion as sacrificing one religion for another, why not imagine it as a process by which to integrate the two? "Maybe this isn't about disavowing Hinduism," Sam explained, "but building onto your worldview." She reminded me that my own Hindu philosophy grants that there may be many paths to God. I had grown up thinking I had it all figured out when it came to my religion. There was a kind of pleasure that came with the certainty of knowing I was Hindu. But perhaps Sam was right. Perhaps there was still more to learn. Sam helped me see conversion not as a sacrifice, but an opportunity to expand and enhance my religious philosophy.

I still wondered, however, how to manage the more contradictory aspects of the two faiths. Hindus and Muslims conceive of God's identity in very different ways. But Sam reminded me that she, being both Jewish and Christian, lives with these contradictions every day. It was then that I realized the intellectual strength and spiritual bravery it takes to be an interfaith person. Contradictions tend to frighten us away, because we're often more comfortable when pieces seem to fit together neatly. It hadn't occurred to me that these contradictions, the striking differences between the two religions, were not actually a problem that I needed to work out or settle in any definitive way. Perhaps their very existence just helps to confirm the complex realities that lie behind religious questions, and that perhaps we don't have all the answers—nor do we need them to be faithful.

Sam was a living testament of this kind of faith. It was the very paradox of her interfaith religion that powered her hyper-awareness that contradiction underlies so many of the ostensible truths (whether religious, ethical, or moral) on which we often rely. Sam's faith is the kind that incorporates what the poet John Keats (2002) calls "negative capability." In Keats's words, she is someone who is "capable of being in uncertainties, mysteries, doubts without any irritable reaching after fact and reason." Conceiving of conversion in this new light, I no longer feared it, but welcomed it with an intense curiosity and interest.

What exciting new thoughts and questions would this new perspective bring me? I was about to undergo changes I could never have anticipated growing up, and embrace a life dramatically different from the one I had been living. I learned from Sam what she had known all along, that I need not fear these changes. Contradictions, conflicts, and differences—whether cultural, ethnic, or religious—don't have to be divisive. In fact, they can do just the opposite: they can bring people together. They brought my husband and me together, and they brought Sam and me together so many years ago.

Sam's inspirational interfaith story gave me the strength to become an interfaith person myself. So I thought, who better to officiate a Hindu–Muslim wedding than a Jewish–Presbyterian? I asked Sam to stand up there with my husband and me on our wedding day, to tell our story, and to marry us. I realized this was a tall order, that Sam was mostly unfamiliar with the customs of South Asian weddings (that her knowledge of such weddings went only as far as the Bollywood films we watched together), and that the complicated, interfaith situation would need to be handled with extreme delicacy. But I knew if anyone had the courage to take on such a challenge, it was Sam. So once again, Sam found herself dressed in a gold and violet *saree*, reciting the poetry of Rabindranath Tagore, joining together my husband's hands with mine, and speaking of the power of human connection. The wedding ceremony was perfect. I had my husband on one side of me, and Sam on the other. Literally surrounded by love, I knew at that point that I could meet the challenges ahead—that with Sam's help, I had all the practice in the world of building and nourishing a relationship across difference.

Reflecting Through Samantha's Eyes

Music and movement were always integral parts of my family's life. Throughout childhood, there were impromptu dance parties, sometimes swaying to my father's Frank Sinatra classics or moving to my mother's Tito Puente Latin hits. We would sing Hallelujahs at church on Sundays, and the *Shema* Hebrew prayer in temple on Fridays. My home was a place to ask questions and share cross-cultural perspectives.

Growing up in an interfaith, interethnic family, we routinely celebrated my parents' varying traditions and holidays. I felt a deep sense of pride in my family's diverse makeup. It was stimulating and colorful. That being said, it was not always easy. I sometimes received piercing pushback from people outside of my immediate circle who told me that I did not "look" Puerto Rican or

Jewish or Christian "enough." At times, I felt self-doubt about articulating my religious identity or feeling like I fully belonged in any of my given cultures.

My hometown was racially and religiously diverse and I became accustomed to having a mixed group of friends. As soon as I arrived at college I was quickly approached by a succession of cultural or religious clubs simply because they saw González or Block in my name. This was jolting because I had never consciously befriended someone because of similar identity markers. Furthermore, having been shunned in the past because of my mixed heritage, I was less inclined to grab hold of a particular group to park my whole identity.

When Mira and I met, I was not drawn to her because I was curious about Bengali culture, or wanted to escape my own. I was simply looking for a friend with an open spirit—willing to accept me in my fullness, who would push me to open my mind in new ways. Mira and I were different in race, culture, and religion—things that might be considered friendship deal-breakers—but these 'identifiers' did not trouble us at all. When we first saw each other in the mirror, we saw two beautiful women, deserving of mutual respect and care. We became curious about each other, deeply generous in our sharing, and fiercely loyal. As a consequence, our friendship soared.

When I first saw this Bengali, Indian young woman smiling back in the dorm bathroom mirror, it could have been easy to make blanket assumptions. *Perhaps she adored spicy food. Perhaps she would never feel comfortable shaking her hips to Latin rhythms.* Within the first few hours of our meeting, I learned that Mira has never been a fan of Indian cuisine. In fact, she hates spicy food so much so that while growing up, her mother had to microwave hot-pockets for her at dinnertime. When I asked if I could show her some Salsa steps at our first college party, Mira jumped right in—moving to the beat with joyful, unabashed intensity. It was as if she had been dancing Salsa her whole lifelong.

I would soon learn that although she had natural Latin rhythm, she loved celebrating her culture through two distinct forms of Indian dance: *bhangra* and *bharatnatyam*. The first time I ever saw Mira dance *bhangra*, I was mesmerized. I was used to moving my hips to all sorts of Latin beats, but this dance was unlike anything I had ever experienced before. The music was explosive and exciting. Mira's feet shot off the ground, and her shoulders cavorted to the beat. She soared across the room with each spellbinding movement.

Before long, she took me by the hand and encouraged me to give it a try. I was clumsy and unbalanced. Mira, patiently molded my arms, positioned my feet, and led the way. Before I knew it, I was a *bhangra* dancing enthusiast.

Wherever there were speakers, Mira and I would pump the music high—and turn even our dorm room into our personal ballroom. We would even fling open our door to invite other hall-mates in for impromptu dance lessons.

A few months into our freshman year, Mira asked me to take part in the Columbia University South Asian dance show. I was hesitant, but she would not take "no" for an answer and assured me that I would be great. When I arrived at rehearsal, I was instantly aware that I was the only non-South Asian there. I could see some of the dance crew looking over at me in surprise that a curly-haired, non-Indian student was eager to perform the moves of their culture. Mira did not seem to notice any tension in the room, and instead expressed her thrill that I would be dancing alongside her. Two weeks later, I found myself on stage, in front of a packed auditorium, feverishly dancing amongst a sea of bright colored *sarees*.

What I came to learn was that *bhangra* was not simply a fun form of exercise for Mira. It was one of the prime ways that she connects with her Indian heritage. Mira also introduced me to *bharatnatyam*, a spiritual and devotional dance that is a sacred way in which Mira shows devotion to the Divine. She explained to me that this kind of dance is actually a form of prayer. Before beginning, the dancer blesses the ground, and each meticulous movement signifies a different divine concept. "This is Ganesh," Mira said, swaying her long arm across the air to represent the trunk of the elephant god. "And this is Krishna," she said as she posed with her body tilted and her hands holding an imaginary flute. It was apparent that this type of dance meant a great deal to her. Mira trusted me with the dearest parts of her life, and despite having no Bengali blood circulating through my veins, I began to understand and wholeheartedly appreciate these vital parts of her being.

Her openness was not one sided. I taught Mira Cha-Cha, Merengue, and Bachata and introduced her to my favorite Latin artists. For me also, social dancing and music are integral parts of my culture, and ways in which my ancestors kept up hope during difficult times. It felt natural to bring Mira into this aspect of my life, since she had welcomed me so graciously into hers.

Dance was only the first step. We both adored musical theater, enjoyed harmonizing to familiar melodies, and even began writing songs together. After showing Mira a few chords on the guitar, she was soon playing the instrument with ease. When attempting to teach her songs from my culture, like the Spanish folk song "Guantanamera," I was surprised to see that Mira already knew the lyrics. She sang joyfully as I strummed the chords. One day, my dear friend playfully asked me to write a song for her. I took her request seriously, and was stunned when lyrics poured out of me in Spanish: "*Mira linda, con los ojos del sol y las manos de la luna. Mira linda, una estrella en el cielo de mi corazon.*" (Mira dear, with the eyes of the sun and the hands of the moon. Mira dear, you are a star in the sky of my heart.) We seemed to be each other's muse—inspiring each other to reach new heights.

Mira and I were also curious and empathetic listeners, and felt comfortable sharing our experiences about the more challenging aspects of being women from minority groups. I confided in Mira that between my ethnically ambiguous features and my Latina-German-Jewish last name, I had experienced being singled out and stereotyped. I told her about once being kept for hours in an airport immigration holding room. When I asked to use the bathroom, the security guard said, "Only with the door open," so as to ensure that I was not carrying drugs. Mira intently listened to my tale and responded that she could relate to airport travel anxiety. "Since 9-11, people who look like me are treated differently," she said. Mira explained her own fears about people labeling her as "terrorist" or "anti-American"—simply because of her tan complexion. She spoke of friends and neighbors who turned against her family after the attacks, and the embarrassment of consistently being "randomly selected" for additional screening at airports. Her honesty opened my eyes and broke my heart.

Sometimes our conversations would shift from the cultural to the spiritual aspects of our lives. Mira always cut straight to the tough stuff, but with a non-judgmental spirit: "How is it that you are both Christian and Jewish? How does that work for you?"

"It's the way I have always known God," I would reply. Then I would ask "In Hinduism do you believe in a whole bunch of Gods?"

"For me, it's different manifestations of one God."

"I love that. We both see God in many forms."

Our respective religions fascinated us, and we made space in our own spiritual and physical lives to welcome the other's in. Mira and I adorned our dorm room with religious symbols and showed each other the different ways we pray. Before any big exam, Mira and I would both make the Christian sign of the cross and then touch our fingers to our head and heart, as taught in Hinduism—just in case. Mira even opened up the most sacred part of her religious practice to me. She invited me to accompany her to a Hindu temple in Queens.

When we arrived, once again I noticed a room of brown faces; I was certainly the only "Jew Rican" there. I felt somewhat self-conscious, but Mira seemed calm and cool. In the center of the bright colored temple was a massive idol of Ganesh—the elephant God. Mira had me sit by myself to fully absorb the experience, while she circled Ganesh exactly a hundred and eight times, praying for love, guidance, and protection. Up until this point, Mira had freely incorporated me into her life, and perhaps that is why, now sitting in a spiritual space so different from my own, I felt at peace. In fact, I felt God's presence alive in that temple.

The next day, Mira invited me to her family's home in Long Island. Shortly after arriving, she took me to her mother's prayer room on the second floor. I was overwhelmed. The cramped space was filled with paintings and statues of different images of God, including Krishna and Ganesh. Then Mira pointed out an image of Jesus Christ. *Imagine my surprise!* "Like I told you, she said, there are many manifestations of God," Mira said. We kneeled down and prayed side-by-side. In that moment, I felt more grateful than ever for Mira. She was comfortable articulating her open understanding of the Divine. Perhaps Mira didn't know this at the time, but she was helping me build up the strength to confidently claim my own interfaith identity. If Mira could see God through multiple lenses, perhaps I should not hesitate to openly express to all how I see God through both a Jewish and Christian lens.

A few years later, I felt called to explore my spirituality even further, and enter into the ministry. While preparing seminary applications, I received a concerned phone call from Mira. At the time, she was preparing to marry a Bengali man of Muslim descent. Since marrying across religion was not typical in Bengali culture, this news did not sit well with some of their family and friends. Mira confided that she was considering converting to Islam, and wanted to know what I thought this could mean for her Hindu faith. "Mira, you are the one who helped me feel confident in my own Jewish-Christian identity. So if you convert, please know that I want you to feel confident in your Hindu-Muslim identity."

Before we hung up, Mira had one more question for me. "Will you officiate my wedding?" Without thinking, I responded with a slew of questions. "Why me?" "I am not Muslim, I'm not Hindu. I'm not even Bengali." "Wouldn't I do more harm than good?" As always, Mira maintained her calm tone and said, "You're the one I want to do this. I know that you are the right person." Without another question, I said yes.

A few months later, I was once again standing in a *saree* looking over a banquet hall of faces different from mine. However, this time, more than ever, I knew I was exactly where I needed to be. I was beside my friend and her love, sharing the story of how their union across difference was both sacred and precious—something that I knew to be true, thanks to my years of friendship with Mira.

Sheryl A. Kujawa-Holbrook (2014) writes that authentic connection across race and religion requires "courageous border-crossing"; each party must be willing to cross over into new territory and open themselves up to being changed. Mira and I consciously ventured into each other's lives, cultures, and religions in this way. Conflict never seemed to arise out of our cultural differences—perhaps because we crossed over into each other's lives with similar enthusiasm, deep curiosity, and genuine love and trust.

When I consider the ways in which Mira has impacted my life—the gifts are too many to count. This friendship, this sisterhood, has undoubtedly opened my eyes to new ways of perceiving and experiencing the world. Mira has awakened me to a particular lived experience that I did not and could not know personally, and she has helped me to nuance my conversations regarding race in America. Furthermore, Mira has given me the deepest friendship I have ever known, and has helped me to find myself and my calling along the way.

Closing Thoughts

Deep and long-lasting friendships across race, religion, or culture are not always easy to find. People often treat differences as barriers too great to overcome, and are unable go deeper with one another. While our little story centers on a friendship between two young women who thrived on these differences, we believe this story has broader, perhaps even global and cosmopolitan implications about the way we believe humans can connect to one another.

When a Christian steps into a Hindu temple, and a Hindu attends a church production, what emerges is a productive cultural exchange that has the power to enhance, deepen, and strengthen a person's individual worldview—either by challenging it or simply by building onto it. If anything, participating in these cultural exchanges can help us open our eyes to the boundaries and limitations surrounding our individual perspectives. By enthusiastically participating in each other's cultural and religious experiences, we presented one another with the uncommon opportunity to take on, even if momentarily, the perspective of another person.

What happens when we stop thinking about racial, religious, and cultural differences as divisive challenges to overcome? This is not to suggest that these differences don't pose challenges. But perhaps what we need culturally is to reorient the way we think about difference. What if instead we were to imagine these differences as the breeding ground upon which real, human connections are made, connections based on mutual understanding, curiosity, and empathy? Our particular story is not one of overcoming cultural, ethnic, and religious differences, but of embracing them with open hearts and minds. We had so much to gain just by inviting one another into our respective cultural and religious worldviews.

Confident that we had something unique and valuable to offer one another, we used our differences to empower each other. We weren't just passive observers of each other's cultures, but we actually stepped inside our very distinct worlds. Through these joint and generous experiences across racial, religious, and cultural boundaries, we grew to deeply appreciate our unique places in this diverse world. At the same time, our friendship allowed us to mature into our own identities with fuller awareness and confidence.

So what do we have to gain by traveling outside our racial comfort zones into unexplored and uncertain terrain? In this increasingly interconnected, yet deeply divided world, we believe it is more important than ever to start viewing cultural pluralism as our greatest strength, rather than our more formidable challenge. If we reorient the way we think about difference in this manner, we can potentially engage those whose religious, ethnic, and cultural views conflict so dramatically with our own. If we attempt to adopt the perspective, even momentarily, of those with competing worldviews, and if we actively participate in the cultural and religious experiences of one another, perhaps we can learn to develop the powerful empathic connections we require to thrive in a world built on the pleasures of cultural pluralism and diversity.

References

Keats, J. (2002). *John Keats: Selected letters*. New York, NY: Oxford World Classics.

Kujawa-Holbrook, S. A. (2014). *God beyond borders: Interreligious learning among faith communities*. Eugene, OR: Pickwick Publications.

· 1 4 ·

SLIDING DOORS, INTENTIONAL CHOICES

Paulette Dalpes and Berenecea Johnson Eanes

Why Is Our Relationship Uncommon?

The fact that we live in a world where our bond is uncommon is at the root of why it is unique and yet tragic. Our story is both distinctive and universal. The choices we made throughout our lives led us to the moment where our friendship was born. It was by chance and yet purposeful. Like moving through a sliding door onto a train leading to the next life moment and opportunity. What sliding doors did we choose to move through or which ones did we let pass? What intentional choices to move forward or stay in place ultimately created the opening where this inimitable friendship became possible?

Relationships between white women and women of color, especially AfricanAmerican women, have a complicated history in the United States given the roots of slavery and white supremacy. Truly deep friendships between Black women and white women can take years to build. Likewise, while relationships between women across sexual orientation are rare, it is even more uncommon when these friendships include differences across race (Galupo, 2009).

Our society and the spaces we grow up in conspire to keep us separate across difference. With regard to race, this conspiracy is built upon hundreds of years of colonization and domination, the legacy of which continues in every facet of our current society. Today, we often live in separate neighborhoods by race (Eligon & Gebeloff, 2016), and our schools are more segregated than during the Jim Crow era (Orfield, 2009). Our childhoods and adulthoods are spent disconnected and apart especially with respect to socioeconomic class and race. Likewise, the experiences of gay, lesbian, bisexual, and transgender communities remain isolated, conscripted, and framed as "the other." The white, male, heteronormative narrative perseveres as the dominant point of reference in our society. The result of these intentional divisions is a persistent unknowing of one another. In the unknowing also lies the presence of fear, objectification, and exclusion.

When we build relationships across race and sexual orientation, we are taking revolutionary action. We are choosing to move through sliding doors into the unknown, to pursue new narratives and to embark on the expansion of what is possible. These revolutionary acts can exact a cost; there are tradeoffs and risks, all of which are measured against the rewards.

Our own personal stories reflect these larger social dynamics. In this chapter, we share the series of sliding doors and intentional choices we made to ensure and solidify bonds across difference. We explore how it is we resisted the conspiracy to keep us apart. How did we forge an uncommon bond across our differences in race and sexual orientation? What persistent messages about who we are and who the other is did we resist and redefine? What personal journeys led us to this relationship and informed our role in this abiding partnership?

We hope to provide a strong message regarding how the gift of our different lived experiences brings brilliant insights, learning, and support to ourselves unlike any other relationship in our lives and especially in our work within the field of Student Affairs and Higher Education. Most importantly, we want to underscore that there were a series of intentional actions and choices we made in our life journey prior to discovering this friendship that make our loving connection possible and are the essence of why it endures. Finally, we hope to inspire you to do the same.

Who We Are

Dr. Berenecea Johnson Eanes:
I grew up as the daughter of a medical doctor and an elementary school teacher in Indianapolis, Indiana. My relationships with my family, church, and community

demonstrated a commitment to love and accept everyone. The ironic part is that I felt my childhood was magical even with the disturbance of my parents' divorce. The community in Indianapolis where I grew up was a rare bastion of AfricanAmerican middle-class life. This community played a large role in my understanding of race and gender and yet it was very heteronormative. I believe the education and life experience of the adults in my life encouraged openness and a sense of needing to know more about the world, absent of judgment. The adults in my community did not want to be judged, so they did not openly judge others.

My grandmother had a second-grade education and picked cotton. I am part of a multigenerational sisterhood of grandmothers, mothers, sisters, and daughters. My mother and her mother demonstrated a strong sense of themselves as women and as AfricanAmericans. I grew in my awareness of race and gender through their example and as a result of my ongoing education. While I felt acceptance within my community, interactions with the larger societal context presented challenges. Each educational space I entered offered learning experiences that opened my mind to the dynamics of race and gender. For example, I knew my skin color was a part of my identity at a very young age because on many occasions I had defining interactions and incidents where my skin color was the topic of discussion. Being a dark skinned girl was not good in the eyes of the dominant white society and I experienced my parents working hard to combat these negative messages.

Studying Social Work in graduate school also focused my learning on racism studies and included a significant amount of self-reflection. As I learned more about power and privilege, I started to see the spaces where I had privilege. I am a heterosexual, AfricanAmerican female married to a heterosexual, AfricanAmerican male. I understand the privileges and position that accompany this identity. While I learned at an early age that people who were gay were considered different, I also witnessed family embrace family across this difference. I knew same-sex relationships were not openly accepted, and as I grew older I had friends who were living with the losses that often resulted when one comes out as gay, lesbian, bisexual, or transgender.

I am aware that I carry my gender, race, and sexual orientation with me into every relationship. Balancing the duality of privilege and marginalization in the context of race is an interesting challenge. Perhaps my good, Presbyterian upbringing helped me navigate these challenges in the messages the church and my family endorsed regarding the importance of loving all people. This helped me to be willing and open most of my life to trust people to be good and true to themselves and to be open in their relationship with me.

Dr. Paulette Dalpes:
I grew up as a white, Catholic girl in a predominantly white, lower-middle-class neighborhood in a suburb of Denver, Colorado. My mother's family worked on the railroad and both of my grandfathers left school by the eighth grade to go to work. My parents completed high school but could not afford to pursue a college degree. My family took pride in our Irish, Scottish, and Austrian immigrant ancestors and this informed my developing ethnic self-identity, but I had no sense of a racial identity. Upon reflection, I can see how race and racism were pervasive factors in my childhood experience, yet I lacked the language or knowledge to talk about these dynamics.

As a growing young girl, I also lacked the language to talk about myself as female and as a lesbian coming out within a strongly religious family amidst a virulently sexist, homophobic community. How I saw myself as an emerging woman and as a same-gender-loving individual was strongly impacted by my family, church, and community. My rebellion against the dominant narrative regarding what it meant to be a woman was inspired during the burgeoning struggle for women's rights in the 1970s. This struggle for a positive feminist identity led to pain and fractures within my family and community. While much healing and resolution have occurred, the challenges of being a woman leader and an out lesbian endure today.

During graduate school, a critical incident raised my consciousness regarding my lack of knowledge of our nation's civil rights legacy and the resulting ignorance I held about race and racism. This experience and the learning I acquired affected choices I made about my first professional position. I selected a job where social justice was a strong focus of the Student Affairs program. Key mentors in my early professional career significantly influenced my understanding of myself across race, gender, and sexual orientation and provided the language and framework upon which to build greater awareness and action. Deep friendships across race also developed at this time. These experiences strengthened my ability to be a better leader. Without this intentional work, the friendship between Dr. Eanes and myself would probably not have been possible.

Attending graduate school, seeking mentors and elders who taught us alternatives to societal messages, and engaging in self-reflection were clear and intentional sliding doors we stepped through to better address questions and inequities we encountered. These actions helped us develop a stronger sense of our privileged and marginalized identities. This self-knowledge and awareness were instrumental in building the foundation upon which we could engage in a friendship across race and sexual orientation in a healthy and enriching manner. Without an understanding of our individual identities and group memberships in the larger societal context, our engagement across difference would lack the depth and insight upon which to sustain a lasting friendship.

The Glue

We were placed in our original space together as Senior Student Affairs Administrators at separate campuses within a large, urban, public university system. We first shared smiling eyes and "amen corner moments" in monthly meetings and then decided to make a plan to have breakfast. It was at this breakfast that the "glue" of our friendship became evident and exciting because we immediately found a common space in our understanding of social justice, oppression, and the work of Student Affairs.

The glue that comes from sharing the same workplace gave us the opportunity to support one another. We also shared a passion for our students who were predominantly students of color from limited economic means, and we had a common commitment to educational access. We joined together in our struggle to be effective senior-level leaders in service to our students. This cemented the glue created between us. Our common passion provided a spark for many long discussions about the work of Student Affairs, which led to longer talks about life, our values, and passions beyond work. These conversations helped us get to know each other in more deep and meaningful ways.

The Blossom

Why this friendship at this time? Why would a Black woman trust a white woman? Why would a lesbian woman trust a heterosexual woman? With life experiences of not being respected and valued, and moments of disappointment and betrayal across race and sexual orientation, why should we try again?

For some reason, our friendship was meant to blossom and we watered it and cared for it the best we could. We became aware that our opinions and shared stories were helping us grow stronger along the road of life in a powerful way. We invested the time when we barely felt there was time and we made a choice to be loyal to the process and the journey.

We intentionally use the term blossom because it describes what happens when a relationship gets what it needs and it grows. It was during this blossoming that the glue of our relationship began to set thicker and stronger.

We made an effort to develop our time and our traditions. We shared our families and real stories with each other.

Berenecea: *One of the most powerful memories I have of this time was when we both happened to be at a common work conference in a lovely resort location. Each of us had our families in tow. In my case, this meant my mother and aunt, the matriarchs of my family; my sister; my husband; and our two children. We travel tight, often in a crew. Paulette and her wife were also at the conference and because we had some glue and I so loved my new friend, I of course said, "Come meet my family!" It was later that I learned that in these kinds of situations very often a lesbian family may feel afraid and/or unsure. It never crossed my mind and it was at that moment that the glue and affection made me blind to the potential discomfort. The fact that it did not cross my mind is evidence of my privilege. I also became aware that I get to these points where I must share my whole self with people that I want to be whole friends. This was our whole self moment!*

Paulette: *The time our families met at a work conference was a turning point and deepening of both our friendship and my personal commitment to our friendship. I distinctly remember the moment when my wife (Kathy) and I arrived at the conference luncheon. We scanned the room to choose the table where we would sit. There were many options of people we could join sitting at tables around the room. The conference attendees were predominately white and there were tables that included colleagues from my current institution. Yet, my wife and I both agreed we would go and sit with Berenecea's family. They were some of the only people of color in the room and they were sitting alone at one of the tables. Kathy and I intentionally made the choice to sit at a table where we could connect across race. In so doing, I was also aware we were taking a risk. Although I knew Berenecea as a colleague and greatly valued our developing friendship, I had never met her family. As a lesbian couple, I am aware that I am hesitant when I meet heterosexual families. I am unsure how they will respond to us. Perhaps this is born of my own internalized homophobia or simply life experience. In this case, we were meeting a whole bunch of her family! How would her husband, her elderly mother and aunt, her sister and children respond when I introduced my wife? I wish I could say this was no longer something I consider, but out of past experience and the desire for comfort, it is always part of my professional social experience. This moment at the conference luncheon stands out in my memory because of the genuine warmth with which we were embraced. Her family welcomed us and our time together was filled with delight, caring, and connection.*

We have probably had millions of moments like this in our relation-ship where a single interaction or conversation could be a trigger; painful, or oppressive in some way. It is these very moments that provide us with spaces to reflect on who we are and what experiences, based on our social group membership, come with us to the relationship.

Today, our relationship provides a safe space to explore our differences. The love and admiration we share afford us room to be free in our dialogue. We both have cultures and families of origin that offer reasons to fear being open about ourselves with one another. It is also second nature to be guarded due to the highly polarized and toxic environment we both experience at work and in society. Yet, we each made intentional choices to move through sliding doors toward deeper honesty and intimacy in our friendship, while simultaneously choosing not to find the exit.

The Armor

"Black women need safe spaces in their lives to take off their armor that they have been wearing since childhood. Armor left on for too long can make a spirit heavy and burdened" (Bell & Nkomo, 2001, p. 260).

There are constant compromises in finding supportive living environ-ments when dealing with racism, homophobia, and sexism. Part of the reason we do not resist segregated lives is because we don't want to go back out into society and deal with the difficulties (constant microaggressions) that pervade our lived experience as people with marginalized identities. Sometimes it is just better to be around people like ourselves who understand us and with whom we feel safe.

We recognize that in each interaction across difference, people from mar-ginalized groups enter with a suit of armor. Creating spaces where this armor can be removed is essential to our well-being. When the workplace is difficult, it becomes harder to extend ourselves in our private life.

Berenecea: *I realized growing up that many people in my life lived segregated lives, perhaps because of the experience of overt racism in the workplace. This means when people left work on Friday their weekend was spent "in the community." People would run to the comfort of being with their own people. I can remember the elders saying, "You must take this time to rebuild." Many of the elders in my life have said, "The only way to survive the world of oppression and racism is to spend time in your community." I was also told, "You can't survive without getting along with* *white people." Therefore, we would spend the weekend and time in church building ourselves up to go back out there and face the white people.*

I am the third generation of women who have learned to take the armor off. My mother has been an example to me of how to build community and develop friendships. My mother's friends hugged each other, talked with each other every day, showed up for important events, and accepted each other. My mother talked with me about trust and what a real friend feels like. I tell my daughter on a daily basis that Nana taught me to be a good friend. My mother also taught me that when my armor is down, then I can rest. I had the gift of having a home where my armor was not needed. My mother also demonstrated a commitment to self-care, doing her hair, laughing loud, and playing in the kitchen. This modeled ways to have fun and relax.

Paulette: *My wife and I intentionally moved to Massachusetts from Colorado to immerse ourselves in a lesbian community. We spent 20 years connected to a vibrant, diverse community where we could remove our armor and be ourselves. Close friendships formed with people we now call family. Lesbian, Gay, Bisexual and Transgender (LGBT) communities often have families of origin and families of choice. It was in this community, this family of choice, where I became stronger in my self-identity as a lesbian. It was also in this community as it overlapped with progressive heterosexuals where I explored and developed a stronger social justice lens, especially with regard to race.*

Moving through spaces to find the right, safe, community is essential in our development as members of marginalized groups. The power of these choices cannot be overemphasized. We are aware that due to many circumstances, not everyone has access to these choices. Yet, we encourage people to find a way to be around your people, immerse yourself in your chosen community, and give yourself the chance to explore, expand, and flourish.

The Privilege

"Before coming together with black women, white women should seek out other white women to talk about their apprehensions and confusion about race, including their own racial membership" (Bell & Nkomo, 2001, pp. 259–260).

It is one thing to understand inequity and discrimination based on race and sexual orientation, it is a whole other matter to actively counteract the ways in which we participate in white, heterosexual privilege and the insidious experience of believing and acting as if we are better because we are white and/or heterosexual. Awareness of internalized dominance is critical to resisting a society that privileges some people over others because of race and sexual orientation. The ideology of supremacy is pervasive and it takes intentionality and vigilance to actively counteract the messages that perpetually tell us we are better than everyone else because of our white skin or our attraction to the opposite sex.

Paulette: *As I grew up, I received societal messages that repeatedly told me I am better because I am white. I had the benefit after graduate school to work at the University of Massachusetts and became involved with the Social Justice Education program, founded by Dr. Bailey Jackson, who wrote one of the first Black identity models in the 1970s (Jackson, 1976). It was through this program that I met Dr. Rita Hardiman who wrote one of the first white identity models (Hardiman, 1982). She and I became close friends and we shared long conversations about being white, white culture, white privilege, and white supremacy. There were many white people during this time that helped me to look deeper at my racism and challenged me by their examples. I learned how important it is to keep these conversations alive, while taking intentional action to resist oppressive dynamics and actively create inclusive and socially just work environments. This is a constant struggle because we never achieve antiracist status.*

Berenecea: *In the AfricanAmerican community people knew there were gay family members but it was not talked about. People were accepted as long as they stayed in the stereotypes, the box society had created. I had more than one gay person in my life growing up and I knew early on that many other people did not see them as normal or acceptable. I don't think I ever had a feeling of homophobia but it may be because of my spiritual walk. I tend to be a realist and I really embraced that we should all love each other. My Sunday School lessons were not lost on me. Furthermore, my parents were social justice pioneers and made it clear we treat all people with love. I did not witness homophobia in my family and social circles so I guess I just never felt it. But I do know because of a dear family friend how much it hurts to hide your life. That moment when you realize that person has separated into another world and only visits the heterosexual world here and there. You know that their families and others are the reason that they keep two identities.*

Intersectionality

We validated one another's experiences as women in leadership and women who are members of more than one marginalized identity. Black heterosexual women and white lesbians share a common intersection of oppression. Michelle Obama, former First Lady of the United States, in her speech at the 2015 Tuskegee University commencement (Obama, 2015) shared that Black women are often judged as "too loud, too angry and too emasculating"—lesbians experience these same criticisms.

In our conversations as executive professional women, we connected in making meaning of similar dynamics and common experiences of being interrupted, denied access to information, and questioned in terms of our credibility. We discovered comparable moments when our opinions were minimized and we were expected to caretake male leaders. We acknowledged to one another that we were often in situations where men wanted to situate us in a role neither of us desired or wanted. Sharing this feminist, social justice lens, and the process of naming our experiences with one another built further common ground and cemented the glue.

Berenecea: *As a woman of color I go into senior administration knowing I will be lonely. There won't be many other senior administrators at the table that look like me. And of those administrators at the table who are not people of color, few will have been in genuine relationship with any person of color. It is rare to gain authenticity across differences. It is trust and authenticity that is needed to have real talk and real friendship.*

Paulette: *It is exhausting and at times frustrating to be the only LGBT person among senior-level administrators. This experience of being the only one increasingly occurs the higher I rise in the profession. During my career, I have found strong connections with heterosexual, women of color and as a result, I feel less alone. I think this is because heterosexual, women of color experience the dual oppression of racism and sexism. They are removed from the white, male power structure in a similar way I am, while white, heterosexual, women still have the experience of benefiting from the privilege of race and sexual orientation. However, in order for the relationships with heterosexual women of color to develop and succeed, there was much work I needed to do, and still do, as a white person, to be a partnering colleague.*

The intersections of our identities also impact our life experience and who we are in our friendship. Some of these intersections go beyond race, gender, and sexual orientation.

Berenecea: *I can remember Paulette and I talking about our families and how we grew up and I had to manage my feelings of pride and shame. We have one deep difference between us and this is related to the socioeconomic class of our families of origin. Last year was the first time we talked at length about my father and his professional identity as a doctor and what it meant in my life as I was growing up. I am so proud of my father but often growing up I had to manage feelings of being proud with other people's discomfort with my class privilege.*

When I was in college, kids would say, "You are living like the Huxtables." Contrary to that belief, we did have a lot, but we are also one generation from the cotton field.

Paulette: *The difference in sexual orientation, education, and the corresponding relationship to upward mobility related to my socioeconomic class has unmoored my relationship with my family in a way that Berenecea has not had to experience. At the same time, Berenecea has had a different experience related to family and health concerns that are consistent with the experiences of AfricanAmerican families in the United States. She lost her father when he died at the age of 71 and her mother has battled breast cancer three times. Meanwhile, my parents remain relatively healthy for their age with no significant health issues as they enter into their 80s. The life expectancy rates across race are definitely exemplified in our own families.*

The most significant sliding door we chose with respect to intersectionality was the intentional act of naming and owning our multiple identities. Recognizing the complexities of who we are is essential to finding deeper connections in our friendships with people whose identities are so significantly different than our own. Sometimes it is not always easy to choose the right doors to move through in these conversations. One has to act with courage and faith.

Owning It

Over the years, we have come to share deeply personal experiences from our past. We talk openly about our relationships with our spouses, our family. We discuss our heartbreaks and successes. We share the moments in our journey when we are unsure if we made the right choices, times when we feel we have failed. There are collective moments of despair, hope, and triumph.

We have grown into owning our relationship. We have pushed passed the choosing to be in it, to owning it. We spend much more time reflecting on the world and how to live in it now than we spent trying to figure out each other in the beginning. We have deeper more challenging conversations knowing that our difference is what enriches the dynamic. We have no filter on our conversation. We are nothing like those two administrators that met at the first professional gathering.

We talk about our dreams, our next big career moves, and we support one another each step of the way. We turn to each other in times of doubt and difficulty to get a different perspective and to learn from one another's experience. We seek out one another for a voice of reason and a sanity check. We compare our experiences and provide guidance on paths one or the other has walked in advance. We seek one another's counsel. We do gut checks. We challenge each other's perspective. We find reassurance and understanding in our shared history and in our different life experiences.

Planning for Long-Term Love

Each of us experiences sliding door moments that may limit or benefit our opportunities to build relationships across race and sexual orientation. The intentional choices we make can be based upon our evolution as professionals in the Student Affairs profession with respect to our own identities. The work we do today to understand dynamics of oppression, power, and privilege can build a foundation and plant seeds for the development of essential relationships in the future.

Paulette: *In the end it comes down to love. Loving myself, all my strengths and imperfections. And loving my friend, all of who she is. I love her by learning more about her culture, her heritage, her story, her family, her goals, her aspirations, her struggles, and her fears. I listen, I nudge, I challenge, I embrace, I celebrate all of who she is. I never forget she is Black, or how being Black informs her experience in the world, especially as an AfricanAmerican woman, married to an AfricanAmerican man and raising AfricanAmerican children in our society today. I do not look past her race, or make an effort to not see her color. Her Blackness, her African heritage, is centered in who she is and therefore it is centered in how I see* her. Likewise, the reality of racism, her experience of living in a society that treats her and her family as disposable, is a dynamic in our friendship never to be minimized or ignored. In fact, we often grieve together about the racism in the world and how it specifically impacts her family. In turn, I try to impact change in my own circle of influence. I try to be present to our friendship. I don't do this perfectly, sometimes I miss things, or I don't understand or cannot see the essence of a circumstance or am unable to track the roots of its meaning. And yet, sometimes it is in the questions, in the staying curious, or in the not knowing that I can offer a gift of reflection, of needing to articulate and verbalize what has gone unsaid. Overall, without question, I am a far better person and a better leader because of the love I share with Berenecea. I am filled with immense gratitude for the gift of our friendship.

Berenecea: The comfort of knowing you have a real friend is priceless, and that I have in Paulette. I am grateful for the love, patience, and honesty. We live busy chaotic lives and the sincere and intentional way that we have found to be friends is not easy to develop. We have such different lives that I know that we often have to remind ourselves how to be in the moment and just be there for each other. My being a working mom in a community that I am dedicated to serving keeps me busy in different ways than her life does. Many of the recent events of our world make me worried and scared for my children. I am worried that they are going to be faced with racism, sexism, and homophobia in a way that does not perpetuate the love I experienced. Paulette is often my ear to listen and my shoulder to cry on when I am immobilized by the amount of hate and racism that still exist in this world. Our uncommon bond provides me with proof that love can transcend race and sexual orientation. I am so grateful to have her in my life. She is full of the kind of pride in being who she is that makes me less scared to face what is the world of today.

It is in the stretching and the pulling, amidst this wonderful, inherent tension across difference that the beauty of creativity happens and the friendship grows. Our differences didn't stagger our intimacy; on the contrary, they enhanced it. If one of us had been less open, less willing, and had not moved forward through the sliding door, then perhaps the moment would have passed, and we would have missed this gift. We are aware of the tremendous loss we would have experienced had this opportunity been overlooked.

We recognize it is hard to feel a loss for that which you do not know. Therefore, we realize many people are not even aware they have missed the gift of a friendship like ours. We believe, when we don't find each other across our differences, we are less than what we could be. Ultimately, our friendship is a reflection of who we are in our deepest and truest sense. It is in the unknown, through the exploration of learning, openness and trust forged with courage and forgiveness that a truly loving uncommon bond endures.

References

Bell, E. L. J. E., & Nkomo, S. M. (2001). *Our separate ways: Black and white women and the struggle for professional identity.* Boston, MA: Harvard Business School Press.

Eligon, J., & Gebeloff, R. (2016). Affluent and black, and still trapped by segregation. *New York Times*, August 20, 2016. Retrieved August 22, 2016 from http://www.nytimes.com/2016/08/21/us/milwaukee-segregation-wealthy-black-families.html?mabReward=A4&action=click&pgtype=Homepage&region=CColumn&module=Recommendation&src=rechp&WT.nav=RecEngine&_r=0

Galupo, M. P. (2009). Cross-category friendship patterns: Comparison of heterosexual and sexual minority adults. *Journal of Social and Personal Relationships*, 26(6–7), 811–831. doi:10.1177/0265407509345651

Hardiman, R. (1982). *White identity development: A process-oriented model for describing the racial consciousness of White Americans* (Doctoral dissertation). Retrieved from ProQuest (No. AAI8210330).

Jackson, B. W. (1976). Black identity development. In L. H. Golubchick and B. Persky (Eds.), *Urban, social, and educational issues* (pp. 158–164). Dubuque, IA: Kendall-Hunt.

Obama, M. (2015). *Tuskegee University commencement speech.* https://www.whitehouse.gov/blog/2015/05/11/case-you-missed-it-first-ladys-powerful-remarks-tuskegee-universitys-class-2015

Orfield, G. (2009). *Reviving the goal of an integrated society: A 21st century challenge.* Los Angeles, CA: The Civil Rights Project/Proyecto Derechos Civiles at UCLA.

· 1 5 ·

RIDE OR DIE

Relationships Beyond Constructs

JLove Calderón

I'm so damn blessed!

My life is filled with the most magnificent tribe of women. I would not be alive and well today were it not for the women in my life, I can say that for sure! Many of my deepest, most important and profound friendships are with women of color.

The oft-hinted (and some come right out and ask it!) question people ask me is how and why do you have so many women of color friends?

Hmmmm. Well. There are many factors to it. But they are definitely not superexciting or earth shattering. In fact, they are plain and ordinary life things. BUT, all together they inform my cultural upbringing in a profound way.

Growing up in Denver, Colorado, I lived in a racially diverse neighborhood and attended multiracial schools. My high school was in a predominately African American and Latino neighborhood.

Sports were a major part of my life. From an early age my Dad (RIP) encouraged me to play and compete. In high school I was on the all Black and Latina basketball team. I also played tennis and partnered with an African American girl. The senior who mentored me in volleyball was Mexican American.

Not sure if ya heard, but I spent a lot of time runnin' the streets! One of my best friends was the first graffiti artist in D-Town and also a founding member of the Rollin 30 Crips. My life of street art was an entrance into both Hip-Hop culture and gang culture, and I quickly became entrenched in both the graff crew and the Crips.

During high school my first real boyfriend lived 10 blocks from me and was a star quarterback and Varsity on the basketball team. Our connection was alive and vibrant. He was African American and I spent hours and hours at his house playing spades with him, his sister, and his mother (when she wasn't working). During spades there was always an easy banter back and forth about race; his sister often poking fun at "white people be ..." and "but you know how Black people are. ..." Collective "um hmms" were heard round the table, lightness, with smiles and laughter. I was experiencing some of the differences of African American culture and, for lack of a better word, white culture.

See, there was great love there. Race was a thing, but it wasn't a thing that was allowed to separate us, to break us apart. I always felt at home. Comfortable in my skin. Fully accepted for who I was.

Oh, and I am a social butterfly. And I'm an Aquarius. And I am an emotional creature. (That matters!)

But why in the world does any of this matter? Well. It actually shouldn't. But we still live in times where a white woman having mostly women of color friends is "a thing." So it's helpful to break it down.

This is how it came to be that I had mostly women of color friendships as a girl and young woman. The confluence of proximity, activities that bond people together (sports, art, crime), Hip-Hop culture (emanating from Black and Brown communities and expressing Black and Brown culture), and longevity (i.e., living together, going to school and parties together, breaking bread together, highs and lows of living, together, etc.) all had an impact on how I developed my friendships.

And this was all before I was 18 years old.

Biggest challenge for me? Navigating the racial divide among my peers, which did peek out its ugly head on the regular. The Black kids, the Latino kids, and the white kids called me every name in the book. Cliques. Daily "Why do you hang out with *them*? They're *so* ..." Fill in the blank, a stereotype for each racial group. It got way crazy once I got my boyfriend. He was the top catch in all of Denver, and not just in my high school. The Black girls were tight! "Get your own and leave ours alone!" The white girls called me a slut.

The white boys told me I was "ruined" and that I could forget ever having a white boyfriend. You know how it is in middle and high school. It was a difficult time in my life, and my refuge was listening to my mix tapes while I poured my crazy out in my journal, painted my pain and rage on the walls, and self-medicated through heavy partying involving drugs and alcohol.

And that was just the kids.

The adults had their own version on this. I was pulled aside on a regular basis. In school, after church, or even driving down the street and being pulled over by cops all with the same message to me that can be summed up like this: "You seem like a nice kid. Don't get mixed up with kids from the wrong side of the tracks." From the majority of adults this was unwarranted and often I wanted to scream at them, at the absurdity of it all ... for in the relationship I was in, I was the white girl gang-banger and my Black boyfriend shunned crime and violence and was a model student and athlete. Racism with its perverse and deadly blinders made no sense at all.

With the cops it was the same ol' racism, but in these circumstances we were doin' dirt. But the ugly I witnessed, time and again, was the willingness and power of cops who determined the fate of teenagers based on who they felt was valuable enough to "save." The world is witnessing how that same narrative of ingrained bias and racism is playing out in society as Black men and boys continued to be killed by police.

So much for adult role models and mentors.

As I moved on to college, being in multiracial relationships was so normalized in my life that the segregated San Diego State campus threw me a major curveball! Fraternities, parties, clubs, all segregated by race. Ninety-nine problems and race is number one. It took time. But conversation by conversation, showing up and being present at events focused on Hip-Hop culture, speaking my truth in classes and around campus, slowly, painfully slowly, I found my tribe. I was surrounded by mostly people of color, and once again I built with the females of color and we rolled deep. There were some other white girls though. White girls who had shared similar experiences growing up as I did. We also became fast friends and our clique was dubbed the United Nations as we rolled to the Palladium nightclub in LA to do what we did!

Those years were definitely my party years, but I also began to get politicized. I majored in African American Studies, and as my knowledge of race in America grew, a slew of emotions hit me hard. It was the first time I really understood the insidious nature and consequences of white supremacy. In each class an explosion of knowledge erupted in my being, and shattered my illusions and ignorance. I was changed forever.

I bounced to NYC. As I moved deeper into movement work, many more challenges rose to the surface. I have been told many times before by female friends of color that it ain't no walk in the park being tight friends with a white woman, especially in movement work. I understood the dilemma, and what it often boiled down to was: am I worth the struggle? Is it worth women of color having to "defend" hanging out with me to others? And what if I say or do the wrong thing? What does it mean to "have my back" as a human being vs. "having my back" in racialized polarized movement work?

I learned quickly that having friends of color in movement was way different than the relationships with my homegirls. With my homegirls, we had loyalty and that ride or die shit that we lived by (to this day my closest friendships date back to age three). Also my homegirls knew all of me, inside and out. We grew up together.

The act of becoming politicized caused a new awareness around identity, equity, and power. My homegirls looked at me as their girl, period. My movement friends looked at me as JLove, and also looked at me as a straight, college-educated white girl.

When I was in my 20s, I lost some of my closest movement friends because of race. Some I still don't speak to today, which is a shame. Looking back, the fractured and damaged relationships with my women of color movement friends were layered with the unexpressed and unaddressed trauma and pain of the intersection of poverty, class, interracial relationships, and privilege. As an independent, out on my own white girl working, living, doing movement work and engaging in communities of color, I had no place to "go" when shit got rough with my friendships.

At that time in my life I brought to the proverbial table an inability to process and express my personal trauma and how it was relating to my lack of emotional maturity to harmoniously negotiate all the alleys, roads, and signs that make up the complexity of intersections of race, class, gender lived experiences, self-esteem and worth, trauma and culture. I was a walking mixed bag of a being "in-process" of building my self-confidence and self-worth, while learning and understanding my political perspective while truly grappling with being in a white body.

What does that really mean?

It means that I messed up! All the time! It matters because regardless of the fact that I was doing my best, at the time my ignorance, my insecurities, my blind spots had real implications and real impact.

I'm sure you've heard the expression hurt people hurt people. At a period when I was attempting to "find my voice," which had been shut down, stomped on, silenced and made invisible, I was silencing the voices of others around me.

Even though it was unconscious and unintentional, the impact was real. My white privilege was messy and ugly and I didn't know what it meant to be accountable and to own my shit. In the collectives and organizations I was part of I was unconscious of the amount of space I took up. I "took over," thinking I was helping the cause when I was really disempowering my comrades. When things got really tough there was the "white girl tears" that, although they felt very real to me, turned the attention toward taking care of me, as opposed to the issues at hand. In one collective I cofounded, when I was asked to leave, the core reason given to me, while sitting in my small bedroom in Bushwick, Brooklyn was, "Your very presence is oppressive."

These were just some of the ways my presence and privilege showed up in the spaces I was in.

It showed up in other ways as well. I was very confident and comfortable being with young people no matter the circumstances, and from my years of experience I became an excellent facilitator. I remember one time we were working at a girl's detention center and I blew it out the water. After, one of my cofacilitators, who was a woman of color, seemed upset. As we chatted briefly on the street corner, before we parted ways she looked me dead in the eyes and said, "I hate how confident you are in front of Black girls." Once she said it, her truth, it was as if she realized she said out loud what she was thinking in her head. I was silent, not sure how to respond. Tears formed in her eyes and she just spun around and walked away from me. My body wouldn't move for a bit. I stood on that corner wondering, how did we get here? And where do we go from here, and where do I fit in this world, in this work?

The sting of that exchange haunted me. Not sure how to take the feedback of, once again, my very presence, I decided to shrink myself. I decided to take myself out of the front of the room, and to stay in the back. At the time it felt like the only course of action to be responsive to the commitment of racial justice and my role as a white person in that. I became unsure of how to be most supportive and helpful in my role as an organizer and to figure out where I fit in. The feeling of homelessness once again flared up and I fought to stay grounded and well. There were so many questions, but no answers evident.

I lost friends whom I loved and who loved me. My children lost out of some really amazing human beings who would have been important people in their lives. This is the cost of not knowing. From a global perspective, white people who don't know are inflicting harm and death on people of color. From daily microaggressions to the killing of unarmed Black and Brown people in the streets. It all matters.

As a youth it was about proximity and shared interests. As an adult it became much more and I had to make intentional decisions about who I was and who my tribe was. To love and be loved. To respect and be respected. To contribute and to be contributed to. What does that all look like and what do I choose to do differently to create that in my life?

I decided that the biggest growth area for me was to become more knowledgeable, more accountable, and more activated.

I learned. I engaged in personal development and transformational work to heal my soul wounds from the past so I could get stronger. I continued to learn and grow as an activist in the movement for racial justice and fought through my unknowing to get to know intimately white privilege, how it shows up, ways to identify and manage it, actions to keep it in check, and my role as a white woman in the world.

And I took time to talk to my friends. Especially the women of color I was closest to, my ride or dies.

As a white woman I had to learn (and I am still learning and growing and I am still deeply flawed, and still sometimes the ugly unconscious privilege reveals itself and must be checked) when to close my mouth and open my ears. I also learned how important it is for me to name privilege when it may or may not be at play and give space for my women of color friends to speak on it or keep it movin. Sometimes that sounds like, "Yeah, J, your blindspot is operating and this is what I need from you in this moment." And sometimes it sounds like, "Nah J that is not comin' up for me at all."

For me, accountability includes being the one naming it, calling it out, then being open and willing to hear what is being expressed, and then making the necessary shifts.

Now the best thing is that we get to listen to each other and bear witness to the hard things. Our deep trust allows us to fully express the complexities that arise.

As a human being I had to learn when I had to stand up for my truth, even with the issue of privilege. I have been bullied before with race as the bullying factor. I have been put down and verbally abused plenty of times where I didn't stand up for myself because I felt like I had no right to my voice in the matter because I was white and the person (s) attacking me were women of color.

Although the milestones in my racial transformations in the past two decades have most often come from pain, what is really beautiful now is that I experience racial transformation with and from joy, triumph, and reaping the incredible benefits of a lifetime of relationships with women of color.

Through my lifelong journey of walking hand in hand in true sistahood with women of color, I do my best to stay true to these ideals:

Through radical honesty and full disclosure of what and how I am feeling combined with the ways in which I express those thoughts and feelings, support continued vibrant sistahood.

Understand through a spiritual and intuitive place when I might need to give more space, sit back, and/or, exactly opposite, when I need to speak up and out and be more supportive.

Ask and listen to the Truth that my women of color friends are expressing, knowing that I will never understand fully because I am a white woman.

Truly, truly believe that our common humanity and liberation is tied together and that one day, although perhaps not in my lifetime, we will all be free.

· 1 6 ·

LETTERS

Roberta Samet and Imani Romney-Rosa

When the two of us are together, there are always three of us—Roberta, Imani, and the work against white supremacy that first brought us together. To say our meeting was improbable is putting it lightly. How did we find ourselves members of the same synagogue? How is it we trust each other completely? How did we come to be sitting together in the same room, on a beautiful spring day, talking about "Undoing Racism" in our Jewish community? These are the questions with which we grappled as we exchanged personal emails over the course of several months. The emails were online conversations about anti-racism organizing that we had been working on together for two years.

September 29, 2015

Dear Imani,

How can I represent the white part of this uncommon bond? It forces me to look at my whiteness in a way that does not come first in relationship to our friendship. The collective message of white superiority is powerful. Let's say, looking at whiteness is an acquired taste. In the right circumstances, I eat it in doses that I can tolerate but can't honestly say I return to that restaurant for comfort food.

I see this friendship as an encapsulated entity with a race analysis surrounding it ... informing, instructing, accompanying.

There is always the personal and the collective. Personally, whatever doubts or questions I have about myself as a leader ... the collective internalized identity of white superiority is more powerful. White people often roll their eyes, assuming that a person of color (POC) is less educated, intelligent, "quota-ed in" and all the rest of that horrible belief system. We are shocked when POC are as good as, better than us, not really different than the notion white people have of "white trash." As in, if with 40 acres and a mule you are still a dirt farmer, then what's up with you? Thinking about this now, there is a white shame when we are outdone, out-thought, out-performed by a POC. Superiority is part of our collective inheritance. And I believe the only, and I mean the only, way to fracture that deeply and often unconsciously imbued belief system is to practice something different. Convert false, unearned superiority to the net gain of an enriched experience, by taking leadership from POC. Superiority is usually assumed, the way you assume your legs will work when you walk and expect that the earth will be under your feet. It's like those GEL inserts that are advertised. A little spring in our walk, hardly noticed, rarely racially experienced. We don't consciously feel superior; we just note what we consider to be inferior. Perhaps this is why in a more homogeneous white country class prevails as a dividing line. But here ... it is race, with class coming in as a second contender. I think that your analogy as a teacher is the closest thing to this. It is through the position of power, not activity. It makes me all the more conscious when I have clients of color. The power differential is so vast, first transferentially, and then add the race mix.

Love,

Roberta

September 30, 2015

Roberta,

We have a common bond. You're right that this is how we should be able to see it, how we should talk about friendship, how it would be, if ... but just seeing each other for who we are wouldn't be enough to cover the legacy of race.

I remember my (white) wife, who went to an integrated high school in the early '70s saying to me, "Until I met the Black people in high school and started to get to know them, I always thought we were the same, that they only had black skin on top."

Yesterday, I was on the phone with my longtime mentor and he said to me, "I ask myself, 'How much time do I have to spend around white people?'" (Even writing this feels like an insult to you and to our friendship. It is a risk. I wonder if you and your kind who know me and my mind realize we can and do feel this way.)

As loved as my daughter is in her home Spanish-speaking child-care situation, when she came home last week saying, "Yo soy bonita, tu eres negrita" ("I'm pretty, you're Black"), no vessel could contain my sorrow and rage. And when I was encouraged by a Peruvian in my mamis group to think of it as a term of endearment (as it and "chinita" and "morenita" are often used), I just shook my head … we can't afford that ignorance here; in the United States we lose the capacity to make innocuous statements about beauty and race in the same sentence.

It is an uncommon bond because I am taught not to trust you. It is an uncommon bond because understanding your culture increases my survival while your understanding mine is optional. It is an uncommon bond because it's a risk and a choice that some people opt out of, sneer at or think is a joke … the way people say (straight) men and (straight) women can never be "just" friends.

Where is the humanity? I think we find it by acknowledging the context, constantly then not letting it define us.

Love,

I

September 30, 2015

Roberta,

My first activist meetings were as a very young child, before I could speak. My parents would take me to organizing meetings—with my mom, I attended meetings in "The Movement" and with my father meetings in support of the emerging Brooklyn College Puerto Rican Studies Department. I love the idea of a movement that is not for the elite, not even "childcare provided," but "come, just come."

How did I come to be co-chair of a Race Work Group (RWG) at Kolot Chayeinu, a progressive, antiracist synagogue in Brooklyn? It started with Amina Rachman, another Black, Jewish congregant, asking, "What is Kolot doing about race?" When the rabbi first asked me to run the working group, I was too busy to take on anything else, let alone sit together with folks I assumed would be mostly white to discuss race. I was a school administrator and teacher, serving on the board of my family's consulting business and in a 12-step program. I was in the process of completing my conversion, landlording, and juggling a new romantic relationship.

The early days of the Race Work Group saw me, in my mid-thirties, hoping to settle down, holding on to the dregs of my romantic relationship with a woman who'd once been my best friend, terrified to do it alone but praying to become pregnant. Later, our being selected as co-chairs coincided with my sitting before the beit din (council of rabbis) and entering the mikveh (ritual bath) for my conversion while six months pregnant. Still later, I found myself nursing my daughter as we sat around the table at "the clubhouse" (Roberta's home) subverting the dominant paradigm and putting ourselves to the task of Tikkun Olam (repairing the world) through antiracist Jewish activism, while job searching to return to classroom teaching after my year home with my baby and intense work on our baby—Kolot's Race Working Group. It felt like circling back to the beginning, but this time I was the mother, not the infant.

October 1, 2015

Imani,

I wonder about that place in a friendship, when one passes through the doorway into deep trust. So, for instance … and this is a big for instance … I trust you fully. I know that what I bring to you will be held gently and honestly in your hands. I don't feel I have to protect myself with you. Likewise, I trust that you will challenge me, my ideas or behavior, with similar care and honesty.

This was achieved only after subscribing to principles that degrade the assumption of white rightness and Black lessness. So to this end, we proposed to dialogue, back and forth, through the process that brought us to this present state of close friendship and deep alliance.

I believe that the most substantial friendships, the ones that stand the test of time and are the most profound, are those in which the friendship has taken on something … being present at the birth of a child, working together, planning a party. The context is larger than the two individual psyches. For our friendship, anti-racism work is the ever-present third.

We became friends co-chairing the Race Working Group (RWG). We had both been through the Undoing Racism Workshop (URW), conducted by the Peoples' Institute for Survival and Beyond. The Peoples' Institute developed and has conducted workshops on structural racism for 35 years. That became our unifying and shared experience. We kept going back to the shared experience. The training became our bridge. The channel. We shared a language. We grabbed on to it. That was our grounding. The clubhouse, my dining room, was where we held our meetings.

For a year I had been pushing the case for the RWG to take the URW. I felt that if we weren't on the same page about our definition of race, we were doomed to ride on retreads of unfinished, incomplete conversations. When I found out that you had taken the training, I felt that wink of, "Ok, a partner. At that moment I knew we could start to steer the direction of the Race Working Group ... from conversations about race to conversations about becoming an anti-racist synagogue.

Love,

Roberta

October 1, 2015

Imani,

It is 1959. I am driving in a 1955 Chevy with my family from Miami to New Jersey. It is hot. We drive through Gainesville, Georgia. My sister and I start singing "We Shall Overcome." Our parents gently silence us. The silencing is confusing. We don't understand danger.

How do I find myself writing this piece with you, Imani, friend, co-anti-racist conspirator? It started long before then and is perhaps over determined.

I am the daughter of civil rights parents. I am a psychotherapist in NYC. I am 65, straight, in a loving relationship. The world of my early life was permeated with social justice as a way of life. I have straddled the world of the inner life and outer life. Sometimes it has felt like a circus act where a woman, standing on the backs of two white horses, makes a series of circles around the inner ring. I stand on the privilege of two white horses.

My Jewish identity is strong yet non-observant. I have found the deepest spiritual practice in indigenous ceremony, while, all the while, participating as a Jew. I became a member of Kolot, in the early days, in affinity with Rabbi Ellen Lippmann, my close childhood friend, who had a vision to create meaningful Jewish practice and community. When Ellen asked me to step into this newly formed group to study race ... I could not say no. Only deep into our race work did we choose to become an antiracist synagogue.

Love,
Roberta

October 2, 2015

Roberta,
I realize that by the time I met you, I stopped looking through/at/with the looking glass self. Wondering who was judging me for not having enough Black friends or Black enough friends. I felt more in my body than before and could receive what was in front of me. This was in part because of time and in part because I'd found a Black group. It is also because one of the lessons I've learned being in the program is that race doesn't always have to be primary: I have met people who share my story to the letter who are of a different race, class, and age, something I never thought possible.

I had heard a lot of great things about the URW and about how magical it was. I would say it was a good training. I had just been promoted to an administrative job and was sailing right along until we got to talking about "gate-keeping"—the power people hold to decide who has access to institutional and organizational benefits. That stopped me in my tracks. That was the first item we talked about and that represented "work" for me—the first module that didn't feel like "Yep, yep, I got this, I know this." One feature of what made that space so helpful for me was feeling like I did not have to take care of white folks in the process. They had their own leader who could help keep them in line, answer their questions, and take care of their fragility.

Imani

October 4, 2015

Imani,
I did the Undoing Racism Workshop because a close friend, a longtime antiracist organizer, said, "Roberta, you HAVE to take this workshop." I thought I had it worked out, having grown up in a civil rights family. I can say that I was weaned on making a social justice difference. I stand on their shoulders. I took the workshop three days after 9/11, at St. Paul's church in Brownsville, Brooklyn. I was one of three white people in a packed room

of St. Paul congregants, a Black activist church in Brownsville, Brooklyn. It changed my life. It was the first time I heard the notion of internalized white superiority. I didn't know then that I would soon be hired by the September 11th Fund to head up their mental health recovery plan. I didn't know that this fledgling understanding of white internalized superiority would guide the work that followed.

Roberta

October 4, 2015

Imani,

Many years ago I fell in love with an African American man. He was a deep love in my life. When I told my parents that he was Black, what ensued was extraordinarily painful. I grew up with civil rights. My parents devoted their lives to this work. The message at home was equality and justice. So I was astonished to find that it was OK to have nationally renowned Black civil rights leaders sit at our dining room table, but not OK to date them.

During the height of the conflict, my father invited me to have lunch at the United Nations (UN). (He had a UN pass as a member of a governmental organization.) I told my parents that my boyfriend was a professional who ran a mental health agency and came from a middle-class Brooklyn family. In an intellectual fashion, my father doubted my judgment in being with this man, further questioned his background. I don't believe he would have asked some of these questions about a white man I was dating. If I'd had more nerve I would have left the table. This from my beloved father. I felt betrayed. All that I had been taught was challenged when it got up close and personal.

Months later, they met him, loved him. We went on vacation together. I did not have a race analysis then. I did not understand that Jim Crow was not ancient history to them. I had no notion of the intergenerational transmission of the race construct. I did not know about the lives of interracial couples that had been threatened and destroyed. My parents were worried about my safety and welfare.

Writing this to you now, my heart hurts all over again. I realize how deeply we are steeped in this illness of racialized fear. We are soaking wet in this. They were guilty and not to blame. We are guilty and not to blame.

Roberta

October 4, 2015

Roberta,
Just read your letter from this morning. It was so painful.
I love your play on words about guilt and blame.
I love you,
Imani

October 4, 2015

Roberta,
Yesterday we did an affinity group activity at my job. The initial groups were people of color, white folk, and a third space for folk who might self-identify there. The third space looked (by my vision and judgment) to be a multiracial group. One woman in the people of color group said she'd like to be in a smaller group for more focused conversation and proposed a Latino group. It only took me a moment, but I knew I would stay with the people of color group. My experience around Latinos ignoring or denying racial identity led me to believe that I'd be better off staying where I was. I have always been Black first. My Black identity trumps my gender, my class, my sexuality, my able-bodied-ness, my Judaism. And I would have been welcome in the Latina, group, but I worry.
Imani

October 7, 2015

Roberta,
Does racial superiority hold up even in mixed gendered groups? And with non-Jews? I'm curious to know how superiority works for you. I know for me, when I think of it in the context of being a teacher with my students, it is nearly invisible to me unless I keep calling my attention to it.
Love,
I

October 8, 2015

Imani,
I'm comfortable in multi-gendered settings. I was brought up to feel equal to men and with the belief that I could do what I wanted to do, achieve what

I wanted to achieve. When confronted with mens' superior/power stuff, my reaction is usually to think they are jerks and challenge them. I am more competitive with men than with women. ... I might defer to them at times in interpersonal relationships, but not generally in the work sphere. This is probably different when I run across a man whom I deem to be truly brilliant, and then, I feel deficient.

As a white Jew, I think there lies an implicit Jewish filter that expresses superiority, intellectually, culturally, all the things that have made us highly achieving and also the stuff that has been a part of being targeted. With non-Jews, I don't experience them as superior. It is not to say that in some settings, with non-Jews, that I don't feel a little of out the mix, but my specialness is a great roadside elixir ... not so included, not really feeling it, but superior nonetheless.

I heard a wild story about two gay men. They liked each other on the phone. They participated in an experiment. They decided that one of them would always be blindfolded when they got together. They spent a year "dating" this way. By the end of the year, they had fallen in love. One was attractive. One was not. They fell in love because they fell in love. There was chemistry there.

So how is this any different from friendship? We are friends because we are friends. There are places we go because we share an antiracist alliance and are willing to go there. There is a depth. But I don't want to discard the fact that we are friends because we wanted to be friends. I am not close friends with every Black or Latina with a shared antiracist analysis.

I don't want to lose the humanity in this. The race aside. I'm not trying to be colorblind. Yes, we were thrown together in an antiracist context and perhaps we otherwise would not have met. I don't pray Saturday mornings like you do. I am always a Jew, but I don't worship.
Roberta

October 11, 2015

Roberta,
I'm still writing you back in my head about racial superiority as I journey to meet you and work on our writing together.

With my white friends, who think of racism exclusively as interpersonal bigotry and not structural, these friendships are destined to be very superficial or one-dimensional. One of my friends has been teetering on the edge for the last year.

I think of the number of friendships that have fallen apart in the face of George Zimmerman, Ferguson or Eric Garner. Even white antiracist activists are struggling to separate themselves from their ignorant white friends.

Just this morning on Facebook, a Black friend wrote, "I am not going to argue with people who think there is reverse racism."

The hashtag "#IJustCant" comes up over and over on the feeds of my Black friends around these issues, issues that have been framed as "our issues" rather than "your" issues or "all our" issues.

Our bond is uncommon … and thank God for it!
Imani

October 14, 2015

Imani,
This reminds me of a lunch meeting I had last summer, after Ferguson. At the time there was an active online debate about unfriending people who posted controversial comments about Ferguson and racism. Some were saying, "de-friend in protest."

Others said that as white people we have to learn to talk about racism with other white people. I'd learned that one of the most important places for white people in antiracism organizing was to work with other white people, not to take the usual route of working in social justice programs, "helping" POC. After all, white people created racism.

So, the lunch. A white friend, who didn't know this man well, introduced us and we went to my favorite Brooklyn restaurant, Madiba, a place owned and run by South Africans. My lunch date was a rather affluent attorney, who, I am sure, considered himself a non-bigot. During the course of our lunch, I felt compelled to introduce the litmus race test, and started talking about the events of Ferguson. What ensued was a conversation that made my blood boil. In a somewhat apologetic way, he talked about welfare mothers and boys in hoodies that made him nervous and similar unexamined comments.

As I quietly persisted in challenging him, he flared, telling me he could be adamant, that he was a law professor—exhibiting male, white, status-born superiority. But committed to attempting to have a difficult race conversation with a white person, I kept my temper in check. Finally I asked him,

"What exactly do you lose in this particular race arrangement?" He was silent, for of course, there is only one answer. Not a damn thing.

So maybe your Black mentor needs to "unfriend." But to avoid checking out, I genuinely tried to not discard this white person, which is what white people often do when political tempers flare and opinions differ. We throw each other away.

How is it that our inter racial, inter generational friendship is saturated with trust, love and dedication to speaking and hearing the truth? What comes from this, when race is acknowledged from the start, rather than being a non-issue (I didn't even notice you are Black) or a progressive fetish (Isn't it cool that I have a Black friend?) when is the friendship firm and safe enough to talk about the hard things? And, when are the racial distinctions too painful to voice (from experiences of walking down the street, seeking medical care, looking for work, reading the Coates book). In this dialogue, we propose our own version of Cornell West and Michael Lerner, as we consciously explore this friendship and how it humanizes our lives.
Love,
Roberta

October 17, 2015

Imani,
What do I do when I take unfamiliar trains to your apartment to work on this piece and find myself the only white person on the train? It is late afternoon. Everyone is tired, and more particularly tired than I am used to seeing. Weary, maybe. What do I do with the thought (read fear) that arises when I see I am the only white person on the train? And with the thought, "will something bad happen to me?" I talk myself down. I remind myself that POC have only treated me with respect and kindness. Something I don't understand but is, nonetheless, true. I talk myself down with this. I think of Michael Moore's graphic scene in *Bowling for Columbine* called "A Short History of the US." Punch line … we kidnap Africans and bring them to America. Millions die on the journey. The rest are enslaved, raped, murdered, worked until they die, and then we arm ourselves against their rightful rage. But what possibly do I do when unfounded fear meets experience, on my way to your house, to write this chapter. I feel so visible.
Roberta

October 17, 2015

Roberta,
Interesting you should write this ... for two reasons. The first is that I just had this *very* interesting realization this year. I love Michael Moore, but never saw *Bowling for Columbine*. I read *Dude Where Is My Country?* So, my recent realization is no wonder white people (cops, I was thinking) are afraid of us, somewhere deep down beneath all the denial and justifications is the very real realization that there were hundreds of years of brutal wrongdoing and, frankly, if it were y'all, you'd be pissed enough to do some damage? It's projection as much as it's anything else really.
Right?
Imani

October 19, 2015

Hey,
The Race Work Group is starting a reading group on race. Starting with the Coates book, *Between the World and Me*. Dec. 1st. Can you come? I'm facilitating ... don't know with whom. Would love to do it with you. Interested? Need to run it by the work group on Thursday.
Love,
Roberta

October 22, 2015

Shit. It's already Thursday. Sorry, I got mixed up with the holiday. I'm on the fence anyway. I've been scared to read the book.:-/

October 22, 2015

Can't you come?

October 22, 2015

Imani,
I pulled the trigger too soon in my response to you yesterday. I really didn't speak to what you said, "that I am afraid to read the book." That is powerful

and I am sorry to encourage you because I want you there. As a white person, as your white friend, there is no way that my experience will be the same as yours … I don't have to be afraid to read the book.

I'm in … and in this work; I can choose to be in. You can't choose to be in. You are in it all the time. Doesn't this create a power dynamic? Why would POC trust white people in this antiracist movement? We can move in and out … as in "I'm tired. I'll take a break." My cells are always on (microaggression) break. My biochemistry is on racial break. My life is easier for nothing I have done to achieve ease. I don't want to fall into the crevasse of white guilt. It is just resistance to getting to this. But what if our cells could talk to each other?

The children of my "world" are afraid of the male children of your world, whose lives are more daily endangered than the children of my "world."

Love,

Roberta

October 24, 2015

Roberta,

I am afraid of reading the book because I don't need any (more) reminders of how powerless we are and how bad things are looking. I don't want to feel the rage and the defeat and the hopelessness followed by the guilt for not being more active, more of an activist. I just want to stay in my sphere of influence doing the most I can do, and some days that's just going to work, staying committed to my 12-step programs, caring for my child, and getting us both into bed.

As for opting in and out of conversations, I realized that the essence of privilege is just that—being about to forget, opt out, ignore any issue. It's hard to start a conversation from such dissonant positions on the game board.

It is a myth, though, for white folk to think they are absenting themselves. Whiteness is happening to white people all the time and the benefits come at a cost—feeling that if you don't measure up it is a personal failing, since the system is set up just for you, isolation, a lack of sense of community (that is centered around race identification.), the guilt you mentioned, which cripples so many, and the murdering of Black and Brown people.

You've seen the Charlie Rose interview with Toni Morrison where she talks about racism. She says, among other nuggets, "There is something distorted about the white psyche … it's like it's a profound neurosis that nobody

examines for what it is and it has as much a deleterious effect on white people as it does Black people."
Talk about turning things on their head!
Love you,
Imani

November 2, 2015

Imani,
I read this on Oct. 25th and am only responding now. It stopped me. I did not want to read this. I did not want to know about your feelings of powerlessness, rage, defeat, hopelessness, and guilt. Not really. I do not want to know because you are my friend and I love you and it hurts to know that you live with all that, just waking up each morning. So I opted out for a week. I carried on with Work Group organizing, upcoming whiteness training, race conversations, but I avoided responding. Here we are, in the thick of it. If white folks knew in their hearts the price to POC, of this racial arrangement, there would be a revolution based on horror. We would wake up, as from a nightmare and shake the sleep off and be compelled to revolt.

Over and over again I learn, on yet a deeper level, what the Peoples' Institute for Survival and Beyond talks about, that the only way to do this work is to build it upon relationship. This conversation is how my white humanity returns. But does this conversation add to your life in any way? I miss you on the Work Group my friend, my partner. And I applaud you stepping out of the work to step more deeply into prayer without the work.
Love,
Roberta

November 5, 2015

Roberta,
Within our relationship, in this conversation, and at the Undoing Racism Workshops are the places where I feel hopeful and safe. I don't mean there won't be friction, disagreement, or hurt feelings, but there won't be suffering. My experiences are valid and valued. I, too, can move from the 3/5th human to wholly human. I don't have to do all the work of patiently educating white people about race and coddle and stroke white fragility. I so appreciate that

the thread began with you catching yourself. I'd simply received your "come, come, come" as enthusiasm. I am used to my feelings around racialized issues being ignored. And I knew you had heard me, so I took your remark on the level of encouragement and an opportunity to work together, then *you* caught yourself. That's powerful.

And your honesty around not wanting to reply to the last email acknowledged my feelings as powerful. Look, I'm not stroking your ego; it's what is expected from a friend who is is empathic and is toe to toe with my pain—to be honest about how it makes her feel—but when race is involved it twists white people and most just never respond, ever, or more often, they defend, say it doesn't exist, criticize our interpretation of the situation (you must have misunderstood), talk about the goodness of the speaker (she's really great ... she has a Black son, you know"). The fact that you said you did not want to read or know what was in the email. In THAT conversation you stood beside me holding my hand. We were in it together. I was no longer holding my pain alone. As Hedy Schleifer says, "You cross the bridge holding nothing but your passport in a transparent bag and you join me in my truth."

It's interesting that you say if white folks knew, there would be a revolution. Even with the death toll rising and with videos of "police" in schools abusing ... not a lot of commentary from my white friends on social media. My sense is only that white folks will revolt when they know the price to themselves. What do you think is the price to white folk?
Imani

November 6, 2015

Sitting at Starbucks, at this ungodly hour, rereading all these words and still stumped by the question "what is the cost to white people." I hear in my head, the stock answer, "our humanity." But what is that composed of? Why do white folk gravitate to expat communities in Panama, Costa Rica, and Mexico? It's partly the economics ... partly the climate ... but so interesting to me that it duplicates the arrangement of race. Poor, mostly Black or Latino people, serving white people.

We are comfortable there. But on a daily basis, what is the cost. The cost is that it does not come naturally, as in emotionally naturally, to be bereft of the awareness that 49% of New Yorkers live below the poverty line. We don't feel it. We believe it is wrong, or we ascribe blame, but we don't feel it. We bemoan how isolated we are. We look for community, a place to walk into where we belong. We raise our children alone. But essentially, our congenital empathy gene has been muted.

L,

Roberta

November 6, 2015

Roberta,

I don't have a lot of experience with that level of self-consciousness in other relationships. It's also what I strive for in myself—walking the thin line that lies between blame and over responsibility. Part of my "it must be me" voice is certainly a product of my interactions with adults as a child, but I suppose another part is my racial inheritance—inferiority, though it's certainly not limited to race-related situations.

(I am challenging myself not to refute/justify/couch/contextualize the superiority comment. Here goes.)

Just this morning I was doing some writing and wrote, "I wish I were more like X who always thinks the other person is wrong and she is right, then I continued by reflecting on how X's self righteousness doesn't bring her any more joy or a deeper sense of connectedness with her spouse (who always does it wrong.)"

I've been thinking about the passage from the Talmud that reads, "Don't be daunted by the enormity of the world's grief. Do justly, now. Love mercy, now. Walk humbly, now. You are not obligated to complete the work, but neither are you free to abandon it" (Talmud 303 Pirkei avot).

Each year during the High Holy Days, we receive a letter about contributing to Kolot Chayeinu, our synagogue, financially and in service. The latter sentence is always somewhere in the letter and each year it strikes me, but recently I came across the quote with even more context. "Don't be daunted by the enormity of the world's grief." Over the last two years, I have been increasingly balancing the two poles of my responses to the televised murders of my people ... paralysis and rage. Many people will say there is nothing new; it's just that now more people know about it.

But if this is true, if what has changed is the dissemination of information then why is change taking so long ... where is the call to "do justly, now?"

"Don't be daunted by the enormity of the world's grief. ..." or my own. I am so grateful that I have you and our friendship and our common understanding

of humility in learning, so that we do not abandon the work and so that I do not feel the burden of completing it alone.
With love,
Imani

References

Moore, M. (2003). *Dude, where's my country?* New York, NY: Warner Books.

Moore, M., Glynn, K. R., Czarnecki, J., Bishop, C., Donovan, M., Heston, C., Danitz, B., McDonough, M., Engfeher, K., & Gibbs, J. (2003). *Bowling for Columbine.* United States: MGM Home Entertainment.

Morrison, T. (1998, January 19). An hour with Nobel Prize-winner Toni Morrison. Interview by Charlie Rose. https://charlierose.com/videos/17664

· 1 7 ·

"THE LADIES SALON"

Building Intellectual and Personal Collective(s)

Rani Varghese, Allia Abdullah-Matta, and Hye-Kyung Kang

Introduction

Cherrie Moraga (2015), in the preface to the fourth edition of *This Bridge Called My Back*, discusses the importance of voice as expressed by women of color writing about their intersecting identities and struggles. She says,

> Still, here in the underbelly of the "first" world, women of color writing is one liberation tool at our disposal. … The very *act* of writing then, conjuring/coming to "see," what has yet to be recorded in history is to bring into our consciousness what only the body knows to be true. The body—that site which houses the intuitive, the unspoken the viscera of our being—this is the revolutionary promise of "theory in flesh"; for its both *expression* of evolving political consciousness and the *creator* of consciousness, itself. Seldom recorded and hardly honored, our theory *incarnate* provides the most reliable roadmap to liberation. (p. xxiv, emphasis in original)

In this chapter, we employ "the very act of writing" as a tool of liberation; our collective bodies express a specific consciousness that signifies and politicizes the experiences of women of color in the academy. Moreover, we use our voices to highlight our distinct and unique journeys to higher education and to co-construct a collaborative narrative that pushes beyond a monolithic or hegemonic construction of interracial friendships that center whiteness.

Much of the writing on interracial relationships has focused on romantic or intimate relationships among whites and other racial groups; the literature that focuses on friendships among adult women of color is limited. In fact, the word "interracial" or "intergroup" is commonly used to signify relationships between whites and Blacks or whites and Latinos, while the term "intraracial" or "intragroup" describes relationships among very diverse groups of people of color. These definitions result in the minimization of specific group differences among people of color and center whiteness. We write this chapter to illuminate and to complicate the narratives of women of color relationships that are left out of the larger conversations about interracial relationships.

This chapter begins with the authors. We situate our socioeconomic, transnational, racial, regional, and ethnic locations. We then chronicle our individual journeys to graduate school, our navigation of higher education, and finally, we discuss the significance of our participation in a group called the Ladies' Salon. In this chapter, we use a common voice in which "we" refers to the authors of this chapter. Other times, we each write from a single voice, identified as Rani, Hye-Kyung, or Allia.

Individual Journeys

Rani: I immigrated to the United States at the age of four from India and grew up in a racially segregated, largely Black (African American) and white Midwestern city. Growing up, I saw myself as a shade of "Gray" and took up liminal space within this dichotomous narrative. In college, my relationships with African American women did not happen organically in the residence halls or in the lunchrooms; they occurred within the context of student dialogue groups that intentionally brought together people of diverse racial/ethnic backgrounds to converse (i.e., Racial Awareness Program at the University of Cincinnati). The idea that simply gathering together diverse groups to live or coexist within the same college and university spaces would result in authentic friendships where people engage in an open and honest dialogue is a myth. On college campuses, intergroup contact can be minimal and does not translate to equitable, positive, or meaningful interactions among groups or individuals (Gurin, Dey, Hurtado, & Gurin, 2002; Hurtado, 2005).

Cross-racial relationships such as the ones I have built with women of color across the African diaspora have occurred based on critical knowledge and awareness. I recognize that my relationships with these women are situated within a sociopolitical and historical context where our relationships were politically and socially discouraged. My relationships with Black women, which are based on shared interests and a deep sense of love and camaraderie, also reflect the relational nature of Black and South Asian women's lives. "We need to recognize not only differences but also the relational nature of those differences" (Brown, 1992, p. 298). While I have different experiences as a South Asian woman compared to the Black women in my life, our histories exist simultaneously and are in dialogue with one another (Brown, 1992).

Lavina Shankar and Rajini Srikanth (1998) offer insight into the ways South Asians have a complex and nuanced relationship to the construction of the Asian American. "South Asians may be 'a part' of the new Asian American banner, but too many differences and divergences keep them 'apart' from the established Asian American identity" (Shankar, 1998, pp. xii–xiii). I have found that in my relationships with *other* Asian women, our bond is not based on our manufactured cultural similarities or constructed solidarity as "Asians." Rather, this bond is constructed by our recognition and engagement with a "brown" consciousness and an empowering identification with the term "women of color." We understand that our *supposed* relationships are dictated by a larger white, patriarchal, and capitalist meta-narrative; however, we decline to ascribe to this mode of thinking.

Hye-Kyung: I am a first-generation immigrant Korean American woman. I identify strongly as a woman of color (among other social locations that include cisgender, straight, bilingual, with a complex class background, etc.), but this was not always the case. In fact, I never really thought about race until I immigrated to the U.S. Having been born and raised in South Korea, where most of the national population identify as Korean, my race and ethnicity were never signifying markers as opposed to my gender and class. My prominent identity was as a twenty-sixth-generation daughter of the Kang family, whose origins traced back to General Kang Min Chum: a 10th-century war hero of the Koryo Dynasty. This changed when I immigrated to the U.S.; from the first day of my arrival, I was identified by my newly assigned marker, *Asian*. As a 17-year-old immigrant, being assigned a racial identity was disorienting. I eventually learned that Asian was the primary classification of people who looked like me in the U.S., regardless of my own conceptualization.

It was not until I took Asian American Studies courses in college that I learned about the complicated history of race in the U.S. I learned that the term "Asian American" was created by Yuji Ichioka as a self-defining political label within the context of the Asian American Movement (Dirlik, 2010).

This was my first introduction to how my racial identity was inexorably polit-ical. After college, I had the good fortune to be a part of community organ-izing and human service agencies in the International District community of Seattle. Known as the only pan-ethnic Asian Pacific American community in the continental U.S., this community has a long history of political and social activism (Chin, 2001).

The historical residential segregation, which kept people of color out of white neighborhoods, is not unique to Seattle. However, the result of the seg-regation was unique in that Asian Pacific Americans and African Americans settled next to each other as neighbors and went to school with each other as classmates (Chin, 2001). In addition, laws preventing the criminalization of miscegenation led to many mixed marriages between Asian and Native American people in Washington State (Santos, 2002). These personal rela-tionships allowed Seattle communities of color to coalesce and support one another during the community activism and mobilization efforts in the 1960s and 1970s (Chin, 2001; Santos, 2002). Since then, communities of color in Seattle have been able to maintain strong and collaborative relationships.

The International District was the center of Asian American community activism in the Pacific Northwest since the early 1970s, and I, like many young Asian American people who were entering community work in the 1980s and 1990s, were greatly influenced by this history and by our activist elders. Thus, my involvement in this community taught me that to embrace my identity as an Asian American meant to take an explicit political position as a person of color *and* to actively stand in solidarity with other people of color.

My personal and social relationships mirrored this political stance; even though the city had only 30% non-white populations (City of Seattle, 2010), most of my friends were people of color. Working and living in mixed-race neighborhoods of color in the 1980s and 1990s, I was as often part of a sister-circle with mostly African American women as I was with "jade sisters" who were Asian Americans of various ethnicities. Most of these women were involved in human services, community organizing, and/or activism, and our shared commitment to racial and gender equity bonded us as women of color. In retrospect, I feel fortunate and blessed to be from a place and time where all of this was possible. It certainly primed me to seek out other women of color and their friendships when I left Seattle and landed on the East Coast.

Allia: *Why is it important for women to define themselves. There is an urgency for women. When you have inherited a construct that names, describes, and practices out an ideology that women are somehow less important, less necessary, then the work of defining yourself carries with it a kind of fury—or Fury* (Christina, 2015, p. 1).

My definition of selfhood begins with my line. I come from a line of African formerly enslaved women, turned African American southern-women workers to northern New York City domestic workers. My mother and aunts were the first *professional* technicians of sorts. They became civil service workers, nurses, and respiratory therapists after their mothers worked in home and school kitchens, as office cleaners, and in other domestic laborer capacities. Their mothers understood the ramifications of their cultural, economic, racial, and social exclusion; they strived to disrupt the ideological construct and practice that names, describes, and positions Black women and women of color as unimportant, less necessary, and significantly invisible, unless in service to others (Christina, 2015, p. 1). They sent their children to public and Catholic schools, purchased homes, and cautioned their grandchildren to go to college.

I went to a small liberal-arts private college (upstate New York), studied abroad in Europe, and graduated in four years. As one of the grandchildren who was encouraged to go to college, my family supported me to the best of their emotional and financial abilities. From their New York City eyes, I was the success story, and I was then tasked to live up to the expectations of being a college graduate. I worked in Social Services, raised children, and then went to graduate school for a master's degree in English. My family was used to my employment and educational shifts because these shifts represented hierarchical movement; education meant more access, so even when I left "a good-paying job" to return to school, it sort of made sense.

My success is predicated on an understanding of my racial, class, and cultural roles. I grew up in a Black and Jewish community. My interracial orientation was constructed based on a Black and white racial dichotomy within my Queens neighborhood in the 1970s. My childhood street consisted of African American, Irish American, Italian American, and Polish American families. I lived across the street from a large cooperative apartment complex that was mostly Jewish, but also consisted of Black and Black-white biracial families. My friends were mostly African American; I knew and played with the white children until about age ten, but they did not go to the local public schools with the rest of us. My predominantly Black middle school was African American with a smatter of recently immigrant Caribbean children;

in this moment, Black folks in the community did not necessarily differenti-ate in terms of immigrant or national locations. Being Black meant you were Black based on the U.S. historical construction of Blackness. It was not up for debate in our neighborhood in the 1970s, nor was there any reason to be concerned about those specific nuances. There were a few Latinos, who lived in the neighborhood because they were a part of the Black foster-care households, and the even fewer white children were from the families that did not participate in white flight and had not chosen to move their children to nondistrict public schools or parochial/private schools.

During high school was the first time I could say that I actually had Latino, Jewish, and Caribbean friends, which I can actually count. My connections to folks in college played out in the same way. The majority of my close friends were Black and Latino—the white folks may have been a bit more diverse in terms of culture and nation, but white meant white, and no South Asians or Koreans were really present to befriend. In addition, had there been a diverse Asian presence, our circles would probably not have entwined.

Navigating Higher Education

Turner (2002), in *Women of Color in Academe: Living with Multiple Marginal-ity*, describes the ways her own social identities, particularly her gender, race, and socioeconomic class impacted her access to and subsequent experiences within institutions of higher education. Drawing on the concept of *lived con-tradiction*, she quotes Padilla and Chavez's (1995) work on the experiences of Latina professors, which exemplifies the experiences of many women of color who are negotiating the higher education landscape in their multiple roles, as students, as faculty, and administrators or staff.

> I am struck by my lived contradiction: To be a professor is to be an Anglo; to be a Latina is not to be an anglo. So how can I be both a Latina and a professor? To be a Latina professor, I conclude, means to be unlike and like me. Que locura! What mad-ness! ... As Latina professors, we are newcomers to a world defined and controlled by discourses that do not address our realities, that do not affirm our intellectual contri-butions, that do not seriously examine our worlds. Can I be both Latina and professor without compromise? (Turner, 2002, p. 75)

Furthermore, she presents the concept of belonging and considers which folks are welcomed and nurtured in academic spaces and which are not. Drawing on this framework, our narratives explore our individual journeys to doctoral programs and the importance of having a community of women, particularly other women of color, who serve as mentors and cheerleaders, who reinforce that your voice, your knowledge, and your particular research are critical and needed within higher education.

Rani: My arrival back in Western Massachusetts to obtain a doctorate in Social Justice Education at University of Massachusetts Amherst happened in the midst of tears and trepidation. I had completed my Master's in Social Work (MSW) in Northampton but had only lived there during the summers. The idea of spending the year and longer in such a homogeneous (i.e., white) environment was both unsettling and overwhelming.

I am the second person in my immediate family to obtain a Bachelor's degree and the first (and only) to obtain Master's and Doctoral degrees. I felt insecure about my abilities as a thinker and a writer. While my Master's degree did, in part, prepare me for graduate-level work, I still did not feel competent and confident. I knew I had the skills to "read" and "engage" people in real life as a clinician, but I felt that it did not translate into reading and analyzing complex theoretical and methodological texts. Furthermore, I did not have the cultural and social capital to understand that I should pretend "to know."

As a first-generation doctoral student who identified as both a woman of color and an immigrant, I did not have the road map (that many of my white peers did) of how to succeed in the academy. While there are many resources and services for students who self-identify as first-generation undergraduate students, such resources are limited for first-generation graduate students and faculty. While first-generation graduate students "possess unique motivations and possibilities for behavior, they are constrained by social context including norms, networks and organizations" and not equipped with the "social capital" needed to maneuver systems of higher education (Holley & Gardner, 2012). I had to work hard to find mentors, to develop a scholarly agenda, and to deepen my skills as a writer, teacher, and researcher.

Feeling untethered and ungrounded, I searched for a community that could meet both my social and academic needs. Through my graduate homes, Social Justice Education and Women, Gender & Sexuality Studies and larger academic and social circles, I made connections with a handful of women who were recent transplants and/or more established in the "Valley." Seeing myself as a social conduit, I brought these friends together, and that particular combination resulted in a combustive reaction, ultimately leading to calling ourselves *The Ladies' Salon*. These women of color and "off-white" woman (i.e., historically marginalized white ethnics) came together to support one another as we negotiated predominantly white institutions. As a doctoral student, my understanding of myself and the landscape of identity was deepened by my friendships with a group of women who represented multiple racial/ethnic identities. I teach my students that learning about issues of social identity and oppression is a lifelong process, and my participation in this group resulted in new lessons about myself and the lived experience of women of color in the academy.

Hye-Kyung: Although I do not remember the specific moment that I decided to pursue a Master's degree in Social Work (MSW) and a Ph.D. in Social Welfare, I know it was an idea that percolated in my mind for a long time. I had always loved learning, and both of my parents had graduate degrees (JD; Doctor of Missiology) from Korea. However, once I started my schooling at an under-resourced urban high school in the U.S., I was discouraged by my high school guidance counselor from pursuing a college education in psychology, which "would be too difficult for [me] as an English-as-a-Second Language student to learn." She told me to pursue something more practical such as cosmetology. If I *really* wanted to go to college, she advised me to study engineering or accounting because "Asians are good at math."

Being a recent immigrant teenager, I did not realize that my counselor's advice was based on gendered and racialized constructions of Asian women. Discouraged, I initially followed her advice and enrolled in pre-engineering courses until I met my first psychology professor, Dr. Les Wong. Dr. Wong was my first Asian American professor, and as a first-generation academic himself, he understood the bewilderment I felt as an immigrant student. He advised me to follow my passion rather than ill-informed advice based on racial stereotypes. He also encouraged me to pursue a Ph.D. in the future even though I was only a freshman in a community college at that time. Years later, after having earned a master's degree and worked in social service and community organizing for more than a decade, I realized Dr. Wong was right; I needed to take a risk and to pursue my educational goal. Although the landscape of academia was unfamiliar and intimidating, I was fortunate enough to find faculty mentors of color in my Ph.D. program at the University of Washington School of Social Work. They taught me to question master narratives and especially those in academia. I was encouraged to build my scholarship on a strong foundation of social justice, anticolonialism, and critical pedagogy. I also learned the importance of alliance-building, mutual support, and mentorship for academics of color. My mentors formed a group for students, faculty, and staff of color within the School called *Bridges of*

Color. Bridges of Color served as a "home base" to build and share power among people of color and created a space for belonging, especially for those of us who were first-generation students and academics. Bridges of Color taught me that it was possible to build solidarity and strategic interracial and intergenerational alliances while recognizing multiple narratives and even competing perspectives.

When I first arrived in Western Massachusetts to teach at Smith College as a tenure-track assistant professor, I wasn't sure if I could thrive—I knew I had survival skills, but to thrive in such a predominantly white environment was another matter. The contrast between the highly diverse and polyglot neighborhoods of New York City where I had lived and taught for the previous 3–4 years and Northampton, a quintessential (read: white) Northeast college town, was stark. I knew that I needed to build my network of support to thrive. I was soon introduced to my sister-friend and colleague, Rani Varghese, who in turn introduced me to an extraordinarily diverse, strong, and supportive multiracial community of color in Massachusetts. All of us were from other regions of the U.S. and away from our families and friendship networks, and this community of color became our family. In this family, I found my sisters of the soul: Allia, Cruz, Diana, Rani, Shelly, Zahra, and Anna Rita. Though we were not related by blood, we recognized what we shared in our cultural DNA: our talents, struggles, brilliance, vulnerability, commitment to social justice, resistance, and grace.

Allia: The ultimate shift of my personal and professional life trajectory was when I decided to relocate and to move toward the doctorate degree, so many years after the first degree. I had surpassed their collective expectations. I risked leaving my family, my community, and a good paying job with a tad bit of status, to earn a doctorate. I was already working in higher education administration and teaching at the college level, so my decision to return to school to get another degree to continue to teach at the college level seemed nonsensical. My family understood cultural and social capital in a very specific way. They could see the merits of my degrees, but could not fully grasp the next move. They were proud, but also wondered if I was in fact a bit out of my mind?

Actually, I was not the first in my family to go to graduate school or to be called Doctor. Three of my paternal great uncles were doctors—one was an MD who died when I was thirteen, one was a doctor of theology and a preacher, and one was a Ph.D. though I am not quite sure what he studied. I just remember that he had retired and lived with my grandparents when

I was an adolescent. I was, however, the first woman in my family to attempt this level of graduate study. I was not out of my mind, and eventually received much familial respect for my choice as a mature African American woman to pursue and to complete a doctoral degree. It had not been nonsensical to redefine and to author myself.

Retrospectively, I realized that I was moving from a place of "Fury" as defined by Christina (2015) in her discussion of the role of the canonical Furies in mythology. The Furies were/are strong women who insisted on justice, operated within the full utility of their magic, were unapologetic in their choices to remedy injustice, and represent the goddess/woman who must author herself (Christina, 2015, p. 2). Christina points to the significance of women authoring as the means "to own the expanse of our voices and our stories, [which] is critical for us as women" (p. 2). The women in my family are representative of Christina's point about the power of the Furies and the work that they do; these women inspired authorship by intentionally constructing their work and familial identities. They exhibited voice and action as the "utterance[s] of unclaimed hallelujahs" (Christina, 2015, p. 3).

Christina's notion of the utterance of the unclaimed hallelujahs connects to Moraga's assertion about the consciousness of what only the body knows to be true. My body and my choice to attend graduate school changed the course of my familial trajectory in terms of access; further, this choice serves as a symbolic utterance of an unclaimed hallelujah. Access somewhat remedies a societal past that had yoked African American women and their families to physical labor; this became more apparent when I moved away from my immediate family and community to Western Massachusetts.

I liked the challenge of graduate study. The coursework was something I could manage. I felt supported by key Africana and Women & Gender Studies faculty members, and I was confident that I could get through the courses and the preliminary exams. My obstacles appeared when it was time to write the dissertation. It felt like I was screening my life through the template of a working-class horror showcase. The shock of this reality stifled my productivity.

Institutionally, the aspects of getting a doctorate as a first-generation Black woman did not compute in terms of fiscal responsibility and familial accountability, which meant that I worked and slept when I needed to write. The pressure to move through a doctorate program in terms of confidence, patience, and respectability, was/is also horrifically challenging to Black/Women of Color. The choice to earn a doctorate in African American Studies led to the ultimate self-definition, [re]expression, and self-authoring. I would earn a doctor of philosophy, study the culture, history, and literature of my people, and focus on the artistic, creative, and literary expression of Black/Women of Color (WOC).

In Western Massachusetts, I connected with a WOC collective that exhibited the power of the Furies, the Ladies' Salon. The Ladies' Salon became my immediate family and community; our bodies created a solid and supportive unit and our collective community served to record and honor our multiracial friendships and our WOC experiences in the academy and the larger society. My accomplishments strategically center my body as an instrument of political and social transformation and form an example of the revolutionary promise of the theory in the flesh (Moraga, 2015); thus, I define, re(create), and author myself, and the support of the Ladies' Salon continues to make this possible; it functions as a roadmap to liberation.

The Ladies' Salon: A Revolutionary Solidarity

The Ladies' Salon ("the Salon"), a supportive creative, emotional, and critically intellectual network and a mutual support and peer mentorship group for first-generation academic women in the Pioneer Valley, MA, started in 2010. This multiracial group consisted of six women of color (African American, Dominican American, Korean American, and South Asian/Indian American) and a first-generation immigrant Italian woman. Our paths crisscrossed and were cemented by our connection to the university and the five-college area; we were graduate students and pre-tenure faculty, and we shared resident women of color status in the valley. The valley offered the potential to connect with women of color across the five college campuses; what was not exactly available was a viable support network for women of color graduate students, and tenure-track junior faculty. Although an interdisciplinary group—representing social work, legal studies, African American studies, economics, English, higher education administration, and social justice education—our mutual interest in social justice and critical pedagogy connected us.

Our aim in creating the Salon was to help us navigate the institutional culture of academia, which was unfamiliar to all of us who lacked cultural and social capital in this arena, and to repudiate the isolation of academic work. We met monthly to share our progress and challenges, to present our current work, and to receive and offer critical feedback and creative solutions. We supported one another toward the achievement of our educational goals;

however, the Salon was much more than an academic support group or a peer mentorship group.

By creating the Salon, we created the space for ourselves outside of academy. Placed on the margins of the academia, we found and nurtured what hooks (1990) called "marginality as the site of resistance." The Salon was that space of resistance that allowed us to support each other, emotionally and intellectually; we held each other accountable to make and meet the goals for our respective successes, and we also created a significant alliance-space that supported the completion of our respective doctoral programs, job search activities, and the journey to tenure. Our Salon ensured that we as women of color could collaboratively produce creative and critical scholarship, and also support our professional endeavors. We did not fall prey to the "divide and conquer" attitude and behavioral patterns that exist and occur in the academy when women of color do not move from the Fury.

Rani describes the experience of being in the Salon this way:

> In the game of Twister, the idea is that you must twist your body, arms, and legs to come in contact with the color you've been assigned. In thinking of my own experiences with relationships, where I had to manipulate my body, detaching or disassembling different parts of myself and my identities in order to be seen, this group has provided me the opportunity to stand in one spot and location and have all parts of myself reflected back through deep connections with women of color of diverse ethnicities and experiences.

Since the inception of the Salon, we have been tremendously productive: six doctoral degree completions, one successful tenure, one career change, and five babies! We are now in various academic positions (one tenured associate professor; one tenure-track associate professor; three tenure-track assistant professors; one high-level academic administrator; and one former professor now pursuing another professional passion.). We are in New York, Western Massachusetts, and Seattle. Throughout these intellectual and professional transitions, our friendships remain strong and continue to grow. As we are spread in many directions, our appreciation for one another and our friendships are paramount. Wherever we are, we've "got all our sisters with us" (Edwards & Rodgers, 1979), and we have each others' backs.

We realize that the Ladies' Salon does not exist in a historical vacuum. We have been inspired by and are continuing the tradition of women of color/ third world feminist collectives such as the Third World Women's Alliance. Similarly, the impact of the Salon extends far beyond its members as we share our lessons with other first-generation college or graduate students of color; we serve as formal or informal mentors, provide resources and support, and function as role models.

References

Brown, E. B. (1992). What has happened here: The politics of difference in women's history and feminist politics. *Feminist Studies, 18*(2), 295–312.

Chin, D. (2001). *Seattle's International District: The making of a Pan-Asian American community.* Seattle, WA: International Examiner Press.

Christina, D. (2015). Our unclaimed hallelujahs. In *This is woman's work: Calling forth your inner council of wise, brave, crazy, rebellious, loving, luminous selves.* Louisville, CO: Sounds True.

City of Seattle. (2010). *Decential census.* Retrieved from http://www.seattle.gov/dpd/cityplanning/populationdemographics/decennialcensus/2010/default.htm

Dirlik, A. (2010). Asians on the rim: Transnational capital and local community in the making of contemporary Asian America. In J. Yu-Wen, Shen Wu, & T. C. Chen (Eds.), *Asian American studies now* (pp. 515–539). New Brunswick, NJ: Rutgers University Press.

Edwards, B., & Rodgers, N. (1979). We are family [recorded by Sister Sledge]. On *We Are Family.* New York, NY: Cotillion Records.

Gurin, P. A., Dey, E. L., Hurtado, S., & Gurin, G. (2002). Diversity and higher education: Theory and impact on educational outcomes. *Harvard Educational Review, 72*(3), 330–366.

Holley, K. A., & Gardner, S. (2012). Navigating the pipeline: How socio-cultural influences impact first-generational doctoral students. *Journal of Diversity in Higher Education, 5*(2), 112–121.

hooks, b. (1990). *Yearning: Race, gender, and cultural politics.* Boston, MA: South End Press.

Hurtado, S. (2005). The next generation of diversity and intergroup relations research. *Journal of Social Issues, 61*(3), 595–610.

Moraga, C. (2015). Catching fire: Preface to the fourth edition. In C. Moraga & G. Anzaldua (Eds.), *This bridge called my back* (4th ed., pp. xv–xxvi). Albany, NY: SUNY Press.

Padilla, R. V., & Chavez, R. C. (1995). *The leaning ivory tower: Latino professors in American universities.* Albany, NY: State University of New York Press.

Santos, B. (2002). *Hum bows, not hot dogs! Memories of a savvy Asian American activist.* Seattle, WA: International Examiner Press.

Shankar, L. D., & Srikanth, R. (1998). *A part, yet apart: South Asians in Asian America.* Philadelphia, PA: Temple University Press.

Shankar, R. (1998). Foreword: South Asian identity in Asian America. In L. D. Shankar & R. Srikanth (Eds.), *A part, yet apart: South Asians in Asian America* (pp. ix–xv). Philadelphia, PA: Temple University Press.

Turner, C. S. V. (2002). Women of color in academe: Living in multiple marginality. *Journal of Education, 73*(1), 74–93.

· 1 8 ·

THE "CRAZY WHITE LADY" AND OTHER ARCHETYPES IN WORKPLACE FRIENDSHIPS, BOUNDARIES, AND POWER

Deinya Phenix

Introduction

While it is my hope that most of the chapters in this book will contain positive examples reflecting women's unique capacity to bridge society's major divides, I share some rather cynical thoughts on a particularly stubborn barrier to such relationships. This barrier is power, and it is especially resonant when we think about authority and control in the workplace. Because many of our relationships are developed at work, collaboration on projects can be a productive way to get to know and bond with colleagues and superiors. But this context can also reproduce and intensify social inequality. The social divisions and hierarchies that exist in our society, particularly gender and race, match up with workplace hierarchies. Positions of high rank, seniority, or supervision within an organization tend to be held by white and/or male individuals.

But the gendered and racial dimensions of these divisions go much deeper than people's official status at work. I argue that there is, embedded in our interactions, a troubling set of processes that muddies the possibility of true reflection, critique, and commitment to social change. Here I can offer a small glimmer of hope for women who want to get past this set of processes and cultivate deep, meaningful friendships.

What Led Me to This Issue and How I Set Out to Find More About It

I must confess to knowing a lot about race as a concept, race as a statistical factor, and race as a lived reality because I am a sociologist. Sociologists scientifically study society. For those sociologists who study American society, race is a major variable. Even as individuals love to say they "don't see color," I have it on good authority that American society is all about race.

But this chapter is not meant to be a paper on social policy or a report on survey results or a controlled experiment with careful statistical models sorting out causation and generalizability. Here, I am writing based on my own experience, based on passively observing interactions, including secondhand musings and stories from my friends. As social science is kind of a reflex for me, I did take the time to interview a small "snowball" sample of individuals willing to talk openly about the subject.

Friendships at Work?

Before I get into the discussion about the main subject at hand, I will make a few general statements about friendships and work in general: There is some pretty solid research showing two seemingly contradictory things about friendships at work:

1. Our relationships at work are mostly arms-length professional. At most, the people we chat with and lunch with at work are acquaintances. Partly because people don't stick around with companies for 40 years anymore, the company is no longer modeled after a big ol' family. Fewer and fewer of us have close friends at work; nor do we aim to make friends at work. The dominant expectation is that interactions at work will be transactional and impersonal.
2. Most American adults make their friends at work because recently we have been spending less of our time in other bonding group situations such as church or civic organizations. After college or high school, there is no other institution in which we have frequent interactions and goal-based group activities. So if you were to acquire a BFF after

the age of, say, 25, you are most likely to meet that person at work. That's where the people are.

So how do we go about making friends in an environment where we are required to spend so much of our waking hours with coworkers while at the same time have an *ick* response when it's time to invite these people into our lives and our hearts? It can be difficult in these situations to foster the trust required to develop friendships. However, despite the rise of telecommuting, modern workplaces still have what sociologists call a *compulsion of proximity*, leading to frequent meetings, even if by video or phone. Work needs to be done in mostly group structures, and people will get to know each other naturally when part of a group with shared tasks. For one thing, the way careers work now, with people bouncing every couple of years, it's important to get to know colleagues' strengths and potential contributions down the road. Every relationship can be considered an investment in an ongoing *alliance*, as the title of a recent book calls it.

One plus side to having to work on teams and get to know at least the basic competencies and personalities of our colleagues is that we tend to drop the cliquish, snobby guards we may have had up in high school or college. At work, we are likely to have frequent interactions and perhaps form deeper relationships with people who we would have had nothing to do with in school. One is likely to be friendly, but not necessarily to the next level. Now, when those relationships do turn deeper, and that person with whom you've worked closely for X months turns out to be a valuable personal asset, you hang on to them.

It can be the most amazing thing to find yourself in a mutually beneficial personal bond in an atmosphere that is by nature increasingly impersonal.

Race Relations at Work

The age of segregation is largely over, right? In fact, as repeated social science observations have shown, people tend to live with and near people who are similar. Popular political humor gets us to laugh about the rarity of interracial friendships, e.g., how unlikely it is that a white person will have more than one or a few Black friends. Social distance is such a real thing that sociologists have a scientific scale for measuring it. Of course, how race and ethnicity play out at a mass scale is different than how these factors play out one on one ... right? Even so, I propose the *One Black/LatinX/Asian Friend* as the first archetype to consider in thinking about how race and ethnicity play out in the social life of the workplace.

American workplaces are increasingly diverse, as our racial caste system is making its slow decline and occupations are no longer legally or formally reserved for one particular race or ethnicity. However, cliques are a reality. Not surprisingly, cliques are influenced by social distance. Some people have been careful about visibly gathering for lunch or leaving at the end of the day with colleagues of the same race or ethnicity for fear of appearing to be too involved in a clique and possibly disqualified for certain informal benefits or opportunities.

Another reality is the demographic patterns in certain positions due to generations of racial domination and due to self-selection. Combined with generations of educational opportunity or lack of opportunity, these social forces have resulted in occupational zones. One of my interviewees observed that there is an entire floor in her mostly white corporation occupied almost entirely by Black people. This was not the executive floor.

So as race and racial domination are realities, let's take deeper a look at how it interacts with gender in hierarchical (boss–subordinate) and other formal work relationships. Rather than make these observations in terms of statistical realities and policy, I find it more useful here to reflect on lived experiences to discuss some of the nuances of how women work together.

Some Observations

I have observed a pattern of interactions that is deeply personal and racialized as it plays out between colleagues. This pattern exists across different types of formal relationships—whether between peers, between a supervisor and subordinate, or between senior and junior colleagues of the same title. The common denominator in this pattern is the informal assertion of power.

Between peers this power dynamic is far more soluble. Ultimately the balance of power is a matter of competition. There is an undercurrent of internalized sexism and gender-based selection of who people are able to work with. A lot of my friends (mostly females of color) have found it easier to work with men, whose competitive strikes are expected and rationalized. Working with other women may be more difficult because women, especially those high up in an organization, can see each other as a personal threat. There may be assumptions about scarcity, as in not enough space for more than one or a few women. There may also be a need to test each other and prove more about their competence on the job, especially in technical fields.

The archetypes *Other Woman* and *Ally Woman* should also be added to our resources for understanding workplace relationships among peers. A common story I've heard is how one can turn into the other. For example, when two of my friends, one white and one Black, started working together in the same position, there was an initial conflict in how they approached the work and how they communicated about it. A huge part of the conflict was cultural and class differences and the cluelessness of one of the women about those differences. These women found the easiest ways to get on each other's nerves. It was only after learning each other's habits and mutual interests that they became friends.

Once the imagined threats are sorted out, a once powerful adversary may turn out to be an ally. The key to this problem is getting to know each other and building on the strengths of each woman and mutual interest. As the experience of my friends has illustrated, Ally Women have assessed each other and found that collaboration—shared power—is more advantageous than competition.

Another pattern, and the one that interests me the most, is how power plays out between senior and junior colleagues. One would think that, as suggested by the idea of a "professional" relationship discussed above, that there would be "nothing personal" in the way people work in their job rank. In my career history and those of my interviewees, I have found neutral professionalism to be something of a myth. As one midcareer professional business consultant put it, "because you spend so much time at work, you have to invest at some personal level. It is impossible not to."

The most interesting phenomenon here is when supervisors and senior colleagues over-personalize their relationships with subordinates. Much of this personalization flows naturally out of the course of work and supervision. For example, when subordinates call in sick, they tend to share details about the illness. This can lead to conversations about the subordinate's health, and these conversations can extend well beyond the acute problem of covering time missed from work. What appears to be friendly concern about a person's health can come off as repeated interrogation.

Personal information such as details of family and children's lives are often shared naturally at a workplace. Once broached, these subjects become repeated topics of conversation. Part of this is due to the precedent and tone set by initial revelations; once those boundaries are compromised, it is nearly impossible to put them back in place and restore professional distance without appearances of being closed off. Thus, people may find themselves stuck in a pattern of personal interactions that they feel ambivalent about. There is a higher cost to the subordinate in pulling back from these interactions.

I have observed a pattern of inappropriate and excessive interest. The unwelcome interest can be personal, e.g., discussion of the subordinate's bathroom use. The excessive interest can also be professional, with numerous examples: In my experience I had a supervisor request to be copied on every email I issued. I've also once had a senior colleague who rearranged the structure of our department to make herself my supervisor rather than just the lead on one of the projects I worked on. An acquaintance of mine told me about being hunted down the hall into another office for an immediate conversation that could have actually happened at any time.

Unwelcome professional interest can focus beyond the scope of a project or shared work and can extend to a subordinate's whole career. It is always appropriate to form alliances and mentor-mentee relationships in a workplace. It is possible, though, for junior colleagues to experience forcible "mentoring" by some senior colleagues, especially those of a certain "mother hen"-type personality.

Supervisors and senior colleagues have the option of working with junior colleagues using a talent management approach, letting collaborations unfold based on each bringing their unique set of skills to a project. Alternatively, these senior colleagues can micromanage and push subordinates to work in very specific ways. I suspect that some of the reason behind overfamiliarity, over-communication, and excessive interest in one's subordinate or mentee is that the senior colleague feels the need to compensate for social distance mentioned above.

Through work, a higher-ranking individual can compel the communication and affective response of those workers with lower status. For example, I have observed mandatory weekly or daily meetings with no agenda in which workers are asked about their hair, their boyfriend, or childbearing choices. As another example, workers have been chastised for their thoughts, apparently revealed through their "face," as those in charge of their work have also taken charge of emotions. I have also seen senior colleagues demand explicit complicity in decisions that the subordinate had no part in—and may even disagree with. Often framed as mentoring or friendly interest, these behaviors often have overtones of control and even policing of the bodies and minds of colleagues.

Several conditions have triggered the behaviors above. One, for example, is the fact that the junior colleague often has a different set of skills or technical expertise required to move a project forward. This need for the work of the junior colleague can pressure the senior colleague to assert dominance and control over such work. The balance of technical versus managerial skill sets creates a pattern of communication in which the work flows in one direction: the commands for labor go to the subordinate or technical worker, and the product of this technical labor goes to the senior worker. Demands from the senior worker, multiplied over the course of a project, can be incessant. Even when these demands are made via email or text on personal phone lines, they must be answered. This is a true imbalance of power.

An illustration of this interaction is a worker who nicknamed her supervisor "Get Me," based on the tone and ceaselessness of the requests. In another example, a young worker, seeing her phone light up during the evening, reacts by saying "that crazy white lady is texting me again." The "white lady" part of this moniker represents the social distance which, as discussed above, is common even in this postracial society. It also represents the audacity of the senior worker to reach out to the worker at seemingly anytime. One would have to be crazy to continue testing routine boundaries. The latter situation also implies a tone-deafness in the senior worker, as she may have missed attempts at establishing boundaries or may have ignored the courtesy of assuming these boundaries. The *Crazy White Lady*, then, is an archetype simultaneously representing distance and violated boundaries.

Another condition is the assumption of youth and inexperience in the junior colleague. This may involve "forgetting" earlier contributions made by the junior colleague, dismissing experience acquired before the relationship or before employment, or extending the timeline by which documentation of achievement and honor are conferred. The disinclination to acknowledge and promote the junior colleague's work may be compounded by assumptions about age. The perception of the junior's age is relative to the senior's age—usually middle age or late middle age, but more importantly may be based on physical appearance and personal style. If the junior colleague appears younger than her chronological age, the price for such youthful appearance is often the assumption of inexperience. On balance, the junior colleague may always be the *New Girl*.

Another, more complex, situation that fosters over-personalization and excessive interest is when the subordinate has true personal needs. For example, some of my friends have received help with school applications, baby clothes, boyfriend stuff, and loans of cash. There have been sponsored outings to the theater and stays at the supervisor's summer home. Taken all together, these illustrate very loose boundaries where the subordinates get a lot out of friendship with someone powerful. In one case, the generosity of the boss was spurred on by the fact that both she and the subordinate were single mothers. In another case, the personal behavior of the superior was duplicitous, always part of a political game of lining up enemies and allies. In yet another case, personal information gathered about a subordinate was used against her.

Many senior colleagues may frame their relationships to subordinates as friendships, and may push for undue depth in those relationships through the behaviors described here. But of particular interest to me is the sincerity with which some of these relationships are managed, even as they are forced. An example of a case of sincerity is an extremely abrasive, overbearing, and much-feared principal investigator at a highly respected research institution. This woman was a pill, known to hound and harass her subordinates even about their sleep habits and continuing education. But the reward for tolerating her quasi-abuse was devoted and fierce protection and promotion of her subordinates' careers. This case illustrates an archetype I'll call *Tiger Mentor*, a true mixed blessing reflecting the wielding of power with a sincere interest in the careers of the subordinate.

I draw connections between the behaviors described above and race relations, both structural in society and particular to workplaces. As mentioned above, much of the privilege that exists outside of work will be reflected in the status of individuals in the workplace. Correspondingly, much of the post-racial and anti-racism rhetoric in larger society will play out in the workplace. Certain actions in the workplace may have the latent purpose of assuaging racial guilt or proof of capacity to get along well with people of color.

As one of my interviewees has noted, race, ethnicity, class, religion, gender, and sexual identity are part of the total package of who we are, and these characteristics combine with professional skills and personal history to inform one's personality. This total package can make a person "cool," i.e., very attractive as a prospect for alliance and possible friendship. Observing that white friends are usually the initiators in the relationships that she has observed, one of my friends attests that modern white people are usually attracted to (the idea of) Black friends. At minimum, it validates one's sense of themselves as liberal and/or open.

Additionally, many white women see themselves and their struggle as on a par with the struggles of Blacks of both genders. Bonding with colleagues of color, especially women, potentially validates this sense of a common ground. However, this assumption can lead to shock or disappointment when women encounter dramatic, culturally based differences in goals and manner. These differences are much more difficult to tolerate when there are (unrealistic) expectations for more common ground. Multiple times, I've fielded some dramatic disappointment when superiors realize that I am not the same as them. The shock and disappointment at the reality of differences might lead to and might even rationalize competitive behavior. There is a high price sometimes for failing to live up to the archetype of *Mini Me*, the easy mentee.

As much as personal and professional relationships are racialized, it is important to acknowledge the importance of other major social factors that can divide us or draw us together. For one thing, class position is also relevant to social interaction. There's some evidence that lower-class, less educated white women have an easier time forming relationships with women of color, especially African American women. This resonates with the peer relationships I mentioned above. Similar conditions, i.e., similar positions in society's hierarchy, can give us a real common ground to start from. The social class example implies that there is a lot of potential for finding such common ground somehow and fostering positive personal relationships at work and beyond. But as some of the examples I've given above indicate, no status—gender or other—automatically entitles us to a good relationship. Good relationships require humble, critical reflection and acknowledgment of all the other social aspects of who we are.

Concluding Remarks

As a global underclass, women share a lot of the same struggle. The solidarity and bond created between women can be an awesome resource for dealing with a difficult world. For this to be actualized, some critical reflection is in order. First, we need to acknowledge that, while meaningful work friendships are useful within and beyond the job, these relationships become further complicated when status on the job is considered. First and foremost, relationships between senior and junior colleagues are tainted by the authority the former has over the latter.

And, as discussed earlier, who ends up at which rank is not random or arbitrary in terms of race, ethnicity or gender, just like the socioeconomic status in our society is not randomly distributed. Surprisingly, race does not play as much a part in the rivalries and tensions among peers, except in the initial problem of social distance. The problem of race comes through in organizational hierarchies, bringing race into the picture of who has control over whom, and this issue of control spreads into the personal realm.

Unintentional as it may be, the reproduction of society's racial imbalance of power is a challenge to sincerity in the personal interactions between colleagues. A deep work friendship may be able to hold up to this imbalance and work to the advantage of both friends if power is acknowledged and carefully wielded. This is the responsibility of the person in power.

The temptation for many young professionals is to consider these workplace social patterns a burden which they should ignore until they are able to escape. Instead, I invite minority workers to leverage these relationships for maximum positive effect on their careers. As hard as it is to shift perspective when you're stuck in an uncomfortable or even oppressive situation, the following observations have helped me remain positive and more in control of my career.

Positive Sides of Each Archetype and Recommendations for Bringing Out the Best in Work Relationships

- One Black/LatinX/Asian Friend is a sign that there is an interest in closing social distance and fostering a real bond beyond the label. We shouldn't take this lightly.
- Other Woman can easily become Ally Woman. The presence of any woman in our workplace should be approached as an opportunity for alliances until proven otherwise.
- Crazy White Lady may actually be Tiger Mentor. Assume it's the latter, make the relationship work for you.
- Mini Me is a myth that will always disappoint. While it is the responsibility of the mentor to respect and leverage differences in style and aspirations, junior professionals critically engage both similarities and differences in navigating relationships with powerful people.
- New Girl is by definition a temporary status. It is the responsibility of mentors and supervisors to acknowledge the experience that subordinates and mentees bring. The absence of that acknowledgment is a signal to move on.

We must do our best to maintain professional boundaries, but at the same time we should value friendships and steer personal interest in a direction that helps us and our careers. Given the shorter "tour of duty" stints that people now have at each workplace, this interest can be very useful later on. Whether the content of workplace interactions are personal or professional, the goal in these should be building as much positive alliance as possible.

As the personal is political, women should not be afraid of taking a critical perspective if we want our "friendships" to be real. Women in superior roles need to be more mindful of the power they have and be more secure in this power rather than playing out a morality drama in their interactions with other colleagues, especially subordinates. In sum, as illustrated here, my own lived history and the lived experiences of the women discussed here include both opportunities for women of all backgrounds to form friendships and barriers/disruptions to those opportunities. Power is the key ingredient in both of these. Acknowledge it and use it for good.

· 1 9 ·

TRUST

Keisha L. Green

On March 14, 2016, I pulled into the driveway of my Northampton, Massachusetts, apartment enthralled by a Northeast Public Radio interview with women's studies scholar, Patricia Bell-Scott, about her recent national best-selling book, *The Firebrand and the First Lady—Portrait of a Friendship: Pauli Murray, Eleanor Roosevelt, and the Struggle for Social Justice*. With the engine still running, I parked my car, listening intently to the fascinating but complex relationship between a highly accomplished Black woman civil rights activist and one of the most well-known first ladies of the United States. I happen to know the exact date of this particular memory because the story, penned by Bell-Scott, compelled me to create a cell-phone memo with notes about the instructive power and lessons learned from an interracial and intergenerational relationship between two dynamic women. The story resonated deeply with me because of my own experience with cross-race/cultural and intergenerational relationships. I was learning about this remarkable "portrait of a friendship" between two history makers during Women's History Month just days after International Women's Day during one of our country's potentially historic (and ultimately bizarre) presidential campaigns, featuring Hillary Rodham Clinton, who, at the time, was projected to be the first U.S. woman president.

The epistolary relationship between the two women, Murray and Roosevelt, was intersectional as it simultaneously centered and traversed race, class, and age. I sat intrigued by this seemingly *uncommon bond*—with significant political implications during a time marked *and marred* by intense racial politics, human and civil rights struggles, and systematic second-class citizenship for Black Americans and specifically for women. How did such an inspirational relationship start and flourish, and what can their story teach us about engaging in *uncommon bonds*? Clearly, the Black-white binary nature of their friendship has a long-complicated racial, historical, cultural, and political backdrop, since the founding of our country, that continues to shape, challenge, or pro/inhibit similar relationships today between Black and white women. The uncommonness of strong ties between Black and white women and the corresponding difficulty establishing interracial sisterhoods is explored in a few of the narratives featured in this edited volume. In these stories, I find traces of my own experiences. As a Black woman, like some of the writers, I find myself at times more comfortably creating friendships with other Black women, and yet race or racial compatibility has neither always been the common thread nor a barrier. I have maintained lasting friendships with many women of color, as well as white women. One of my closest friendships of nearly 20 years is with a white woman who on paper shares eerily similar background details with me. In fact, the two of us affectionately refer to one another as "twins" because our lives have been fantastically intertwined since the day we met. Notably, we would discover that as undergraduates we both attended small liberal arts colleges serving as student government presidents. We would eventually live in Brooklyn apartments on the same street, enriching our faith at the same mega-church, marrying Caribbean men, and completing doctorate degrees in education. After being in one another's weddings, bearing witness to the birth of our daughters, and tragically losing our mothers too soon, we now both call Western Massachusetts our home, where we work in higher education. Beyond the similar biographical checklist, what are the goods of our friendship that make it strong and enduring?

This two-decade-long friendship between a Southern Black woman and a Northeastern white woman has persisted for mainly two reasons: authentication and shared worldview. Regarding authentication, my friend has demonstrated that I can trust she appreciates the salience and complexities of social identity, particularly race. I met her shortly after first noticing her establishing what seemed to be authentic interactions with undergraduate students of color on the campus where she worked. These student relationships were extensions of the close relationships she had with other women of color in her life. She navigated historically Black spaces—including neighborhoods, churches, parties—with an authentic appreciation for the culture that created those spaces and actively sought to contribute what she could without muting any other woman's voice. Her personal and professional leanings are toward examining her own white privilege. She voted for Hillary and helped organize with the Clinton for President campaign; supported the Women's March when women en mass protested President-Elect Trump's politics and behavior; and in raising her two daughters, she is affirming them as unapologetically Black girls.

Uncommon bonds among women historically have been fraught with tensions. Importantly, what do such attempts at sisterhood look like at a much broader national or global level? What are the political implications of solidarity or lack thereof among women? If we know healthy friendships among women are often the life source needed to face a dysfunctional family; toxic work environment; or racist, patriarchal, sexist, and heteronormative society, in what ways have or can a sisterhood among women of diverse backgrounds, class strata, and age be transformative? Perhaps the recent U.S. presidential election results, Women's March, and the #BlackGirlsRock movement provide both insights and cautionary tales.

Black Women Vote for Clinton; White Women Vote for Trump

In the 2016 U.S. presidential race, national exit poll results revealed that Black women voters were nearly unilateral in their support of Clinton, contrasting the more fractured support from white women who ultimately favored Trump at 53%. Despite the "white pant suit nation" and the cadre of liberal feminist women, Trump still garnered a large portion of the women's vote. This phenomenon is significant because it points to a long history of mistrust between Black and white women. Black women voted 96% for Clinton in past elections and not necessarily because of an overwhelming or blind support of her policies. In fact, some Black women served up a helping of side-eye about Clinton's infamous "super-predator" comments related to the fear that exists when it comes to Black children's bodies. This "super-predator" myth was made popular by political scientists and criminologists in the 1990s as a way to explain youth violence in large cities. The racially coded term pathologized and dehumanized youth of color framing them, specifically Black youth, as morally depraved, subsequently contributing to the mass incarceration of African Americans. Clinton has expressed regret for her remarks indicating that rather than criminalizing Black youth, we need to acknowledge structural racism and systemic failure to provide necessary resources to support these same youth. And many of us will certainly remember her comments during the 2008 Presidential campaign, suggesting that then-candidate Barack Obama did not embody "fundamentally American" values or have the experience to be president.

Still, in spite of the theory that Candidate Trump's brash misogyny alone should have disqualified him from the race, Clinton was more than just the lesser of two evils. As potentially the first woman president of the U.S., she represented a historical benchmark in electoral politics that could be rivaled only by the election of the first African American president eight years prior. Black women demonstrated the strength, resolve, and soul to stand up for that chance at history, simultaneously standing against an opponent who had already shown not only chauvinistic, but white supremacist tendencies. Voting against their own self-interest, white women aligned with conservative white men believing, however falsely, that such a move might signal increased personal power and economic gains. Whatever the case may be, it is apparent that an overwhelmingly large portion of white women were able to justify electing the candidate that was most likely to make Black communities the target of state-sanctioned economic, educational, and environmental violence. The stark difference in the exit poll numbers contributes to Black women's continued lack of trust of white women, an indication that when difficult times arise, white women can be comfortable siding with their husbands before they stand with their sisters. How could women disagree on something so fundamental as the common bond of womanhood? The election results were an assault on women. If we can't agree on the significance of these common bonds, what can we agree on?

Women's March

The postelection energy was electrifying, particularly among self-proclaimed "Nasty Women" wearing "pussyhats" who marched for human rights, gender equality, and to protest Trump's election, which came as a stunning surprise to mostly white liberal women baffled that a racist, sexist, bigoted campaign won. And it was this white liberal feminist shock and awe that was behind the organizing of thousands of other women, many of whom were conspicuously absent from previous marches in the name of #BlackLivesMatter or silent in response to the #SayHerName movement. This passivity has not gone unnoticed by Black women and other women of color who continue to express frustration by the lack of inclusiveness among white women conveners of the many marches for women's rights, equity, and social justice. If at the heart of the protests was a desire for all women to stand in solidarity against patriarchy, sexism, racism, and oppression, why were white women seemingly taking the lead, and why weren't more Black women marching? I suspect many Black women were keenly aware that white women were not unified in their opposition of Trump and all that his administration represents, and perhaps questioned white women marchers' commitment to ending racism or protesting the violence against Black women and men with as much fervor as their fight for gender equality and women's rights. Furthermore, Black women have long been using intersectional identities, lived experiences, and leadership skills to organize and fight for Black families and communities of color. Although, such work is often portrayed differently. For example, the Women's March in D.C., predictably, was treated like a civil protest, while the protest activities by women of color in places like Ferguson and elsewhere were treated like military combat zones. Ultimately, past and present sentiment among many Black women is a desire to prioritize issues related to race *and* gender with an intersectional approach, and an understanding that our voices should be central in the struggle for human rights.

Black Girl's Rock

This is the anthem for Black and Brown girls and women everywhere, particularly in the U.S., where Black women experience multiple forms of oppression and are, according to Zora Neale Hurston (1986) in *Theirs Eyes Were Watching God*, "de *mule* uh de world so fur as Ah can see." In contrast, social media campaigns and empowerment projects like #BlackGirlsRock, created by former DJ and model, Beverly Bond, and #ProfessionalBlackGirl started by professor and producer, Dr. Yaba Blay, place Black women's trailblazing impact on culture and all-around excellence at the center of the conversation. These themes are more than just popular hashtags; they represent convenings across the country and mark a unique moment of progress, as Black women are experiencing a renaissance, so fittingly encapsulated by another hashtag, #BlackGirlMagic. Shonda Rhimes, Ava Duvernay, and Issa Rae are producing award-winning film, television, and internet content; Gabby Douglas, Simone Biles, and Venus and Serena Williams have triumphed consistently within gymnastics and tennis, respectively, for years; and there are currently a record number of Black women in the U.S. Congress (21). And, perhaps one of the most recognizable #BlackGirlMagic icons is Michelle Obama, widely considered one of the most graceful, stylish, and educated First Ladies ever to walk the halls of the White House.

Ultimately, much of what stands in the way of authentic relationship building between Black and white women is a matter of trust. Because of the historical complexities related to economics and class that have hovered over the relationships between white women and Black women, there are many reasons to be distrustful. If I can't trust you to vote in our shared and common interest; if I can't trust you to include me in your organizing or to organize on my behalf; if I can't trust you to celebrate my culture, or at least stand back as I celebrate with other Black women—then how could I possibly be in an authentic relationship with you? And if you don't trust my political analysis, my emotional intelligence, or my societal contributions, why would you want to be in relationship with me? These moments—this election, this demonstration, this celebration—are significant because they remind us of our racial history. This history is inescapable, no matter how far removed. The Movement for Black Lives, highlighted by the hashtag #BlackLivesMatter, is a contemporary response to the most recent and most violent occurrences of Black bodies being seen as subjects to be feared and deemed so untrustworthy that we should be exterminated. And even in this context, Black women rise into leadership roles, initiating the movement in self-defense and self-actualization. The resilience of African American women has created a wellspring of wisdom that inspired yet another hashtag: #trustBlackwomen.

Conclusion

Often strong bonds among women are formed as a product of common culture, interests, employment, children and schools, and of shared time and space. Much of our time is spent engaging in culturally specific rituals and traditions (familial or otherwise)—at least for women of color. These life experiences cement the bonds, which is why, understandably, many women form friendships with women of the same race. However, cross-race and cross-cultural relationships among women are possible. In the end, Murray and Roosevelt developed an enduring friendship that came to be characterized by honesty, trust, affection, empathy, support, mutual respect, loyalty, acceptance, a commitment to hearing the other's point of view, pleasure in each other's company, and the ability to pick up where they'd left of, irrespective of the miles that had separated them or the time lapsed. (Bell-Scott, 2016, p. xix)

While race may not be *the* salient factor in a bond between two women of different racial backgrounds, race certainly *still* matters. There is no time or space for color-blindness. Cross-racial friendships work because there is acknowledgement and appreciation of difference. White friends are good friends when they do the self-work to become aware of the race-related personal boundaries, cultural fault lines, and political trigger points and can navigate those spaces with not just good intention, but also with genuine care. Black women are good friends when we allow ourselves to be vulnerable in relationship with white women, in spite of deep-rooted instincts that keep guards raised. This kind of earnest appreciation and courageous communication creates opportunities for uncommon bonds.

The ease and comfort that I have experienced maintaining select cross-race and cross-cultural relationships friendships is primarily because of an intentional effort to humanize the "other" and to connect through common life experiences both personal and professional. After all, what and who are we women if not a sum of our varied life experiences. What binds two or more women together might be a shared journey such as the loss of a parent; juggling challenges around fertility, pregnancy, and motherhood themselves; or remaining single in a world that assumes all women want to be married with children. The quest for genuine connection comes from our souls searching for our reflections, and hearts yearning for love and acceptance, or our spirits seeking validation and needing to be seen and understood. Such life source—life-sustaining relationships—can be found in unlikely places and spaces, including beyond our cultural boundaries or racial confines. In particular, as we are living this "new" America where a person like Donald Trump can become president, it is all the more reason to seek friendships that help change the world. Through our personal relationships we sway the hearts and minds of a people.

References

Bell-Scott, P. (2016). *The firebrand and the First Lady: Portrait of a friendship: Pauli Murray, Eleanor Roosevelt, and the struggle for social justice.* New York, NY: Knopf.
Hurston, Z. N. (1986). *Their eyes were watching God: A novel.* London, UK: Virago.

AFTERWORD

Crossing

Jamila Lyiscott

Yesterday, her skin, a border
That she was not allowed to cross
She toed the line and touched its seams
To calculate what it might cost

Yesterday, you, a crooked glare
Confined her hope with no remorse
She conjured courage for shelter
From the sting of your excessive force

Today
Love is thicker than water
And you are offended by a sisterhood
Thicker than skin
The audacity of Freedoms to forged itself across boundaries
Meant to let no one in

Today
Your vexation is our victory
For the uncommon bonds she found
When she conjured pillars out of your margins
To lift her up and hold her down

CONTRIBUTORS

Allia Abdullah-Matta is an Associate Professor of English at CUNY LaGuardia Community College. Her scholarship primarily focuses on twentieth- and twenty-first-century African/African Diaspora literature and visual culture. As an educator and writer, she strives to address the power and the politics of creative expression and voice as essential instruments of social justice practice and transformation.

Felice Belle is a poet, playwright, and pop culture enthusiast. She holds a B.S. in Industrial Engineering from Columbia University, an M.A. in Individualized Study from New York University's Gallatin School, and an M.F.A. in Creative Writing from Long Island University.

Amber Buggs lives in Southern California and is a higher education professional within the University of California system. She is a proud alumna of the University of California, Santa Barbara, with a Bachelor of Arts in English Literature and New York University where she earned a Master of Arts degree in humanities and social thought.

JLove Calderón is an art-ivist, author, and conscious TV, film and digital producer and director who has spent over two decades working on issues of social justice, race and gender.

Paulette Dalpes has 30 years of experience as a Student Affairs professional, including 18 years working at community colleges. Her career in student affairs includes senior-level and systems administration; facilitating federally funded TRiO grant programs; training and development on issues of diversity and inclusion; and work in residential life at large universities. Dr. Dalpes is the coeditor of *The Handbook for Student Affairs in Community Colleges* and a forthcoming special issue on Student Affairs for the *Community College Journal of Research and Practice*. Dr. Dalpes attended Colorado State University as a first-generation college student, earning a bachelor's degree in psychology and a master's in college student personnel administration. She earned her doctorate in education at the University of Massachusetts. She and her wife, Dr. Kathy Obear, recently relocated back to Colorado after 8 years in New York City and over 20 years in Massachusetts. They celebrated 30 years together in 2016.

Robin DiAngelo is a former Associate Professor of Education. Her scholarship is in white racial identity and race relations. In addition to her academic work, Dr. DiAngelo has extensive experience as a workplace consultant in issues of race relations and racial justice. She has numerous publications and books, including *What Does It Mean to Be White?: Developing White Racial Literacy*. Her work on *White Fragility* has influenced the national dialogue on race and been featured in Alternet, *Salon*, NPR, the *New York Times*, the *Atlantic*, *Slate*, and Colorlines.

Joicelyn Dingle is a writer and photo editor/producer of 18 years. After receiving her degree in Marketing from Hampton University, she worked in management and marketing for Spike Lee's 40 Acres and a Mule Merchandising and then, Russell Simmons's Phat Farm. She is the cocreator of *Honey* magazine and the columnist for Ebony.com's The Coolest Black Family in America series. Joicelyn lives and works between New York City and Savannah, Georgia.

Stacey Gibson is a parent, educator, and consultant who teaches English in the Chicago-land area and works to help students and adults understand how oppression is covertly normalized and replicated. In addition to presenting at numerous conferences, her writing has appeared in Lee Mun Wah's *Let's Get Real* and her antioppression curricula for the PBS documentary *American Promise* can be found at Teaching Tolerance. She would like to thank the nameless ones who preceded her as she knows she could not be without them.

Reverend Samantha González-Block serves as the Associate Pastor at Grace Covenant Presbyterian Church in Asheville, North Carolina. A graduate of Barnard College and Union Theological Seminary in the City of New York, Samantha has focused her studies on interreligious engagement, interfaith families, and education. She has worked in a number of different fields in the United States and abroad, and continues to use Latin dance as a medium to bring people together. Samantha is the recipient of the Auburn Seminary Maxwell Fellowship for promise of excellence in parish ministry.

Keisha L. Green, Ph.D., is Assistant Professor of Secondary English Education at the University of Massachusetts, Amherst, and her publications appear in *Race, Ethnicity and Education*, *Equity & Excellence in Education*, *Reading African American Experiences in the Obama Era: Theory, Advocacy, Activism*, and *Humanizing Research: Decolonizing Qualitative Inquiry With Youth and Communities*

Jessica Havens is an educator and consultant who works with youth and adults to develop their critical consciousness about identity, power and privilege. She holds a B.A. in Secondary Education and an M.A. in Women & Gender Studies with a focus on antiracist feminisms. In all her work, Jessica aspires to integrate love and mindfulness as essential tools for social change.

Millicent R. Jackson is a fiction writer based in Western Massachusetts. The recipient of the 2008 Archie D. and Bertha Walker scholarship at Fine Arts Work Center in Provincetown, her work has been published in *Today's Black Woman*, *The Power to Write* by Caroline Joy Adams *and Peregrine* (literary journal).

Berenecea Johnson Eanes enters her fifth year as Vice President for Student Affairs at California State University, Fullerton, and 28th year as a professional in higher education. Responsible for running a division that supports the personal, social, and academic development of a diverse institution with nearly 39,000 students, Dr. Eanes has served as an executive at several universities, including John Jay College of Criminal Justice, Hamilton College, Columbia, and Morehouse College. Dr. Eanes, a member of the Presidential Cabinet at CSUF and leader within multiple student affairs professional associations, earned a Ph.D. in Social Work from Clark Atlanta University, a Master of Social Work from Boston University, and a Bachelor of Science in Public Health from Dillard University in New Orleans.

Hye-Kyung Kang is an Associate Professor and Director of the Social Work Program at Seattle University. Dr. Kang's research focuses on postcolonial social work practice, community organizing and mobilization in immigrant communities and communities of color, cultural citizenship, and critical pedagogy. She is concerned with the interconnection between personal struggles, environmental problems, and societal oppression and inequalities, and continues to teach clinical social work practice that integrates multiple contexts and narratives.

Jamila Lyiscott is currently a visiting Assistant Professor of Social Justice Education at the University of Massachusetts, Amherst, where she also serves as an affiliated faculty member of the W.E.B. Du Bois Afro American Studies department. Coupled with these appointments, Jamila was recently named a Senior Research Fellow of Teachers College, Columbia University's Institute for Urban and Minority Education (IUME). Across these spaces, her research, teaching, and service focus on the intersections of race, language, and social justice in education. The recently awarded Cultivating New Voices among scholars of color fellow also serves as a spoken-word artist, community organizer, consultant, and motivational speaker locally and internationally. Her scholarship and activism work together to prepare educators to sustain diversity in the classroom, empower youth, and explore, assert, and defend the value of Black life. As a testament to her commitment to educational justice for students of color, Jamila is the founder and codirector of the Cyphers For Justice (CFJ) youth, research, and advocacy program, apprenticing inner-city youth, incarcerated youth, and preservice educators as critical social researchers through hip-hop, spoken word, and digital literacy. She is currently preparing a book manuscript about her work within Predominantly White Institutions across the nation, helping educators to confront white privilege within and beyond the classroom.

Christina Marín, Ph.D. is Professor of Theater/Drama Director at Central Arizona College. She is an Applied Theater practitioner who works in diverse communities in the United States and abroad.

Jennifer M. D. Matos holds a doctorate in Education with a concentration in Social Justice Education from the University of Massachusetts at Amherst. She is a founding member of the Social Justice at Work Consulting Group, an agency that provides social justice training and resources to K-12 schools, colleges, and private organizations. Currently, she is a Lecturer at Mt. Holyoke College in South Hadley, MA, where she teaches in the department of Psychology and Education. She resides in Western Massachusetts with her wife and their daughter.

Nelle Mills is a New Orleans–based writer, educator, and activist. Currently, she teaches creative writing at 826-New Orleans to youths aged 6–16 and serves as the lead writer of "Alleged Lesbian Activities," a play about New Orleans's disappearing dyke bars.

Eman Mosharafa, Ph.D., is an Associate Professor at October University of Modern Sciences and Arts (MSA), which is located in Cairo, Egypt. Before joining MSA in the Fall of 2016, she taught for six years at The City University of New York (CUNY). Dr. Mosharafa is an expert on Middle Eastern and Islamic cultures and their media portrayal. She worked in news, advertising, and drama production. Her research interests include mass communication, political and cultural communication, and new social media. Her current project is an exhibit in New York City called "Beyond Sacred: Unthinking Muslim Identity." She is fluent in English, French, and Arabic. Dr. Mosharafa aspires to graduate ethical and skilled mass communication students and to create bridges between American and Egyptian media professionals.

Thembisa S. Mshaka is a 25-year veteran of the entertainment industry and a multiple award-winning creative campaign writer/producer. Ms. Mshaka is the author of the career guide *Put Your Dreams First: Handle Your [entertainment] Business* and contributed to the anthologies *Icons of Hip Hop* by Mickey Hess and *Sometimes Rhythm, Sometimes Blues* by Taigi Smith. She is now writing, directing, and producing for TV and film.

Professor Emerita of Language, Literacy, and Culture, College of Education, University of Massachusetts, Amherst, **Sonia Nieto** has devoted her professional life to issues of equity, diversity, and social justice. She has written extensively on multicultural education, teacher education, and the education of students of diverse backgrounds. Her most recent books include *Why We Teach Now* (2015), and *Finding Joy in Teaching Students of Diverse Backgrounds: Culturally Responsive and Socially Just Practices in U.S. Schools* (2013), as well as a memoir, *Brooklyn Dreams: My Life in Public Education* (2015). She is the recipient of many awards for her scholarship and advocacy, including six honorary doctorates.

Gail E. Norskey holds a doctorate in Microbiology from the University of Massachusetts at Amherst. For over two decades she led Smith College's outreach and community engagement efforts, and was the founding director of the college's Center for Community Collaboration. A highlight of Norskey's work was the Smith College Summer Science & Engineering Program for high school girls, promoting the advancement of over 2,000 young women from around the globe in science study. She resides in southern Maine and Florida with her husband, and is the proud mom of two daughters.

Deinya Phenix, Ph.D., is a sociologist and quantitative criminologist who has worked alongside policymakers, community organizers, and other change agents. Her career passion is diving deep into the social forces behind human behavior, including culture, life course development, and urban policy.

Imani Romney-Rosa is a founding trainer with Romney Associates and an educator and school administrator with more than 15 years of experience working in public and independent schools. Ms. Romney-Rosa's focus is on creating safe and inclusive learning environments. She also served as co-chair of the Race Task Force at Kolot Chayeinu: Voices of Our Lives Synagogue in Brooklyn, NY. Ms. Romney-Rosa received her undergraduate degree in Communication Education and Performing Arts from the University of Massachusetts, Amherst, and her Master's in Spanish Philology from Middlebury College, Madrid, Spain.

Marcella Runell Hall is the Dean of Students at Mount Holyoke. She is a social justice scholar and accomplished author. She previously spent seven years at New York University, where she was the founding codirector for the Of Many Institute for Multifaith Leadership and served as a clinical faculty member in the Silver School of Social Work. She was the recipient of the NYU 2013–2014 Dr. Martin Luther King, Jr. Faculty Award. She has edited three award-winning books and she has written for Scholastic Books, the New York Times Learning Network, VIBE, and various academic journals, including Equity and Excellence in Education. She and her husband live in the Pioneer Valley with their two young daughters.

Roberta Samet is a social worker in private practice in NYC. She is a second-generation antiracist and stands on the shoulders of her father, Seymour Samet, who was a civil rights pioneer and activist. She is the cochair of Kolot Chayeinu's Task Force on Race and is an active member of the Anti-Racist Alliance of New York. She formerly was the mental health program director for the September 11th Fund, where she developed the mental health recovery plan for NYC. Prior to that she was an AIDS activist, developed new housing for People With HIV/AIDS in the Lower

East Side and developed mental health programs when she was a consultant to the NYC Department of Mental Health.

Joni Schwartz, Ph.D., is an Associate Professor of Communication Studies,
social activist scholar, and founder of three NYC adult learning centers.
She is coeditor of *Swimming Upstream: Black Males in Adult Education*,
reflections editor for *Dialogues in Social Justice* and author of numerous
journal publications. Her documentary, *A New Normal: Young Men of
Color, Trauma and Engagement in Learning*, is utilized in college classrooms,
and she is the executive producer for an upcoming documentary about
post-incarceration and learning. ePortolio: https://lagcc-cuny.digication.
com/joni_schwartz_ph_d/Welcome.

Mira Sengupta graduated from Barnard College, where she studied English
and Religion before earning a Master's in Literature at City College
(CUNY). She is now pursuing a Ph.D. in 18th-Century British Literature
at Fordham University, where she teaches literature and composition, and
is currently writing her dissertation entitled "Devilish Thoughts: Echoes
of Satanic Persuasion in the Eighteenth-Century Novel." Her articles
have appeared in *The Marvell Society Newsletter* and *ANQ: A Quarterly
Journal of Short Articles, Notes, and Reviews* (forthcoming).

Kersha Smith, Ph.D. is an Assistant Professor in Psychology in New York.
Her primary research investigates curricula and pedagogies responsible
for the construction of critical knowledge and transformative learning.
Kersha has been published in various edited books and in journals such as
Pedagogy, Culture & Society and *The Journal of Social Issues*. She is a recipient of the Spencer Foundation's Discipline-Based Studies in Education
Fellowship. She was granted the Calvin W. Ruck award, which recognizes
scholars committed to social justice, and The Larry Murphy Award by the
Adult Higher Education Alliance for her work on transformative learning
in non traditional student populations. She lives in Brooklyn, New York
with her husband and two young sons.

Liza A. Talusan, Ph.D., is a mother, writer, educator, facilitator, and teacher.
She earned her B.A. in Psychology from Connecticut College; her M.A.
in Higher Education Administration from New York University; and her
Ph.D. in Higher Education from the University of Massachusetts, Boston.
Liza's work spans nearly 20 years in educational settings in both K–12 and
higher education as well as public and private institutions. Liza identifies
as Filipina American and as a partner in an interracial and interreligious
marriage. As the mother of multiracial children, Liza has learned to speak

openly about identity and the impact of identity on our lives. To learn more about Liza, please visit www.lizatalusan.com.

Jodi Van Der Horn-Gibson, Ph.D. is an Assistant Professor in the Department of Speech Communication & Theatre Arts. Her research focuses on intercultural communication, and the representation of race in film and theatre.

Rani Varghese is an Assistant Professor at Adelphi University School of Social Work. Given her training in clinical social work; women, gender, and sexuality studies; and social justice education, she brings an interdisciplinary approach to her teaching, consulting, and research. Her research focuses on clinical social work education, social justice practices and principles, and intergroup dialogue.

S. Lenise Wallace, Ph.D., is a motivational speaker, college professor, and public relations professional. She is an Associate Professor teaching communication courses in New York City. Her research interests include public relations and race, gender, and sexuality in mass media. Due to her prominent work in the field, Dr. Wallace was featured in editions of *The Practice of Public Relations* by Fraser Seitel, one of the nation's leading public relations textbooks.

WWW.UNCOMMONBONDSBOOK.COM

Please visit the website for *UnCommon Bonds* for additional resources and more information, including updates on events and appearances.

Follow on Facebook: https://www.facebook.com/uncommonbonds
Follow on Twitter: https://twitter.com/uncommon_bonds

Studies in Criticality

General Editor
Shirley R. Steinberg

Counterpoints publishes the most compelling and imaginative books being written in education today. Grounded on the theoretical advances in criticalism, feminism, and postmodernism in the last two decades of the twentieth century, Counterpoints engages the meaning of these innovations in various forms of educational expression. Committed to the proposition that theoretical literature should be accessible to a variety of audiences, the series insists that its authors avoid esoteric and jargonistic languages that transform educational scholarship into an elite discourse for the initiated. Scholarly work matters only to the degree it affects consciousness and practice at multiple sites. Counterpoints' editorial policy is based on these principles and the ability of scholars to break new ground, to open new conversations, to go where educators have never gone before.

For additional information about this series or for the submission of manuscripts, please contact:

Shirley R. Steinberg
c/o Peter Lang Publishing, Inc.
29 Broadway, 18th floor
New York, New York 10006

To order other books in this series, please contact our Customer Service Department:

(800) 770-LANG (within the U.S.)
(212) 647-7706 (outside the U.S.)
(212) 647-7707 FAX

Or browse online by series:
www.peterlang.com